Islam and Tolerance in Wider Europe

Edited by
Pamela Kilpadi

OPEN SOCIETY INSTITUTE

Published by

International Policy Fellowships
Open Society Institute–Budapest

Október 6 utca 12, H–1051 Budapest, Hungary
Tel: (+36 1) 327 3863
Fax: (+36 1) 327 3809
Email: fellows@osi.hu
Website: www.soros.org/initiatives/ipf

Open Society Institute–New York

400 West 59th Street
New York, New York 10019 USA
Website: www.soros.org

Distributed by

Central European University Press
Budapest – New York

Mail: H–1397 Budapest, P.O. Box 519/2, Hungary
Tel: (+36 1) 327 3138
Fax: (+36 1) 327 3183
Email: ceupress@ceupress.com
Website: www.ceupress.com

Central European University Press

400 West 59th Street
New York NY 10019, USA
Tel: (+1 212) 547 6932
Fax: (+1 646) 557 2416
E-mail: mgreenwald@sorosny.org

Library of Congress Cataloging-in-Publication Data

Islam and tolerance in wider Europe / edited by Pamela Kilpadi.
              p. cm.
         Includes bibliographical references.
         ISBN-13: 978-1-891385-52-0 (pbk. : alk. paper)
         ISBN-10: 1-891385-52-6 (pbk. : alk. paper)
         1. Muslims--Europe--History--21st century. 2. Europe--Ethnic
relations--History--21st century. 3. Islam and politics--Europe.
4. Islam and state--Europe.   I. Kilpadi, Pamela, 1968-   II. Title.

D1056.2.M87I73 2006
305.6'97094--dc22

                                        2006027999

Cover design and cover photo by János Mészáros • Aula.info
Typography and layout by Judit Kovács • Createch Ltd.
Printed in Hungary by Createch Ltd.

Policy Perspectives · International Policy Fellowships Program

Islam and Tolerance in Wider Europe

Series editor Pamela Kilpadi

CONTENTS

Policy Perspectives

About Us

International Policy Fellowships

The International Policy Fellowships (IPF) program supports analytical policy research in pursuance of open society goals such as the rule of law, democratic elections, diverse and vigorous civil societies, and respect for minorities. IPF seeks to enhance the quality of policy research, advocacy, and analysis in countries where the Soros Network operates and supports fellows in promoting open, transparent, and responsive public policy processes that are critical to effective democratic governance. The IPF alumni network is an alliance of some 250 open society leaders in over 40 countries.

www.soros.org/initiatives/ipf

Open Society Institute

The Open Society Institute works to build vibrant and tolerant democracies whose governments are accountable to their citizens. To achieve its mission, OSI seeks to shape public policies that assure greater fairness in political, legal, and economic systems and safeguard fundamental rights. On a local level, OSI implements a range of initiatives to advance justice, education, public health, and independent media. At the same time, OSI builds alliances across borders and continents on issues such as corruption and freedom of information. OSI places a high priority on protecting and improving the lives of marginalized people and communities.

Investor and philanthropist George Soros in 1993 created OSI as a private operating and grantmaking foundation to support his foundations in Central and Eastern Europe and the former Soviet Union. Those foundations were established, starting in 1984, to help countries make the transition from communism. OSI has expanded the activities of the Soros foundations network to encompass the United States and more than 60 countries in Europe, Asia, Africa, and Latin America. Each Soros foundation relies on the expertise of boards composed of eminent citizens who determine individual agendas based on local priorities.

www.soros.org

Center for Policy Studies

IPF is also affiliated with the Center for Policy Studies (CPS) in Budapest. CPS is an academic unit within the Central European University that is dedicated to improving the quality of governance in the region by the provision of independent public policy analysis and advice. The Center strives to share relevant experiences of post-socialist transition with a sound appreciation of local policy contexts. The CPS Policy Documentation Center (PDC) online database includes hundreds of policy studies by International Policy Fellows (source IPF).

www.ceu.hu/cps
http://pdc.ceu.hu

IPF also collaborates with the Woodrow Wilson International Center for Scholars in Washington, DC and the Centre for European Policy Studies (CEPS) in Brussels to provide policy fellows with further opportunities for joint scholarship and research dissemination activities in these policymaking capitals.

Woodrow Wilson International Center for Scholars

The Woodrow Wilson International Center for Scholars aims to unite the world of ideas with the world of policy by supporting pre-eminent scholarship and linking that scholarship to issues of concern to officials in Washington. The Center is not an advocacy think tank developing specific policy recommendations, but a nonpartisan center for advanced study, a neutral forum for free and open, serious, and informed scholarship and discussion. IPF and the Wilson Center's East European Studies Program provide several policy fellows with International Junior Public Policy Scholar Fellowships at the Center each year.

www.wilsoncenter.org

Centre for European Policy Studies

The Centre for European Policy Studies is an independent policy research institute dedicated to producing sound policy research leading to constructive solutions to the challenges facing Europe today. The Centre strives to achieve high standards of academic excellence and maintain unqualified independence; provide a forum for discussion among all stakeholders in the European policy process; build collaborative networks of researchers, policymakers and business across the whole of Europe; and disseminate CEPS findings and views through a regular flow of publications and public events.

www.ceps.be

The Authors

Rutvica Andrijašević (International Policy Fellow, 2004–5) is an Economic and Social Research Council (ESRC) Postdoctoral Fellow based at Oxford University's Centre on Migration Policy and Society (COMPAS). During her IPF year she was based at the Centre for European Policy Studies (CEPS) in Brussels. Her main areas of interest and specialization are trafficking in women, gender and migration, European enlargement, and externalizations of asylum. She earned her PhD in women's studies from Utrecht University. Further information about her research is available from the IPF websites: http://pdc.ceu.hu (Source IPF), www.policy.hu/andrijasevic, and http://www.compas.ox.ac.uk/about/biog/rutvica@ceps.be.shtml. E-mail: andrijasevic @policy.hu or Rutvica.Andrijasevic@compas.ox.ac.uk.

Pavel Bayov (International Policy Fellow, 2005–6) heads the Irkutsk regional government's research and information division for the Cultural Affairs Committee. He also teaches courses on religion, culture and sociology as Associate Professor at Irkutsk State Technical University. His research focuses primarily on the role of religion in transforming society. Pavel studied history at Irkutsk State University and earned his PhD in sociology from Buryat State University. Further information about his research is available from the IPF websites: http://pdc.ceu.hu (Source IPF) and www.policy.hu/bayov. E-mail: bayov@policy.hu.

Amel Boubekeur is Research Fellow at the Centre for European Policy Studies (CEPS) in Brussels. Her current research explores contemporary transformations of Islam in the West (Europe/USA), and focuses on issues including the new Islamic elite, Muslim women leadership, and political Islam. She is also conducting research concerning the European Neighbourhood Policy toward the Arab countries. She is the author of *Le Voile de la Mariee. Jeunes musulmanes, voile et projet matrimonial en France.* She earned an MA in sociology from Ecole des Hautes Etudes en Sciences Sociales-Paris and is currently a PhD candidate in social sciences at Ecole Normale Supérieure-Paris. E-mail: amel.boubekeur@ceps.be.

Aldo Bumçi (International Policy Fellow, 2001–2) was sworn in as Albania's Minister of Justice in September 2005. Formerly he served as the director of the Albanian Institute for International Studies and a professor at Tirana University's Faculty of Social Sciences. He gained his MA in international relations from Bilkent University in Ankara, Turkey. Further information about his research is available from the IPF websites: http://pdc.ceu.hu (Source IPF) and www.policy.hu/bumci. E-mail: bumci@policy.hu.

Ihsan Dağl (International Policy Fellow, 2001–2) is Professor of International Relations at Middle East Technical University in Ankara, Turkey, specializing on human rights, democratization, Islam and politics, and EU-Turkey relations. He has published research articles in journals including *Middle Eastern Studies, Mediterranean Quarterly, Critique, Turkish Studies, Journal of Southern Europe and Black Sea Studies*, and *Perceptions*. In addition to his IPF award Ihsan has received research fellowships from Fulbright, the Carnegie Council on Ethics and International Affairs, NATO, the Turkish Academy of Sciences, and the European Commission Jean Monnet Projects. He earned a PhD in politics and international relations from Lancaster University. Further information about his research is available from the IPF websites: http://pdc.ceu.hu (Source IPF) and www.policy.hu/dagi. E-mail: dagi@policy.hu.

Michael Emerson (IPF Group Advisor) is Senior Research Fellow at the Centre for European Policy Studies (CEPS) in Brussels. He served as European Union Ambassador to Moscow from 1991 to 1996. His primary research interests focus on pan-European institutions, political economy of Wider Europe, European security policy, and EU relations with Russia, Ukraine and the Northern Dimension, Turkey, and Cyprus, while his secondary areas of research expertise include the economics of transition to a market economy, EU politics, enlargement of the EU, European Monetary Union, democratization in South Eastern Europe, EU relations with the Caucasus, and EU–US relations. He earned an MA from the University of Oxford and honorary doctorates from Kent University and Keele University. E-mail: michael.emerson@ceps.be.

Simeon Evstatiev (International Policy Fellow, 2005–6) teaches Middle Eastern and Islamic History at St. Kliment Ohridski University and serves as Research Director for the Centre for Intercultural Studies and Partnership in Sofia, Bulgaria. His current research and teaching focuses on political and religious movements in Arab world, tradition and innovation in Arab society and Islamic culture. He earned his MA and PhD in Arabic and Islamic History from Sofia University. Further information about his research is available from the IPF websites: http://pdc.ceu.hu (Source IPF) and www.policy.hu/evstatiev. E-mail: evstatiev@policy.hu.

Archil Gegeshidze (International Policy Fellow, 2005–6) is Senior Fellow at the Georgian Foundation for Strategic and International Studies (GFSIS). His professional expertise lies in the fields of regional security, cooperation in the South Caucasus, and political risk analysis. Prior to joining GFSIS, he was a Fulbright scholar at Stanford University. Archil worked for the Georgian government from 1992–2000, with his most recent post as Head of the Foreign Policy Analysis Department of the State Chancellery (office of the President). While working in the government, he also served as Assistant to the Head of State on National Security and Chief Foreign Policy Advisor to the President. Currently he lectures on globalization and development at Tbilisi State University. He holds a Candidate of Science degree from Georgian State University in Economic and Social Geography, and achieved the diplomatic rank of Ambassador Extraordinary and Plenipotentiary. Further information about his research is available from the IPF websites: http://pdc.ceu.hu (Source IPF) and www.policy.hu/gegeshidze. E-mail: gegeshidze@policy.hu.

Alexey Gunya (International Policy Fellow, 2006–7) is Senior Researcher at the Russian Academy of Sciences' Institute of Geo-graphy in Moscow and Institute of Computer Sciences and Problems of Regional Development in Kabardino-Balkaria (North Caucasus). The main focus of his research is the sustainable development of mountain areas. Since the early 1990s, he has organized and participated in various expeditions to the mountainous regions of Central Asia and the Caucasus, co-ordinated international projects concerned with the sustainable development of Caucasian and Central Asian transitional societies and lectured at Russian and foreign universities. He earned his Candidate of Science and Doctor of Science degrees from the Russian Academy of Sciences' Institute of Geography. Further information about his research is available from the IPF website: www.policy.hu/gunya. E-mail: gunya@policy.hu.

Fariz Ismailzade (International Policy Fellow, 2006–7) is political analyst based in Baku, Azerbaijan, and a lecturer in political science at the Western University in Baku. Since 2003 he has chaired the US-educated Azerbaijani Alumni Association, a 1200-member strong organization. Fariz has conducted research at the Center for Strategic and International Studies in Washington, DC, and also worked at the Embassy of Azerbaijan in the US. He worked for six years in the NGO sector in Azerbaijan, mainly on issues concerning youth, refugees and civil society. His research focuses on the geopolitics of the Caucasus region and CIS affairs. He is a regular correspondent for *Eurasianet.org, Transitions Online, Jamestown Daily Monitor,* and *Central Asia-Caucasus Analyst* and has written on the politics and economics of Azerbaijan and the Caucasus region for the East-West Institute, Institute for War and Peace Report, Analysis of Current Events, Freedom House, CaucasUS Context, and Azerbaijan International and Collage. He holds an MA in social and economic development from Washington University in St. Louis and a BA in political science from Western University in Baku with one-year interim studies at Wesleyan University in Connecticut, US. Further information about his research is available from the IPF websites: http://pdc.ceu.hu (Source IPF) and www.policy.hu/ismailzade. E-mail: ismailzade@policy.hu.

Nüket Kardam (IPF Senior Associate) is Associate Professor at the Graduate School of International Policy Studies, Monterey Institute of International Studies and spends part of each year in her native country, Turkey. Her main areas of expertise are gender and development, development theory and practice, international organizations, Turkey and Central Asia, and she has conducted research on organizational change in donor agencies, problems of collaboration between donors and recipient, and more recently on global women's human rights norms and their implementation at local levels. She has advised the United Nations Development Program and other international organizations on gender mainstreaming strategies, gender and good governance programs and participated in a training program at OECD on the same topics. Her recent book is entitled *Turkey's Engagement with Global Women's Human Rights.* She earned a PhD from Michigan State University and MA from the University of British Columbia. Website: http://policy.miis.edu/faculty/faculty.html?id=33. E-mail: nkardam@miis.edu.

Dilek Latif (International Policy Fellowships finalist, 2005) is Senior Lecturer in international relations at the Near East University in Nicosia, North Cyprus. Her particular scholarly interest lies in the area of peace operations, focusing on international strategies toward establishing peace and reconciliation in ethnically divided societies. She has been involved in internationally sponsored bi-communal peace projects in Cyprus as a consultant. Currently, she is involved in the International Peace Research Institute of Oslo's (PRIO) research project 'Reconciliation in Cyprus.' She gained her PhD from Middle East Technical University in Turkey. E-mail: dilekl@hotmail.com.

Irina Kouznetsova-Morenko (International Policy Fellow, 2004–5) is Assistant Professor at the Department of History and Sociology of Kazan State Medical University, Russia. Her research activity focuses on issues of social justice, ethnic relations and religion, as well as social aspects of health. She holds a Candidate of Sciences degree from Kazan State University. Further information about her research is available from the IPF websites: http://pdc.ceu.hu (Source IPF) and www.policy.hu/morenko. E-mail: morenko@policy.hu.

Mladen Momčilović (IPF Recruitment and Training Manager, 2000–3) is Parliament Program Manager at the USAID-funded National Democratic Institute for International Affairs (NDI), Belgrade Field Office. He served for two years as NDI Serbia Deputy Director of the Security Sector Reform Program. Previously he worked as IPF's Program Coordinator and later Recruitment and Training Manager, as well as Managing Editor of the East European Constitutional Review (EECR) at the Constitutional and Legal Policy Institute (COLPI) in Budapest. Mladen's current research focuses on security sector reform issues in Southeast Europe and the challenges of strengthening the parliament's affairs of the executive in Serbia. He earned his BA in Political Science from the School of Slavonic Studies in London and London School of Economics, and MA in Political Studies at the Central European University in Budapest. E-mail: mladenm@ndisrbija.org or mmladen@gmx.net.

Algirdas Petkevicius (International Policy Fellow, 2003–4) is Local Government Officer with the Organization for Security and Cooperation in Europe's Mission to Georgia. He has worked with the OSCE since 2004 in its local offices including Kosovo. Prior to his OSCE engagement, Algirdas worked in the Lithuanian Ministry of Public Administration Reforms and Local Authorities and as an independent consultant. Algirdas's research expertise lies in the area of social responsibility and global governance, the role of local and regional decision-makers in economic development and the policy implications of the EU enlargement. Algirdas holds an MSc in Development Management from the London School of Economics and LLM in Comparative Constitutional Law from the Central European University, Budapest. Further information about his research is available from the IPF websites: http://pdc.ceu.hu (Source IPF) and www.policy.hu/petkevicius. E-mail: petkevicius@policy.hu.

Eduard Ponarin (International Policy Fellow, 2006–7) chairs the Faculty of Political Science and Sociology at the European University at St. Petersburg. His academic interests focus on statistics and nationalism and include issues of post-Soviet political and social transformations and Islam. Eduard received his first degree, in psychology, from Leningrad (now St. Petersburg) State University, and a PhD in sociology from the University of Michigan. Further information about his research is available from the IPF websites: http://pdc.ceu.hu (Source IPF) and www.policy.hu/ponarin. E-mail: ponarin@policy.hu

Nicolae Popescu (International Policy Fellow, 2005–6) is currently a researcher based at the Centre for European Policy Studies (CEPS) in Brussels and also serves as the editor of Eurojournal.org and as a political analyst on post-Soviet affairs with the BBC World Service Romanian Section. In 2005 he was a Visiting Research Fellow at the Institute for Security Studies of the European Union, Paris. His main areas of expertise are the European Neighborhood Policy, conflict resolution, Russian foreign and security policy, Europeanization, and theories of European integration. He earned his MA from the Central European University in Budapest where he is a PhD candidate. Further information about his research is available from the IPF websites: http://pdc.ceu.hu (Source IPF) and www.policy.hu/npopescu. E-mail: npopescu@policy.hu.

Jiří Schneider (International Policy Fellow, 2002–3) is Program Director of the Prague Security Studies Institute (www.pssi.cz) and previously held various positions at the Czech Ministry of Foreign Affairs including Political Director and Head of Policy Planning Department. From 1995–1998 he served as the Czech Ambassador to Israel and from 1990–1992 as a member of the Czechoslovak Federal Parliament. He has lectured in international relations at Charles University (Prague), Masaryk University (Brno), New York University and Anglo-American College (Prague). Jiří holds graduate diplomas from Czech Technical College and the University of Cambridge. Further information about his research is available from the IPF websites: http://pdc.ceu.hu (Source IPF) and www.policy.hu/schneider. E-mail: schneider@policy.hu.

Ekaterina Sokirianskaia (International Policy Fellow, 2005–6) is Assistant Professor of Political Science at the Chechen State University in Grozny and works as a researcher for the Russian human rights organization Memorial in Nazran, Ingushetia where she is in charge of projects on enforced disappearances in Chechnya. She received her MA from the Political Sciences Department at the Central European University, Budapest where she is currently a PhD candidate. She defended her Candidate of Sciences degree at the Department of Public Administration at St Petersburg State University. Further information about her research is available from the IPF websites: http://pdc.ceu.hu (Source IPF) and www.policy.hu/sokirianskaia. E-mail: sokirianskaia@policy.hu.

Natalija Vrečer (International Policy Fellow, 2000–1) is an associate at the Institute for Ethnic Research in Ljubljana, researching human rights, migrants and refugees. From July 2006 she will work as a researcher and a policy adviser at the Slovene Institute for Adult Education focusing on issues of adult education as well. She holds a doctorate in social anthropology from the Institute of Humanities at Ljibljana University. Further information about her research is available from the IPF websites: http://pdc.ceu.hu (Source IPF) and www.policy.hu/vrecer. E-mail: vrecer@policy.hu.

Islam Yusufi (International Policy Fellow, 2002–4) is founder of Analytica, a think tank in Macedonia (www.analyticamk.org). Until recently he served as Assistant National Security Adviser to the President of Macedonia. Following his tenure with the presidential administration, he worked on various portfolios with European Union institutions in delivering assistance to countries of the western Balkans. His research interests include governance, security sector reform, and European integration of the western Balkans. He received his MA in International Relations from Bilkent University, Ankara, post-graduate degree from the University of Amsterdam, and is currently a PhD candidate at the University of Sheffield. Further information about his research is available from the IPF websites: http://pdc.ceu.hu (Source IPF) and www.policy.hu/yusufi. E-mail: yusufi@policy.hu.

The Editor

Pamela Kilpadi joined the Open Society Institute in 1994 as a research associate for the Forced Migration Projects in New York, where she researched and wrote articles for OSI publications and academic journals on forced migration in the former Soviet Union. She established the Projects' Budapest office in 1996 and was appointed to run the International Policy Fellowships program when it was launched two years later. Pamela worked as a journalist and editor in Boston and Moscow from 1989 to 1994, writing features on Russia's political and social transformation for publication in English and Russian. She earned a dual degree MA from the Columbia University School of International and Public Affairs and an advanced certificate from the Harriman Institute, Columbia University.

Introduction

Introduction

Pamela Kilpadi

What makes this volume unique is the fact that its authors have not only spent many years conducting field research investigating the issues presented, but that throughout this time they have participated actively in the democratization of their transforming societies. As representatives of a new generation of open society leaders, their policy perspectives benefit from a uniquely 'inside out' rather than the usual 'outside in' orientation found in most English-language information about their communities. The results are illuminating.

The authors live and work primarily in what has come to be known as Wider Europe—an area loosely referring to Europe's eastern and southern neighbors, or perhaps all of geographical Europe beyond the borders of the recently enlarged European Union. Like the concept of Europe itself, Wider Europe lacks a commonly understood definition, not to mention a common identity.

In its articulation of EU values and the conceivable limits of the Union's borders, the European Commission avoids drawing attention to the fact that its eastern neighbors are largely Orthodox Christian and its southern neighbors largely Muslim, not to mention the fact that the EU's Mediterranean neighbors have served time as European colonies. The new Russia—once an imperial and later Cold War threat to Western European powers—is now an acknowledged player in EU affairs.

While such delicate diplomacy is perhaps advisable on the part of European politicians, ignorance about the political abuse of religion in the context of nation and empire building has long clouded understanding between the West and its eastern and southern neighbors. "For many Americans, for many Westerners, and for many policymakers, the experience of political Islam caught them completely off guard. Most development theories never foresaw anything like it: not only Islamic resurgence, but also what is taking place globally today—a religious resurgence manifesting itself fairly consistently across the world in terms of religion and nationalism, religion and ethnicity," Georgetown University professor and the founding director of the Center for Muslim-Christian Understanding John L. Esposito noted ten years ago.

"Even for many Middle East experts, the study of Islam was not seen as anything you do very seriously... In a context in which there is relative ignorance, we got a number of headline events... If you are an American policymaker and your experience with political Islam is Americans held hostage during the Iranian Revolution, the slaying of Anwar Sadat, and hijackings, if you are living behind barbed wire embassies, how are you going to feel about this thing called Islam? What if you were there when the World Trade Center blew up? The understanding of "Islamic fundamentalism" or political Islam was mediated through headline events… The demonization of Iran in America is second only to the demonization of America in Iran."[1]

Despite increasing global awareness about the abuse of religion to justify repression, these words from 1996 eerily echo today's reality. This would not have surprised renowned Palestinian American scholar Edward Said, whose work so eloquently demonstrated how the reproduction of prejudices and stereotypes in the western media and the academic discipline of Middle Eastern studies called "Orientalism" helped sustain Western imperial hegemony over the Middle East. The all-too-familiar western construction of Islam and the Orient from a perspective that takes Europe as the norm is also described and lamented by the contributors to this volume, especially those in Russia.

Islam and Tolerance in Wider Europe attempts to illuminate the complex interplay between religion, nationalism and expansionism in an increasingly globalized world, as revealed by a new generation of open society leaders working to build a more tolerant Europe. Each chapter—focusing on Western Europe, the Caucasus, Russia, Turkey, Central Europe, and the Balkans—includes several essays by authors involved in the dynamic policymaking processes transforming their respective countries. Taken as a whole, the compilation offers insightful insider stories and comparisons across countries and regions.

The chapters are not arranged in any particular geographical order, but rather begin with the European Union—the current continental agenda-setter—and roughly follow a path through those regions of Wider Europe that are perhaps most characterized by interfaith and interethnic tension, through areas with relatively less tension (but perhaps as much if not more misunderstanding), and ending with some lessons from a region torn apart by multiple conflicts. In an attempt to do justice to years of evidence-gathering, extensive references are included for essays incorporating new investigatory research on controversial issues.

In the first chapter on Europe's transforming identity, Centre for European Policy Studies fellow and former EU Ambassador to Russia Michael Emerson explores whether the EU can claim a common set of values that distinguish the Union from other global powers. The remaining two essays in this section then investigate whether the EU is succeeding in upholding these values, especially as regards the Muslim communities and migrants under its jurisdiction. It is exceedingly difficult to demand adherence to common values from non-EU neighbors aspiring to join the club when current EU members are failing to meet club criteria. As regards the treatment of its Muslims, the EU appears to be largely failing its own tests.

The second chapter on ethnic (and religious) relations in the Caucasus highlights the continued legacy and impact of Russian colonial expansion in this volatile region. A first-hand account of the Beslan primary school hostage-taking that claimed the lives

---

[1]   Esposito, John L. "Political Islam and U.S. Foreign Policy," *The Fletcher Forum of World Affairs*, Vol. 20:2, Summer/Fall 1996, pp.119–132.

of over 300 people including nearly 200 children explains how this tragic event—in reality linked to the war in Chechnya—was incorrectly associated with a local territorial dispute, leading to the persecution of Ingush Muslims. The essay describes how Russian colonization has created stable patterns of relations between 'reliable' Orthodox Christian empire-builders and often 'unreliable' Muslim communities in the Imperial and later Soviet states. This and subsequent essays, which cover Georgia as well, emphasize that the creation of artificial borders shifting long-established interethnic power balances (such as the division of Chechnya and Ingushetia) contributed to outbreaks of violence. Dispelling myths of collective guilt and restoring a more equitable distribution of political and economic resources, therefore, will go a long way toward easing tensions among Caucasus communities.

In the third chapter, political ideology and religious tolerance in Russia is explored at a time when Russia appears to be re-exerting its 'near abroad' influence. The first essay asserts that the Russian Orthodox Church has somewhat paradoxically become the torch-bearer of Russia's Communist legacy, subsuming the role of the former Communist Party in the monopolization of an often xenophobic 'purely Russian' popular ideology that attempts to shut out all 'nontraditional,' 'alien' religions. Apparently, as the influence on U.S. policymakers of both the 'war on terror' and the Christian right agenda grows, so does the convenient cooperation between Russian policymakers and Church hierarchs. Subsequent studies, including one which involved the first public discussion and cooperative initiative ever organized between journalists and Muslim leaders in the Russian Republic of Tatarstan, examine how Moscow's political rhetoric and influence play out on the ground in Russian republics as well as the Russian-influenced secessionist entities of Georgia and Moldova.

The fourth chapter on political identity and human rights in Turkey investigates the journey taken by Turkey's religious and political elite away from an anti-western Islamic identity toward a pro-EU secular identity striving to adopt European values and join Europe. The need to rethink and revitalize approaches to promoting human rights and civil society within Muslim societies is also addressed by the studies in this chapter, portraying a quite optimistic picture about the possibilities for positive and peaceful political and social transformation in some predominantly Muslim countries.

Islam and policy in Central Europe is the focus of the fifth chapter. Although not technically within the confines of Wider Europe, East Central Europe is nevertheless still considered by many Western Europeans as a bloc of "new" European or even Eastern neighbor countries. With the exception of largely urbanized and Europeanized Muslims from the Balkans, the majority of Central Europeans have had relatively little exposure to more traditional Muslim communities. The fear of unknown Muslim traditions and practices is common in the region, as illustrated in the essays by sometimes irrational opposition to public projects associated with Islam and Muslims, such as the construction of mosques.

The sixth and final chapter examines lessons from the post-war Balkans—a region exhausted by the political manipulation of religious and ethnic tensions which ripped the former Yugoslavia apart in a series of bloody battles in recent decades. The region's wounds are slowly healing, with the post-war ethnically divided societies host to multiple international experiments in the promotion of tolerance. A key lesson that runs through many of the essays harkens back to findings from the Caucasus, which show that more equitable political representation among ethnicities as well as distribution of economic resources will pave the road toward lasting peace.

The authors of this volume are fellows and colleagues of the International Policy Fellowships program—an initiative of the Open Society Institute that has attempted to combat 'brain drain' while at the same time developing policy research capacities, initially in emerging democracies of the former Soviet sphere where concepts such as 'policy' and 'fellowship' often remain virtually untranslatable. Since its establishment in 1998, some 250 of its most active alumni and current fellows have grown into a working network of open society leaders spanning more than 40 countries on nearly every continent.

Now nurtured by a variety of local and international donors as well as Soros programs and foundations, the new network of open society policy researchers has grown in influence, with alumni fellows launching their own research institutes and national policy fellowships. According to the results of a recently completed multi-year impact evaluation by the Global Development Network's Bridging Research and Policy Project (available at www.gdnet.org), by contributing new, locally interpreted and "owned" knowledge to the "knowledge value collective," the International Policy Fellows encourage reforms within their country and organizational contexts, which is beneficial to their societies as well as their own performance as researchers.

In their search for new knowledge, fellows have demonstrated that the more we strive to view the world from other perspectives, the more we succeed in finding solutions to common problems. The lesson for good governance is that the more states open their policymaking processes to critical and minority opinions, the better their chances of ensuring the security and prosperity of their societies.

Nevertheless, open society has its enemies. Following a brief period of post-Cold War openness, Russian and other former Soviet and Eastern European officials have begun cracking down on civil society. At times bolstered by an increase in oil prices and a decline in western moral authority following the war in Iraq, authoritarian leaders around the world are flexing their muscles, and even winning approval on occasion via the ballot box.

As a consequence, in addition to thanking those listed in this volume for both their editorial and intellectual insights, I wish to extend special thanks to those colleagues who cannot be named in these pages.

part one

Europe's Transforming Identity

What Values for Europe?

Michael Emerson

T his is not to compete with Moses, whose Ten Commandments addressed the domain of personal morality and have earned the respect of Christians and Muslims alike. Here the concern is for the values and system of the European public domain. Nor does the present contribution claim originality, since it is based on the content of the draft European Constitution.[1] But the European Union would do well to follow the example of the universally honored prophet in offering a clear, concise presentation of message. The Constitution was meant to do this, but its ten commandments are to be found literally all over the place in the 481-page draft, which is indeed more of a bible, open to various interpretations. To be carved into a tablet of stone, brevity is required.

The Ten Commandments of the European Union

The ten commandments set out herewith are an entirely Euro-centric personal attempt to capture what currently seem to be the values and ideals of the European Union. This of course does not imply that the system of EU values is better than others, simply that these values are all either explicit or implicit somewhere in the draft Constitution.

The European Union considers itself to be values-based and driven. Undoubtedly the dominant gravitational force on the European continent, the EU has quite surprisingly become the world's most powerful magnet, with strict conditions for membership based on values that have transformed the periphery in line with the model of the center. Former communist states in Central and Eastern Europe have looked to the EU as the fastest and surest way of achieving the transition into the modern world of liberal democracy and open society. Yet the EU draft Constitution was rejected in the May 2005 referenda in France and the Netherlands. The negotiation of the draft by an impressive constituent assembly was still a major achievement, and its rejection in the referenda was for a host of reasons. But were some of these reasons signaling rejection of some of the proclaimed values? To this we return later.

Michael Emerson, IPF Group Advisor for the Wider Europe working group, is Senior Research Fellow at the Centre for European Policy Studies (CEPS) in Brussels. From 1991–1996 he served as European Union Ambassador to Russia.

The draft Constitution devoted its Article 1–2 explicitly to 'The Union's Values.' But this turns out in any case to be a disappointing text, with a whole dictionary of words, as follows:

> *The Union is founded on the values of respect for human dignity, freedom, democracy, equality, the rule of law and respect for human rights, including the rights of persons belonging to minorities. These values are common to the Member States in a society in which pluralism, non-discrimination, tolerance, justice, solidarity and equality between men and women prevail.*

Values of the EU vis-à-vis the other global powers

Let us go through the draft Constitution articles briefly, one by one, and consider how the other global actors—the United States, Russia and China—rank by the same value-based criteria. This could be a guide to the possibilities for harmonious foreign policy, or to the difficulties that will have to be managed.

The Preamble to the draft Constitution starts by clearly marking out commandment 1 about *democracy, human rights and the rule of law*. Here the US is on the same page. Russia, as Council of Europe member, should also be on the same page, but in practice it is currently de-democratizing and performing poorly on the rule of law. China makes no pretence to being a Western democracy.

The four freedoms of movement (commandment 2), are provided under Article III-130 of the draft Constitution. The US is on the same page again. Russia and China would say the same, but in Russia there remain some residual restrictions—such as the *propiska* system of residence registration—on the freedom to choose where to reside.

Social cohesion, whether it be economic, social and territorial (commandment 3), can be pulled out of Article 1–3. The US, Russia and China would all say they provide for social cohesion. The US certainly has a more austere regime of social security and higher interpersonal inequality, but would argue that the EU on the other hand has an unsustainably heavy system, and will therefore converge more toward that of the US in due course. Russia's system of social security, be it at

THOU SHALT BE
TRULY DEMOCRATIC
AND RESPECTFUL OF HUMAN
RIGHTS AND THE RULE OF LAW

THOU SHALT GUARANTEE
THE FOUR FREEDOMS OF
MOVEMENT (GOODS, SERVICES,
CAPITAL, LABOR)

THOU SHALT PROVIDE
FOR SOCIAL COHESION
BETWEEN PEOPLE, REGIONS
AND STATES

THOU SHALT ENSURE
SUSTAINABLE ECONOMIC
DEVELOPMENT FOR THE
BENEFIT OF FUTURE
GENERATIONS

THOU SHALT REJECT
NATIONALISM AND FAVOR
THE MULTIPLE IDENTITY
OF CITIZENS

the interpersonal or interregional levels, is in a state of virtual ruin. For China the phenomenal rate of economic growth is the mechanism for lifting people out of poverty.

Sustainable economic development for the benefit of future generations (commandment 4) comes from Article 1–3. In practice the Kyoto protocol represents the EU's leading contribution for trying to save the world from global warming. Russia has signed on to this. But the US has famously rejected it, while continuing to be world's most extravagant CO_2 polluter. China cites the need for economic catch-up as the reason not to join Kyoto at present.

The abhorrence of nationalism (commandment 5) is implicit in the Preamble of the draft Constitution, where it emphasizes the need to overcome bitter experiences of the past and look forward to a common destiny while remaining proud of national identities. This is reinforced in Article 1–2 which underlines tolerance, non-discrimination and pluralism; and in Article 1–10 which is explicit about citizenship of the Union complementing national citizenship. Nationalism becomes worrying when it invokes patriotism to the point of justifying intolerant discrimination at home and threatening policies abroad. Post-9/11, the patriotic political discourse in the US has registered a distinctly nationalistic tone, but this is quite mild compared to Russian or Chinese nationalistic discourse.

Multi-tier governance (commandment 6) is explicit in Title III with its detailed provisions governing the distribution of competences between EU and member states—

between the exclusive competences of the Union, shared competences and those where the Union is only providing coordinating or complementary action. This is reinforced in Article 1–11, which enunciates the principle of subsidiarity. The US is, for its part, one of the classic federal democracies. Russia, on the other hand, is currently de-federalizing, as part of its de-democratizing tendency. China can be considered as tending toward an asymmetric federation, with a variety of regimes, from the extreme case of Hong Kong to the substantial degree of autonomy of many provinces.

Secular governance and multiculturalism (commandment 7) seem to flow from the reference to pluralism in Article 1–2, elaborated in the preamble and inspired by the cultural, religious and humanist inheritance of Europe. The debate during

THOU SHALT ASSURE FEDERATIVE MULTI-TIER GOVERNANCE

THOU SHALT ASSURE SECULAR GOVERNANCE AND FAVOR MULTICULTURAL PLURALISM IN SOCIETY

THOU SHALT PROMOTE MULTILATERAL ORDER IN INTERNATIONAL AFFAIRS

THOU SHALT ABSTAIN FROM THREATENING OR USING FORCE AGAINST OTHERS WITHOUT JUST CAUSE

THOU SHALT BE OPEN, INCLUSIVE AND INTEGRATIVE TOWARD NEIGHBORS THAT ADHERE TO THE ABOVE the Convention was far more explicit, with serious tensions over whether there should be references to God or Christianity. The Pope himself intervened, strongly supported by several devoutly Catholic states, including Poland. However the weight of opinion in favor of uncompromisingly secular governance and not referring to just one religion prevailed. Turkey's candidature will be the real test, with ominous indications from leading politicians in Germany, France and Austria that would exclude Turkey from full membership. Meanwhile the ethno-religious violence of 2005, from suicide bombings in London to the burning banlieues of Paris, convince most Europeans that they must try harder to make a success of multiculturalism. Everyone except far-right sympathizers understand that the immigrant communities will never return home. The US is arguably succeeding better at multiculturalism than the EU, but its secularism is slightly colored by the apparent political influence of Christian evangelist movements. Russia is certainly secular and substantially multicultural, but the relative harmony between mainstream Russia and the Volga Muslim communities stands in contrast to the deepening conflicts and ungovernability of the Northern Caucasus. China is officially secular and multicultural, but Tibet exemplifies authoritarian rather than democratic multiculturalism.

> **Europeans must try harder to make a success of multiculturalism. Everyone except far-right sympathizers understand that the immigrant communities will never return home.**

Multilateralism (commandment 8) is explicitly endorsed by the European Security Strategy adopted in 2003/4, while the Constitution in Article I–3 commits to the strict observance and development of international law. The US is clearly resistant to any multilateral legal encroachments on the sovereignty of Congress. Russia's idea of the multilateral order is strongly related to its role as permanent member of the UN Security Council, giving its exceptional diplomatic leverage to require consensus on given issues. Yet Russia's role in the OSCE and Council of Europe reveals its disinterest in values-based multilateralism. China's position is similar to that of Russia.

Commandment 9 about *the use of force* is not explicit in the texts. There is a normatively neutral remark in the European Security Strategy: "we need to develop a strategic culture that fosters early, rapid and when necessary robust intervention." But it is evident enough that the EU collectively would not achieve consensus to go to war without an indubitably just cause. Individual member states may be more willing to go to war where the justness of the cause may be more controversial, as Iraq has shown, but at the EU level the requirements of consensus to undertake forceful action will continue to be very strenuous. As for the US, the post-9/11 environment has seen a revision of security strategy in the direction legitimizing preemptive action, justified by the proliferation of weapons of mass destruction combined with the new hyper-terrorism. However the Iraq war was highly contested according to 'just cause' criteria. Russia has shown a continuing inclination toward unprincipled pressurizing behavior with its former Soviet Union neighbors, but without threatening war. China openly threatens to use military force to take Taiwan, which the West does not consider to be a just cause.

An inclusive and integrative European Union (commandment 10) follows from Article 1–58 of the Constitution, stating that the Union shall be open to all European states which respect its values. In addition Article 1–57 envisages special relationships with neighboring countries. Even if the EU's further enlargement is now on slow or stop, its new efforts to develop a neighborhood policy is fashioned as a mechanism for extending the EU's values. The US, on the other hand, does not have the same possibilities to integrate its neighborhood, apparently because its political structure and own demos is too strongly formed to make the progressive integration of its neighborhood feasible for either party. Russia wishes to reintegrate the former Soviet space to the maximum extent, but lacks normative political attractiveness at least to its European CIS neighbors to do this, as recent developments in Ukraine have shown. China develops a Greater China concept in east and southeast Asia, but since China is not democratic it had to find alternative methods to promote bottom up rather than top down integration through deepening trade, investment and personal relations between mainland China and the Chinese diasporas in the region.

What values for Europe?

What picture do we have then of EU values compared to those of the US, Russia and China? A simple count shows the US sharing 6 out of 10 EU values. Russia's showing is very bleak, with unqualified commitment to hardly any of the commandments. China is more convincing on a few accounts. But does the EU live up to all the ten commandments itself? On two accounts—multiculturalism and openness for further enlargement—there are now some doubts, to say the least.

Of course this has so far been an utterly Euro-centric approach to matters that are to a degree only subjective perceptions, and the rest of the world can indeed claim that they have indeed a different value system, without that meaning a lesser one. This is a question that we must now dwell on.

The US parts company with the EU on four accounts: lesser commitment to multilateralism in general and to sustainable development, a greater preparedness to use force, and a lack of an integrative regime for including the neighbors. The US can certainly and does make the argument that its lesser multilateralism is just a reflection of the impracticability of much of the UN system, with its membership crowded with so many weak states. It also argues that its greater preparedness to go to war is no more than facing up to the world's actual security challenges, which the EU runs away from. Finally the US can point out that lack of an integrative regime is hardly a lack of values, but just a structural political fact. Together these arguments can be a rebuttal to European sermonizing about their superior value system.

That is not an end to the story, however, since the question remains: **Which system is going to attract more support in the world?** Whose is the closest to what may

> It is not clear whether the US has any new instruments of leverage on authoritarian Arab regimes or Putin's Russia. Nevertheless an EU and US 'good cop, bad cop' act can indeed work, as long as both cops are working from the same rule book.

become the global reference model? The US weaknesses, according to our Euro-centric reference, are part of the explanation why the US's international reputation as global actor has suffered serious damage under President Bush. Polls show this clearly, and the US is obviously uncomfortable with it. The message of the second Bush administration appears to be softening the anti-multilateralism at least in diplomatic tone. Whether the Iraq war has surely stiffened domestic political resistances to embarking on risky wars is not yet known, and as of now it is also unclear whether the military option as a possible ultimate response to the growing Iran crisis is on the table. The other side of this coin is the evident success of EU integrative policies in achieving the democratic transformation of the former communist states of Central and Eastern Europe. President Bush makes striking speeches about the cause of global democracy, but it is much less clear what the instruments are to be. The war in Iraq has been too costly and uncertain in its consequences to be presented as a model. Elsewhere it is not clear whether the US has any new instruments of leverage on authoritarian Arab regimes or Putin's Russia. Nonetheless the combination of the very different strengths and slightly different values of the EU and US can be seen as complementary assets. A 'good cop, bad cop' act can indeed work in practice, as long as both the cops are working from the same rule book.

Which system is going to attract more support in the world? Are the EU's set of values gaining increasing weight and recognition as a pre-eminent global reference?

The very poor Russian performance according to the EU system of values poses a different question, namely whether the present Russian political regime is sustainable alongside that of the EU. Russian political discourse is all about the pursuit of Russian national interest, rather than 'obeying the West' as they say happened in the early post-Soviet years. Maybe Russia can conceivably turn in on itself for some years at least, just selling gas to the EU, and buying consumer goods and holidays in the sun in exchange. But there is also the question whether Russia's current foreign policy priority, to secure reconsolidation of the post-Soviet space, is sustainable. In recent years, Russia's diplomacy has lost one goal after another, as clumsy pressurization of its neighbors drives these states even faster in a West European direction. Russia may choose for the time being a very different values system for its 'near abroad' foreign policy, based on a restrained realpolitik. It is restrained in the sense that no-one expects Russia to invade Ukraine or Moldova to get the leaderships it prefers. Yet the combination of clumsy realpolitik without a credible threat of invasion is a sure loser. Since the neighbors know that they will not be invaded, the pressurization only pushes them away even faster. Russia's choice of a divergent value system in its near abroad policy, compared to that of the EU, is working contrary to its declared national interest.

These considerations bring us back to the question whether the EU's set of values—the ten commandments—is just the preference of one region of the world. Or is it more than a parochial West European affair, gaining increasing weight and recognition as a pre-eminent global reference? At least this proposition is now being discussed.

Note

[1] The draft Constitution has been ratified by about half the member states, but rejected in referenda in France and the Netherlands in May 2005, and therefore not adopted. However for the purpose of this article the draft Constitution, prepared by a lengthy Convention of political representatives, is taken as giving indications of European values.

The Role of Islam in Europe: Multiple Crises?

Amel Boubekeur and Samir Amghar

A car is blazing after it was set alight by rioters in the La Reynerie housing complex in the Mirail district of Toulouse, southwestern France. ▪ Remy Gabalda, AP

Over time, virtually all social problems involving European Muslim communities have been reconceptualized within the framework of Islam as a crisis phenomenon. Questions of Muslim political and social integration have become inextricably tied to the 'Islam crisis.' Traditional ideas of a 'clash of civilizations' and the consequent need for intercultural policies to prevent crises involving Islam have dominated recent public debates surrounding the headscarf, French rioting, and cartoon controversies. European policymakers engaging in these debates are finding it difficult to agree on whether Europe's Muslim citizens should be defined as minorities, immigrants, or new Europeans.

The contemporary history of Muslims in Europe extends over 50 years. Until the early 1980s when a new generation of young Muslims born in Europe began rising to prominence, their presence was not particularly visible and European public policies tended to categorize them as temporary immigrants. Policies intended to curb discrimination and unemployment and respond to social discontent and rioting were elaborated along ethnic lines (in particular French migration and social policies affecting the 'beur' children of immigrant parents from North Africa), sparking social discontent and rioting. Beginning in the 1990s, public discourse increasingly identified Islam as a major part of the problem. Developments including the terrorist attacks in Europe (Paris,

Amel Boubekeur is a Research Fellow at the Centre for European Policy Studies (CEPS) in Brussels and a sociologist studying the contemporary transformations of Islamism in the West (Europe/USA). Her current research focuses on the new Islamic elite, Muslim women leadership, and political Islam. She is the author of *Le Voile de la Mariee. Jeunes musulmanes, voile et projet matrimonial en France.* **Samir Amghar** is a sociologist at the Ecole des Hautes Etudes en Sciences Sociales (EHESS) in Paris, studying the radicalization of young European Muslims. He has edited the *Islamismes d'Occident*.

Madrid, London), Rushdie controversy in the United Kingdom, process of the 're-Islamization' of young people born in Europe, questions about the separation of religion and poli-tics (laïcité), struggles against anti-Semitism, and even concerns about delinquency in poor districts predominantly inhabited by Muslims reinforced the view that a new phenomenon—a 'crisis of Islam'—called for drastic policy prescriptions.

These 'multiple Islam crises' and controversies are reflections of the existing gap between Europe's policy elite and Muslims citizens living on the social periphery. The apparent failure of 30 years of European social policies to integrate Muslims is directly related to the lack of Muslim political participation in European affairs at both national and local levels on issues other than security and terrorism. Although the radicalization of Islam is an important and urgent issue, the policy relevant concerns of most Muslims in Europe instead involve day-to-day problems of Islamophobia; worship management; and social, cultural and political exclusion—problems that tend to be ignored or poorly articulated at the policy level.

To better understand the real role of Islam in European social crises, it is necessary to examine both its European roots and external influences of Muslim countries. Any balanced analysis should also question whether the ghettoization of Muslim communities, or their *communautarisme,* often seen as a basis for radical Islam, actually leads to political radicalization and violence.

> The apparent failure of 30 years of European social policies to integrate Muslims is directly related to the lack of Muslim political participation. Muslims in Europe are most concerned with day-to-day problems of exclusion that tend to be ignored at the policy level.

The external influence

Islam is now considered a European religion. Crises involving Muslim populations in Europe are often blamed on influences from 'foreign' Islam, with blame most often assigned to two types of external phenomena.

First is what has been called 'consular' Islam. During the 1970s and 1980s, the first Muslim immigrants to Europe (mainly from Algeria, Morocco and Turkey) effectively organized worship, mosques finances, imam activities, and Koranic teaching through their countries' consulates. The consulates were intent on diffusing Muslim protests or crises in Europe carried out in the name of Islam.

More recently a second phenomenon —transnational or 'foreign' Islamic movements—have begun to compete for control over Muslims in Europe. These include the Tabligh from Pakistan, the Salafi movement from Saudi Arabia, and the Muslim

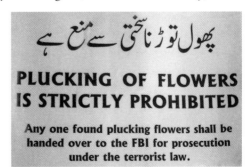

PLUCKING OF FLOWERS IS STRICTLY PROHIBITED

Any one found plucking flowers shall be handed over to the FBI for prosecution under the terrorist law.

Sign greeting visitors at a hill station guest house in Pakistan's North-West Frontier Province near Kashmir. The Urdu translation: "It is strictly forbidden to pick the flowers" ▪ Pamela Kilpadi, IPF

Brotherhood organized by an Islamist elite in exile from Middle Eastern and North African countries.

'Consular Islam' and these 'imported' groups employ various means in their attempts to influence the ideological and normative landscape of Islam in Europe. During the 2003 elections to establish the French council of Muslim worship organized by conservative French politician Nicolas Sarkozy, for example, Moroccan and Algerian consulates in France tried to influence the voting process. The goal was to secure a kind of national political majority among Muslim leaders from these countries via the elections. The Turkish diaspora has played an important role in advocating for Turkey's accession to Europe. After fatwas were issued related to the Iraqi and Israeli-Palestinian conflict from Youssouf Qaradawi (an Egyptian-Qatari theologian with the Muslim Brotherhood movement), many European Muslims chose to oppose to the war by boycotting Israeli and American products. Foreign violent videos advocating for religious war (jihad), foreign fighter narratives, and websites from the Middle East also target young European Muslims.

Nevertheless the European roots of these crises are also crucial, since a small minority of Muslims in Europe resort to violence in response to what they perceive to be injustice directed against them via European policies. Such frustration is of course more often acted upon peacefully, as demonstrated by the decisions of more and more young Salafis to leave the Europe of their birth in search of a better life—and most importantly a 'bourgeois' standard of living which Europe failed to provide—in Saudi Arabia and other Gulf countries.

> **Movements promoting violence can serve as an outlet for disenfranchized and frustrated European Muslim youth seeking upward social mobility. While most vent their frustrations via peaceful means, a small number choose jihad.**

European responses to 'foreign' Islam

The incursion of 'foreign' Islamic discourse has led European policymakers to search for external solutions to European crises involving Islam. For example, in an attempt to fight radicalization, France, the United Kingdom, Germany, Austria and the Netherlands have launched expulsion campaigns against foreign imams to their countries of origin (Morocco, Algeria, Turkey). During the headscarf controversy, Nicolas Sarkozy traveled to the Al Azhar University in Egypt to obtain a fatwa from the Egyptian mufti Al Tantawi requiring girls to remove their veils at school. During the recent riots, French media described the "young Muslim" rioters as foreigners leading an "intifada des banlieues" with France becoming "Baghdad," while some US commentators asserted that France was paying the price for its pro-Arab policies. Such clichés only serve to further convince political actors in the Muslim world of the need to develop opportunities for influencing policymaking affecting Muslims in Europe. Following Sarkozy's Egyptian trip, Islamist movements led demonstrations against the veil law.

Experience has shown that Muslim religious leaders are not able to diffuse social crises or even adequately represent Muslims in Europe. Public debate surrounding the controversy over Islamophobic cartoons, for example, revealed that the views of Muslim religious leaders describing the cartoons as evidence of the West's hatred of Islam were not shared by European Muslims, who largely perceived the issue in terms of the need for equal respect for Muslims as European citizens. In fact, most European Muslims rally around European values in such cases. During the veil and cartoon controversies, European Muslims turned to their local judiciaries and the European Court of Human Rights in support of values of freedom of belief, muticulturalism, and even secularism. In the same spirit the French rioters, who were not mainly practicing Muslims but rather various groups sensitive to French Islamophobic attitudes, did not have clearly defined proposals because they were not contesting the French model of integration, but rather seeking its effective implementation.

Islamic religiosity, politics and violence

The religious factor is also relevant to the process of Muslim radicalization in times of crises. Three distinct groups of activist Muslims can be distinguished according to their views on the relationship between religion and politics: Muslims who develop a 'religious citizenship,' those who reject all non-Muslim political systems, and an ultra-radical minority that places jihadist Islam at the core of their political commitment.

For the first group, Islam is their starting point for a sense of citizenship and commitment to European society. Demonstrations against the veil law, for example, were for them a political negotiation emphasizing the need for citizens' participation to build a common society where Muslims act as a positive minority. They vote, engage in traditional secular political parties, and participate in European political events such as the referendum on the European Constitution, organized events related to globalization, etc. European Muslim leaders such as Tariq Ramadan contributed to the development of the concept of religious citizenship.

> During the veil and cartoon controversies European Muslims turned to the courts in support of European values of freedom of belief, multiculturalism and even secularism. French rioters were not contesting the French model of integration, but rather seeking its effective implementation.

We find the second group among Salafi and Tabligh disciples. Their conception of politics does not lead to violence, but rather a withdrawal from all political processes and institutions based on non-Muslim concepts. For them, commitment to a secular state is not relevant; they do not conceptualize themselves within the framework of a non-Muslim political system. Withdrawal is considered preferable to participation in light of their stigmatization as Muslims and their social exclusion as ethnic minorities and poor people. This group was not concerned by the demonstrations against the veil law or the publication of cartoon caricatures of the Prophet.

The last group is the jihadist one. Although they do not share any particular social status, they do share the experience of social decline and displacement. Their reasons for resorting to violence have more to do with painful personal experiences of social and political injustice as Muslims in Europe than belief in radical Islam. They trust that Islam will defend Muslims from European/Western threats against them. They place jihad at

> **We need to identify the common interests of European institutions and EU Member States so that European Muslims do not feel trapped in a tug-of-war while Europe struggles to discern its changing identity.**

the core of their religious beliefs and rely on violence as the only way to provide Muslims a voice in European policymaking. They believe that terrorist acts such as the London and Madrid attacks are the only way to successfully achieve certain political objectives such as the withdrawl of UK and Spanish troops from Iraq.

Integration rather than confrontation

The role of Islam in Europe's 'multiple crises' is as complex as the various Muslim communities living in Europe. To better address such crises we need to understand the common interests shared by European institutions and EU Member States. Currently these interests rarely converge, leaving European Muslims feeling trapped in a tug-of-war while Europe struggles to discern its changing identity. Muslim groups can be categorized according to their mode of political protest during European crises involving Islam, but they are extremely diverse. The single feature they have in common is their disappointment over European policies affecting their everyday lives in Europe.

More than ever, Europe has a role to play in rethinking what can be proposed to its Muslim citizens in terms of real political representation and participation rather than occasional solicitation. To minimize the likelihood of social crises, Europe needs to create and make visible an alternative and common public space that provides its Muslims with a voice just as it does its Christian and Jewish communities, especially concerning questions related to Islamophobia, inclusion, religious radicalization...

The strength of the foundations of a new Europe will depend upon the extent to which Muslims are allowed to participate in the construction of a new European identity.

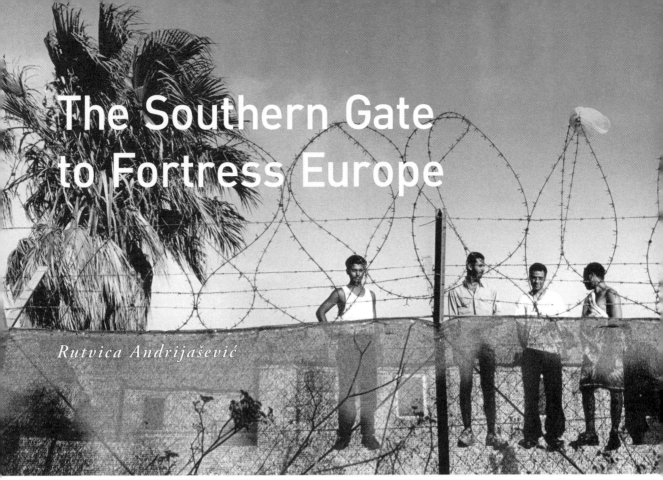

The Southern Gate to Fortress Europe

Rutvica Andrijašević

Migrants behind barbed wire at the 'holding center' on the southern Italian island of Lampedusa ▪ Matias Costa, Panos

I t is the last day of August 2005 and on the airport runway in Lampedusa, a small Italian island situated south of Sicily, yet another deportation of 'undocumented' migrants from Africa and the Middle East is taking place. Two planes parked approximately twenty meters away from each other are waiting for passengers. A group of tourists pours out of the airport building and strolls toward the Air One airplane, an Italian tourist carrier. The adjacent Air Adriatic plane, a private Croatian air company, is boarded by a group of passengers walking in fixed formation. Four police officers (one in back, one in front, and one on each side of the procession) wearing civilian clothes and large black protection gloves lead the group of ten migrants from the detention camp to the airplane. The plane is parked only fifteen meters or so away from the barbed wire that separates the runway from the camp. From the perspective of an informed observer, the ordinariness of the event exacerbates its violence.

Rutvica Andrijašević is an Economic and Social Research Council (ESRC) post-doctoral fellow at the Centre on Migration, Policy and Society (COMPAS), University of Oxford. Her 2004–6 research as an International Policy Fellow benefited from comments by Thierry Balzacq, Sergio Carrera and Elspeth Guild of the Centre for European Policy Studies (CEPS) in Brussels where the policy study was initially drafted, as well as Julia Harrington of the Open Society Institute Justice Initiative. Further information about her research is available from the IPF websites: http://pdc.ceu.hu (Source IPF) and www.policy.hu/andrijasevic.

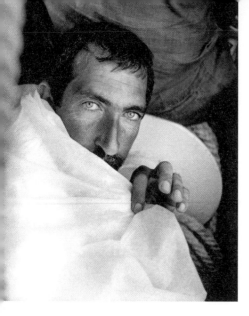

No information is available concerning the whereabouts of migrants and asylum seekers expelled from Lampedusa to Libya. Human Rights Watch believes that the majority are detained in Libyan detention camps, where migrants and asylum seekers in particular are often the victims of arbitrary detention, inexistent or unfair trials, killings, disappearances and torture ▪ Matias Costa, Panos

Seven groups of ten men are led to the plane. The migrants boarding the plane are all dressed the same: they wear dark blue sports trousers with a matching jacket and carry a white plastic shopping bag. Behind the barbed wire there are several hundred migrants seated in small groups on the soil. When the plane takes off most of them are on their feet, waving.

Earlier the same day another group of migrants is escorted by police from the detention center to the port just down the hill and transferred by a ferry operated by a company called Siremar, first to Porto Empedocle and then on to the detention center in the Southern Italian town of Crotone. This time, following a rigorous 20-minute march from the camp, the migrants were made to sit on the ground behind a large van while tourists boarded the ferry and enjoyed their last unperturbed glimpse of the town of Lampedusa. Dressed in the usual dark blue sport outfits and carrying white plastic bags, the migrants were transferred from the pier to an isolated space in the lower part of the ferry, while police blocked access to the port and prohibited any filming or photographing.

Between Libya and Sicily: The criminalization of migration

Positioned some two hundred kilometers south of Sicily and three hundred kilometers north of Libya, in 2004 the island of Lampedusa became the main point of arrival for boats carrying undocumented migrants and asylum seekers from Libya to Italy. The 'temporary stay and assistance center' (CPTA) in Lampedusa is one of eleven existing migration holding centers, most of which are located in the south of Italy. Migrants typically depart from Libya in overcrowded, makeshift boats and undertake the perilous sea journey which can last up to several weeks. Once in the Italian waters near Lampedusa, the boats are intercepted by Italian border guards and migrants are transferred to the Lampedusa holding center. After staying in the center for a period that usually varies between five and forty-five days, the majority of migrants are transferred to CPTAs in Sicily or southern Italy and others are expelled to Libya.

The Italian-Libyan partnership agreement initially signed in 2000 to fight terrorism, organized crime and illegal migration was extended in 2003 and 2004 to include a migration readmission agreement, training for Libyan police officers and border guards, and Italian-funded detention and repatriation programs for irregular migrants in Libya. The aim of these schemes is to deter irregular migration and prevent further migrant deaths at sea by combating smuggling networks. Paradoxically, research described here suggests that these policies may actually 'illegalize' the movement of certain groups of migrants, thereby increasing rather than decreasing the involvement of smuggling networks in human trafficking.

Due to pressure from the Italian government, the European Union (EU) lifted the arms embargo on Libya on October 11, 2004, allowing Libya to purchase (from Italy) technological surveillance equipment and speedboats, and run training programs initiated by Italian policemen. Only recently it has emerged (following the European Commission's report on its technical mission to Libya in December 2004) that Italy is moreover financing the construction of three detention camps in Libya as well as the deportations of 'irregular' migrants from Libya further to Sub-Saharan Africa and Egypt.[1] The deportation from Italy to detention camps in Libya followed the signing in August 2004 of an agreement between the two countries on combating illegal migration into the EU. Despite repeated European Parliament, UN Human Rights Committee, and NGO requests to make the agreement public, its contents continue to remain undisclosed.

In 2004, a total of 10,497 migrants, including 412 minors and 309 women, transited through the Lampedusa CPTA.[2] No official data is available on the Lampedusa migrants' countries of origin or reasons for migrating. While the United Nations High Commissioner for Refugees (UNHCR) points to the presence of refugees and asylum seekers fleeing persecution among those detained at Lampedusa as well as among those expelled to Libya, the Lampedusa authorities refer to those held at their center as 'illegal migrants' and claim that there are virtually no asylum seekers present among migrants who depart from Libya. The authorities also assert that the majority of third-country nationals at the center are economic migrants of Egyptian nationality.[3] However, data gathered at Lampedusa by Médecins sans Frontières and the Italian nongovernmental organization ARCI identifies the migrants' primary regions of origin to be the Middle East (Iraq and Palestine), Maghreb (namely from Morocco, Tunisia and Algeria), Horn of Africa (including Sudan), and Sub-Saharan Africa.[4] Despite the continuity of migratory flows from North Africa to the south of Italy since the end of the 1990s, more consistent data on migrants' countries of origin and the nature of their journeys remains unavailable.

The Italian navy arrests a group of migrants after intercepting their boat off Lampedusa ▪ Matias Costa, Panos

The detentions and deportations at Lampedusa came to the attention of the wider public in early October 2004, when more than one thousand 'irregular' migrants were expelled to Libya on military and civilian airplanes. These collective deportations occurred in a highly charged political atmosphere surrounding the proposal advanced by German Minister of Interior Otto Schily and Italian Minister Giuseppe Pisanu to establish refugee processing centers in North Africa. Apparently, Germany, Italy and the United Kingdom backed the project, while France and Spain were opposed. The proposal—initially put forward by the UK and rejected during the 2003 Thessaloniki Summit—envisioned the establishment of 'regional protection zones' and 'transit processing centers' located outside the external borders of the European Union.[5] Under this proposal, asylum-seekers and refugees would submit their EU asylum claims and wait in these centers until their applications were processed.[6] Even though the proposal for 'processing centers' was rejected by France, Spain and Sweden in October 2004, the EU informal Justice and Home Affairs Council considered five pilot projects proposed by the European Commission (EC) and co-funded by the Netherlands. These projects aim to upgrade existing 'processing' facilities and develop asylum laws in Algeria, Libya, Mauritania, Morocco and Tunisia.[7]

European governments in support of such schemes consider expulsions to Libya a necessary measure to counter 'the emergency' represented by the influx of boat-people from Libya and the urgent need to deter 'a million' waiting in Libya from reaching Italian shores.[8] The European Commission claims that detention and deportation are indispensable measures for countering undocumented migration and ensuring a credible and effective Europe-wide immigration policy.

Available research and analysis raise serious doubts about the validity of these claims, however. Existing data shows that the majority of irregular migrants have entered Italy with a valid visa and become undocumented only after the visa expired or after they overstayed their residence permit. Only 10 percent of undocumented migrants currently residing in Italy entered the country 'illegally' by sea.[9] Furthermore, Libya's migrant population is made up primarily of labor migrants from neighboring African countries who have played a key role in Libya's informal economy for several decades, while irregular migrants who transit through Libya on their way to Europe represent only a small segment of the country's migrant population. In other words, reducing Libya's current migratory patterns to an unprecedented surge of 'illegal' migration is erroneous and misleading (Pliez 2005). The use of terms by European politicians such as 'the emergency' recap the fantasy of 'the invasion' of Eastern Europeans into Western Europe following the fall of the Berlin Wall—now commonly referred to as 'the invasion that never happened.'

Libya's migratory reality is far from being, as suggested by the image of 'a million illegal migrants' sailing to Europe from Libyan shores, a country of emigration or a transit route for clandestine migrants from Sub-Saharan Africa to Italy. On the contrary, Libya is primarily a country of destination and immigration for the Maghreb (the region of Africa north of the Sahara desert and west of the Nile). Foreign nationals constitute approximately 25 to 30 percent of Libya's total population. Large-scale economic and social development schemes in the 1970s, launched thanks to petroleum industry

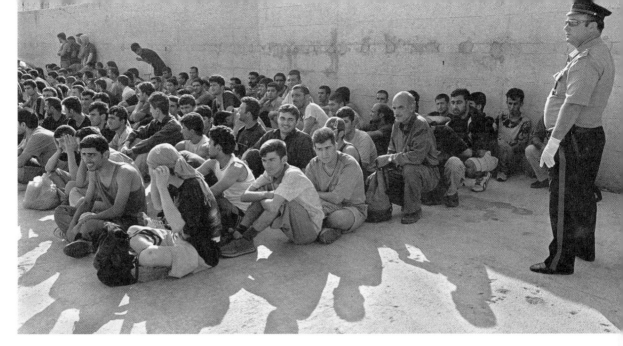

NGOs claim that the signing of the bilateral agreement between Libya and Italy in August 2004 led to widespread arrests in Libya of individuals from sub-Saharan Africa and the death of 106 migrants during subsequent repatriations from Libya to Niger ▪ Matias Costa, Panos

revenues, relied in the first instance on migrant laborers from Egypt. Egyptian nationals, employed mainly in the agriculture industry and education, constitute the largest migrant group in Libya today.[10]

Libya is home also to a large Maghrebi community from Morocco, Tunisia and Algeria,[11] and the country's economic development relies on cheap and seasonal labor from the neighboring Niger, Chad and Sudan.[12] The influx of migrant workers from sub-Saharan states is prompted by Libya's reorientation away from pan-Arab and toward pro-African policies[13] and its active role in the foundation of the Community of Sahel-Saharan states (CEN-SAD), an economic project aimed at greater regional cooperation and integration via the free circulation of people and goods between member states.[14] Migrant workers from Sudan, Chad and Niger, facilitated by Libya's open border policy towards sub-Saharan Africa, are generally temporary and pendular laborers working in sectors such as agriculture, tourism and local trade rather than, as commonly assumed, the source of irregular migratory movement to Europe.[15]

Nevertheless, stoking the public's fear of an immigrant invasion serves Italy's political interests. Under discussion since 2002, Italy has failed to pass an organic law on the right to asylum along with most other European states, and is especially reluctant to admit asylum seekers and refugees onto its territory. A study of migratory patterns in 2004 indicates that refugees fleeing African conflicts in countries such as Sudan and Somalia are likely among the migrants who transit Libya.[16] Because the Libyan government does not recognize asylum seekers and the authorities of the Lampedusa holding center allegedly classify the majority of migrants as Egyptians without investigat-ing their nationality, there is no way to identify individuals who may be fleeing persecution.

The existing data on the number of deportations from the detention centers further questions the argument that detention is indispensable to assure an effective removal policy. A recent report shows that out of 11,883 irregular migrants detained in Italian 'temporary stay and assistance centers' in 2004, less than half were deported while the rest were released or escaped.[17] As regards asylum seekers, the 9,019 asylum applications filed in Italy in 2004 translate into the country receiving roughly 16 asylum seekers per 100,000 inhabitants.[18] Even if doubled, the total number of requests for asylum in Italy would be of 34 per 100,000—still far below the EU average of 60 asylum seekers per 100,000 inhabitants.[19] While this increase is hypothetical, it helps illustrate the gap between asylum trends in Italy when compared with other EU countries and highlights Italy's reluctance to assume its share of asylum responsibilities in Europe.

Over the past decade, European governments incapable of harmonizing a common or coherent immigration policy and faced with growing public intolerance toward largely Muslim economic migrants have increasingly invoked the alleged existence of an 'asylum crisis' and have substituted national asylum programs for formal immigration schemes.[20] The 'asylum crisis' strategy has proven successful in garnering public support for European governments to contract out their asylum responsibilities to less capable government structures in developing countries. While Europe's actual asylum situation is certainly less acute now than in past decades and cannot be described as a crisis, Europe is experiencing a far less publicly visible 'human rights crisis.' Long-standing precepts of refugee protection in Europe have been seriously eroded, further exacerbating intolerance toward immigrants who are more frequently categorized as 'illegal.'

As recent research on human traffick-ing has repeatedly shown, border controls, detentions and expulsion practices do not prevent people from moving from their countries of origin, nor from reaching Europe, but rather they increase the costs and dangers of migration. The EU's enlargement eastward has demonstrated that tightening border and visa controls enhances migrants' vulnerability and furthers the interests of smuggling networks. If arranging a visa is not cheap and easy, migrants are not able to access (even when available) formal governmental channels for migration.[21] Instead, they resort to irregular channels that exploit migrants' legal vulnerability by charging higher fees for travel and documentation or profiting from migrant labor at various points during the journey.[22] Stricter immigration controls aimed at preventing trafficking do not necessarily protect migrants from abuse but can increase the vulnerability of migrants to violence during travel while increasing the costs of 'doing business' for traffickers[23] and leaving ample space for third party profiteering and abuse.

European officials and civil society united in outrage

Since the much-publicized mass deportations, Lampedusa has been repeatedly denounced for alleged procedural irregularities and human rights violations. Consistent and numerous allegations of degrading treatment of third-country nationals in detention, difficulties for asylum seekers in gaining access to the asylum determination process, and large-scale expulsions to Libya prompted the European Parliament (EP), European Court of Human Rights (ECHR), and United Nations' Human Rights Committee (UNHRC) to call on Italy to respect the rights of asylum seekers and refugees to international protection and to refrain from collective expulsions[24] of asylum seekers and irregular migrants to Libya—a country that has no asylum system, has not signed the Geneva Convention on Refugees, and practices the kind of large-scale expulsions of undocumented migrants in which 106 people recently lost their lives.

No information is available concerning the whereabouts of migrants and asylum seekers expelled to Libya.[25] Human Rights Watch believes that the majority are detained in Libyan detention camps.[26] Investigations by Amnesty International (AI) document that the Libyan government engages in the incommunicado detention of migrants and possible asylum seekers as well as suspected political opponents, torture while in detention, unfair trials leading to long-term prison sentences or the death penalty, and the 'disappearance' and death of political prisoners in custody. Migrants and asylum seekers in particular are often the victims of arbitrary detention, non-existent or unfair trials, killings, and disappearances and torture in the detention camps.[27] Once they are detained in Libya there is virtually no way for NGOs to assist them or verify the conditions of their detention and relative expulsion procedures. The Libyan detention centers are, in fact, almost inaccessible to international organizations or human rights groups. The UNHCR is unable to access people returned from Lampedusa to Libya, since it is

impossible for the organization to operate according to its protection mandate in Libya. On January 20, 2005 as well as in successive open letters to the Council and the Commission,[28] Amnesty International urged the Commission to publicly distance itself from the actions of the Italian authorities and to carry out an independent investigation regarding Italy's compliance with international legal obligations as part of the EU *acquis*.[29]

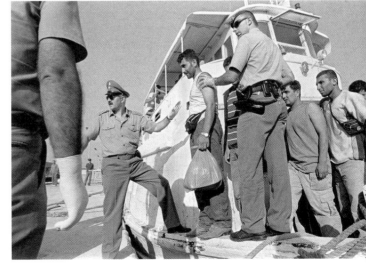

An Italian coastguard vessel brings 202 migrants ashore in Santa Maria di Leuca after intercepting their boat
▪ Matias Costa, Panos

NGOs claim that the signing of the bilateral agreement between Libya and Italy in August 2004 led to widespread arrests in Libya of individuals from sub-Saharan Africa[30] and the death of 106 migrants during subsequent repatriations from Libya to Niger.[31] NGOs point out that the improvised identification of large numbers of migrants as Egyptians at the Lampedusa holding center is the basis for forced collective removals of migrants, first to Libya and later to Egypt, a country with which Libya collaborates on matters of illegal migration.[32]

Nevertheless, collective deportations from Lampedusa to Libya resumed in March, April, and June 2005. By August 2005 mass deportations were conducted on a nearly weekly basis after the International Organization for Migration (IOM) signed an agreement with Libya aimed at deterring irregular migration from and into the country.[33] As deaths of migrants increased at sea during the crossover to Italy and in the desert as a consequence of deportations from Libya, social movements, several NGOs and European institutions mobilized in order to spread information and put an end to these collective deportations. La Rete Antirazzista Siciliana (The Sicilian Antiracist Network) video-recorded and circulated images of deportations at the Lampedusa camp,[34] and a number of activists organized a protest on April 2, 2005—the European Day for Freedom of Movement—in front of the offices of the Italian charter carrier Blue Panorama in Rome, which succeeded in halting the company's deportation flights.[35] Following the October 2004 events, ten European associations of NGOs working on migrant rights issues organized joint actions and filed a complaint with the European Commission against Italy's collective expulsions of migrants to Libya.[36] Moreover, Amnesty International urged the Commission on several occasions to halt the deportations and to investigate the detention practices of Italian authorities, while briefing Members of the European Parliament (MEPs) on the human rights situation of migrants and asylum-seekers in Lampedusa.[37]

In its 'Resolution on Lampedusa' in April 2005,[38] the European Parliament called on Italy to refrain from collective expulsions, grant UNHCR access to the Lampedusa center, and guarantee the individual examination of asylum. On 15 and 16 September 2005, a delegation of twelve MEPs working with the Committee on Citizens' Freedoms and Rights, Justice and Home Affairs (LIBE) arrived at Lampedusa to assess the center's

The Lampedusa holding center does not fulfil its main functions: it facilitates only a nominal amount of expulsions and perpetuates ill-treatment rather than offering assistance. To ensure that detention procedures and practices are in conformity with existing domestic and international standards, one short-term objective would be to mandate an independent monitoring body to make regular, unrestricted and unannounced visits to the center
▪ Matias Costa, Panos

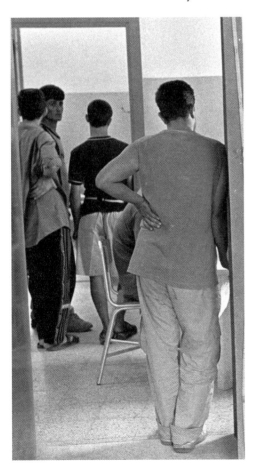

Migrants being photographed for identification purposes at L'Orizonte refugee camp in Squinzano. Independent monitors are not allowed access to the Lampedusa holding center
• Matias Costa, Panos

procedures, treatment of the detainees, and the overall running of the Lampedusa center. As regards the conditions of detention, the Lampedusa camp was denounced for inadequate accommodation, poor hygienic conditions, and the use of coercive and violent police methods toward migrants during police-run removal operations to Libya. The overcrowding of the center, which has a maximum legal capacity of 180 persons, is such that the average number of migrants detained during the summer months in 2005 was between 300 and 400 and sometimes reaching up to 1,000 persons.[39]

Based on the evidence, ten European NGOs have taken legal action against the Italian Government, filing a complaint with the European Commission[40] and calling on the Commission to sanction Italy for:

- Violation of the right of defense and of all parties to be heard[41] and hence the right to asylum as recognized by the Amsterdam Treaty

- Violation of the prohibition of torture and inhuman or degrading treatment, provided for in article 4 of the European Charter of fundamental rights and article 3 of the European Convention for the protection of human rights and fundamental freedoms[42]

Intended to coincide with a high-level EU Justice and Home Affairs visit to Libya in June 2005, a coalition of 13 European NGOs[43] proposed to EU Member States and the Commission a number of core principles to be applied during migrant repatriations to ensure that the policies fully respect the needs and dignity of individuals.[44] In the complaint filed with the European Commission concerning the expulsions from the Lampedusa holding

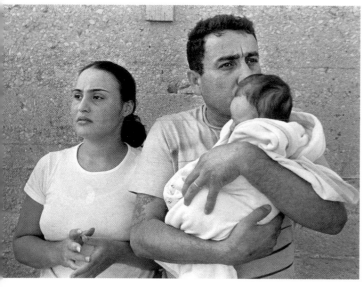

center to Libya, the NGOs called on the Commission to sanction Italy for:

- Violation of the prohibition of collective expulsions provided for in article 4 of the 4th Protocol of the European Charter of Human Rights (ECHR) and Fundamental Freedoms, article II-19-1 of the Charter of Fundamental Rights, and article 13 of the International Covenant on Civil and Political Rights

- Violation of the *non-refoulement* principle[45] prescribed in article 33 of the 1951 Geneva Convention on Refugees and Article 3 of the Convention Against Torture[46]

In its observations on Italy during the 85th Session of the UN Human Rights Committee in Geneva in November 2005,[47] the Committee raised the issue of the right to international protection and recalled the right of each person not to be expelled to a country where he/she might face torture or ill-treatment. Along similar lines, in its *Resolution on Lampedusa* the European Parliament called on Italy to refrain from collective expulsions to Libya and took the view that these expulsions constitute a violation of the principle of *non-refoulement*. The Parliament also called on Libya to allow access to international observers, halt the expulsions and arbitrary arrests of migrants, ratify the Geneva Con-vention, and recognize the mandate of the UNHCR.

Italian authorities have responded to allegations of collective expulsions by invoking article 10 of Law 189/2002 of the new Italian Immigration Act—in parti-cular procedures regarding the refusal of entry (*respingimento alla frontiera*). The authorities claim that removals from the Lampedusa center are not expulsions but rather refusals of entry determined on an individual basis. An expulsion needs to be decided by the judge and prohibits entry into Italy for ten years, while a 'refusal of entry' is an administrative measure that does not ban the migrant from entering Italian territory in the future.[48] Irregular migrants reaching Lampedusa are served refusals of entry and returned to Libya because they have transited Libya prior to reaching Italy. Italian authorities insist that the refusals of entry are determined on a case-by-case basis and that since the majority of migrants reaching Lampedusa are economic migrants rather than refugees, Italy is not in violation of the *refoulement* principle nor in breach of the Geneva Convention.[49] The Italian government has explained its refusal to disclose the content of the bilateral agreement with Libya by saying that making the agreement public would diminish the success of countering smuggling and trafficking networks res-ponsible for organizing and profiting from irregular migration from Libya into Italy.

Italy is developing future detention and expulsion schemes in collaboration with the IOM, a key partner for both the Italian and Libyan governments.[50] Italy was scheduled to fund an IOM pilot project in Libya starting in August 2005.[51] As far as Libya is concerned, following the agreement signed on August 9, 2005 for the opening of an IOM office in Tripoli,[52] IOM and Libya defined a program of activities supporting the Libyan government in countering illegal migration and developing a long-term migration management approach under the *Programme for the Enhancement of Transit and Irregular Migration Manage-ment* (TRIM).[53]

Who are the gate-keepers of Europe?

Current European discourse on Libya and the EU's immigration policies of detention and removal of undocumented migrants points to a series of ongoing transformations in Europe. A sound understanding of the implications of these transformations is crucial for academics, activists and policymakers alike.

The proposal to establish extraterritorial migrant processing centers and the construction of Italian-funded detention centers on Libyan territory, deportations to and from Libya, and joint Italian-Libyan police patrolling of the Libyan coastline are all instances that de-localize the EU's external border from South Italy into Libyan territory. Consequently, they all challenge the idea of the EU's external border as a firm border between Italy and Libya and show that the southern EU border, rather than being a linear and stable geographical demarcation, is a discontinuous and porous space encompassing the area between southern Italy and Sub-Saharan Africa.

This reading of the border calls into question the common assumption that the state regulates people's entry/stay into its territory. States certainly play a crucial role but the example of current migration projects in Libya suggests that non-state actors such as the IOM partake, shape and determine state policy on migration. Questions arise regarding state sovereignty and the ways in which non-state actors regulate and manage a state's migratory movements—functions traditionally reserved for the nation-state.

There is currently wide consensus among scholars, activists and policy analysts that the tightening of immigration policies and strengthening of border controls has resulted in a reduction of legal channels for migration into the EU so that illegality has become a structural characteristic of modern migratory flows. From this perspective, detention camps for undocumented migrants in Italy (and in Europe) are not seen as institutions geared toward deportations, but rather sites producing the conditions of 'deportability' which function as filter mechanisms and allow states to selectively admit certain groups of migrants (Karakayali and Tsianos 2004, Mezzadra 2004). Effective scholarly scrutiny and policy interventions depend upon the further development of analytic frameworks better able to grasp the ways in which detention centers create and uphold conditions for the hierarchization of access to labor and citizenship in Europe.

The ruins of boats used by migrants on the clandestine journey from North Africa, dumped half-submerged in the harbor of Lampedusa ▪ Matias Costa, Panos

Contracting out European sovereignty and human rights protection

The state practice of 'contracting out' also raises serious questions about IOM interventions and ability to adequately protect the rights of migrants on behalf of states. In the case of the repatriations of irregular migrants and asylum seekers expelled from the Lampedusa holding center, IOM and states cooperate in obstructing asylum seekers' right to asylum. Moreover, the fact that irregular migrants and asylum seekers are deported from Lampedusa without knowing that they are being transferred to Libya, that the removals are executed by force and that once in Libya migrants are again detained in police-guarded structures, raises serious doubts that the IOM-run repatriations from Libya can be identified as voluntary. When decisions to return are made under duress or as an alternative to state-run forced expulsions, 'voluntary' seems to designate an absence of viable options rather than a deliberate choice. IOM cannot be held responsible for the rule of law in the same way as sovereign states. However, in deporting irregular migrants and asylum seekers from Libya, IOM is to be seen as assuming joint responsibility for any violation of fundamental rights that asylum seekers and irregular migrants might suffer.

Furthermore, the current Italian–Libyan partnership on migration indicates a new reorientation of Libyan politics from a pro-African to a pro-European stance, with profound implications for Sub-Saharan migrants. Libya's consequential tightening of its borders with Sub-Saharan neighbors is likely to clash with the long-established principle of the free movement of people that has been a cornerstone of regional cooperation and integration in the Sahel-Saharan region. This shift could destabilize current political relations between Libya and neighboring states and may further 'illegalize' movements of large groups of Sub-Saharan nationals.

Policy Recommendations: Legitimacy, transparency, accountability and in the management of state borders

Given the fact that available data regarding the detention and deportation of irregular migrants and asylum seekers in Lampedusa and Libya are often contradictory and incomplete, bilateral agreements on irregular migration remain undisclosed, and the European Union framework offers Member States wide discretion in applying restrictive exceptions in national legislation, clearly defined principles of legitimacy, transparency, and accountability are needed to guide the EU and Member States undertaking migration management partnerships with neighboring countries.

Legitimacy

Migration holding centers are instruments facilitating the effective repatriation of third-country nationals who have entered Italy illegally. The Lampedusa holding center does not fulfil its main functions, however: it facilitates only a nominal amount of expulsions and perpetuates ill-treatment rather than offering assistance. To ensure that detention procedures and practices are in conformity with existing domestic and international standards, one short-term objective would be to mandate an independent monitoring body to make regular, unrestricted and unannounced visits to the Lampedusa holding center. The closure of the Lampedusa holding center should constitute a longer term objective.[54] Since the Lampedusa holding center is classified as a clearing station, Italy is likely to disregard established minimum procedural and legal safeguards on return, removal and custody provided under the EU Return Directive. The closure of the Lampedusa holding center would prevent future procedural violations and ensure that the rights of migrants and asylum seekers are not sidestepped by the Italian authorities.

Transparency

Whether carried out by the Italian and Libyan states or by the IOM, policies and schemes countering irregular migration from and into Libya are all characterized by a lack of transparency. Independent access and the transparency of information, programs and agreements between Italy and Libya regulating migration management are needed before an accurate assessment can be made of the situation regarding detention, expulsion and asylum along the EU's southern border. Information regarding the number, frequency and destinations of the return flights from the Lampedusa holding center, the content of relevant Italy-Libya bilateral agreements and between Libya and the IOM, and the content of the contract for the TRIM Program cofunded by the EC must be made public in order to achieve a transparent EU policy on asylum and immigration.

Michael, age 32, who is Eritrean, lies in a bed in a converted church which serves as an immigration reception center. He arrived in Lampedusa after a three-day long journey in a small fishing boat and has been waiting at the church for his residence permit for eight months ▪ Alfredo D'Amato, Panos

Accountability

The EU must provide leadership and take a stand in upholding the protection of human rights within contexts of third-country partnerships on migration and asylum programs. Divergent interests between national and EU competencies over borders, asylum and immigration should not permit Member States to violate the principles of the EU Return Directive and disregard minimum safeguards on return. In cases where Member States or the EU 'contract out' migration management to the IOM, this must not exempt the EU, Italy or Libya from their international legal obligations under established norms prohibiting *refoulement* and protecting human rights.

The lack of safeguards and control mechanisms protecting the established human right to seek asylum and Italy's tendency to circumvent its responsibilities on matters of asylum require an intervention from the European Parliament. The EP is directly involved in the decision-making process on European asylum and immigration policy and should propose amendments to the Return Directive and the Action Plan on Libya requiring the observance of international human rights standards. In the absence of any EU monitoring mechanism in Libya, the EP should urgently visit those detention centers in Libya where detention and repatriation programs are funded by the EU and Italy. The EP's intervention would play a crucial role in achieving a transparent and democratic procedure working toward a common European asylum policy and help steer the debate away from a control-based and toward a rights-based approach.

The implementation of detention and expulsion schemes that illegalize migratory movements and erode the rights of migrants to seek asylum brings into question the political responsibility of all actors involved, whether they be governments, supranational bodies, or agencies. The Italian and Libyan governments, the European Union, and the International Organization for Migration all need to assume their share of responsibility for human rights violations resulting from the procedures and programs they implement both inside and outside the borders of the European Union.

Notes

[1]   The European Commission report *Technical Mission to Libya on Illegal Migration 27 Nov - 6 Dec 2004* is found on http://www.statewatch.org/news/2005/may/eu-report-libya-ill-imm.pdf.

[2]   See European Parliament, *Report from the LIBE Committee Delegation on the Visit to the Temporary Holding Centre in Lampedusa*, EP/LIBE PV/581203EN, p.2.

[3]   Ibid., p.3.

[4]   See ARCI, *Il diario del presidio ARCI a Lampedusa,* 2005a; ARCI, *Lampedusa Watching*, 2005b.

[5]   The letter from British Prime Minister Tony Blair to the Greek presidency proposing transit processing centers can be downloaded at http://www.statewatch.org/news/2003/apr/blair-simitis-asile.pdf.

[6]   For a brilliant analysis of legal and theoretical issues raised by transit processing centers and protection zones, see Noll 2003.

[7]   For a more in-depth overview of the events and actors, see Schuster 2005.

8   This number was provided by Italian Ministry of Interior G. Pisanu. See *il manifesto* 22nd April 2005, p.9 or http://www.ilmanifesto.it/Quotidiano-archivio/22-Aprile-2005/art74.html. (consulted on 25/04/2005).

9   Ministry of Internal Affairs, quoted in Cuttitta (2005)

10   Hamood, S., *African Transit Migration through Libya to Europe: the Human Costs*. The American University on Cairo, Forced Migration and Refugee Studies, 2006.

11   Boubakri estimates that 2 to 2.5 millions foreigners live in Libya, or 25 to 30 percent of the country's total population, including approximately 200,000 Moroccans, 60,000 Tunisians and 20,000–30,000 Algerians. Boubakri, H. "Transit Migration between Tunisia, Libya and Sub-Saharan Africa: Study Based on Greater Tunis," Regional Conference *Migrants in Transit Countries: Sharing Responsibility for Management and Protection*, Council of Europe: MG-RCONF (2004)6e; p.2.

12   Boubakri, H., ibid., and Pliez, O., ibid.

13   Disappointed by the lack of support from Arab countries, isolation from the international community due to the bombings in 1998 of flights over Lockerbie in Scotland and in 1989 over Niger, and the 1992 UN Security Council arms embargo on Libya, Colonel Mu'ammar al-Qaddafi reoriented Libya's foreign policy away from Arab countries and toward its sub-Saharan neighbors.

14   Libya is a key member of the Group of Sahel-Saharan States and of the African Union. The Group is also known as CEN-SAD (the Community of states bordering the Sahara and the Sahel) and was established in 1998 in Tripoli. Its members are: Egypt, Djibouti, Libya, Morocco, Somalia, Sudan, Tunisia, Senegal, Eritrea, Chad, Central Africa, Gambia, Mali, Niger, Burkina Faso, Nigeria, Togo and Benin. The African Union was founded in 1999 by the Organization of African Unity, whose main objectives were to "rid the continent of the remaining vestiges of colonization and apartheid; promote unity and solidarity among African States; coordinate and intensify cooperation for development; safeguard the sovereignty and territorial integrity of Member States; and promote international cooperation within the framework of the United Nations." http://www.africa-union.org/.

15   Pliez, O. ibid.

16   Pliez, O. "La troisième migratoire, les conséquences de la politique européenne de lutte contre les migrations clandestines," paper written for Asia-Europe Foundation workshop *The Management of Humanitarian Aids and of Transnational Movements of Persons in the Euro-Mediterranean Area and in South-East Asia*, 2005.

17   The exact percentage is 48,1. Quoted in the 2005 report by Corte dei Conti available at http://www.corteconti.it/Ricerca-e-1/Gli-Atti-d/Controllo-/Documenti/Sezione-ce1/Anno-2005/Adunanza-c/allegati-d3/Relazione.doc. (consulted on 12 September 2005)

18   Asylum levels in Italy are in fact among the lowest in Europe and in 2004 reported a fall of 26 percent, which is 5 percent above the average drop in EU asylum levels. These numbers are extrapolated from the UNHCR's 2005 report on *Asylum levels and Trends in Industrialized Countries 2004. Overview of Asylum Applications longed in Europe and non-European industrialized countries in 2004*. Population data unit/PGDS: UNHCR Geneva. http://www.unhcr.ch/statistics.

19   This calculation does not take into consideration that out of 9,019 requests for asylum filed in 2004, only 781 were approved, i.e. the hypothetical increase calculated above concerns only requests for asylum rather than the allocation of actual asylum status.

20   See for example Helton, A. and P. Birchenough (Kilpadi), "Forced Migration in Europe." *Fletcher Forum of World Affairs*, Vol. 20(2), Summer/Fall 1996, pp.89–100.

21   Anderson, B. and J. O'Connell Davidson, *Needs and Desires: Is there a Demand for "Trafficked" Persons?*, Geneva, IOM, 2003.

22   See for example research on trafficking in women in Europe including Andrijasevic, R. "La traite des femmes d'Europe de l'Est en Italie" *Revue européenne des migrations internationals,* Vol. 21(1), 2005, pp.155–175.

23   Salt, J. and J. Stein, "Migration as a Business: The Case of Trafficking." *International Migration,* 35(4), 1997, pp.467–491.

24   According to the European Court of Human Rights, collective expulsions are defined as "any measure by which foreigners are forced, due to their membership of a group, to leave a country, apart from cases in which this measure is adopted following and based on a reasonable and objective assessment of the specific situation of each of the individuals composing the group."

25   The data provided by the Italian authorities specify that 1,153 migrants were returned to Libya between 29th September and 8th October 2004 and another 494 between 13th and 21st of March 2005 (EP/LIBE PV/581203EN, p.2). Italian authorities provide no data for later expulsions. The numbers reported here come from NGO sources.

26   Human Rights Watch, World Report. Events of 2005, p.373.

27   Amnesty International's report quotes testimonies of hundreds of Burkinabé nationals as well as several Eritrean and Nigerian migrants who were expelled from Libya to their country of origin after their documents and possessions were confiscated. They testified to having been detained in inhumane conditions without adequate water, food or medical care. Amnesty International, *Libya: time to make human rights a reality,* 2004, AI INDEX MDE 19/002/2004.

28   Amnesty International letter to JFS Commissioner Franco Frattini, dated 21 March 2005 (B456); and AI appeal to the EU regarding expulsions from Italy to Libya, dated 28 June 2005 (B472).

29   In particular with regard to Italy's obligation under articles 5 (information), 6 (documentation), 7 (residence and freedom of movement), 13 and 15 (material reception and health care) of the directive 2003/9/EC laying down minimum standards for reception conditions for asylum seekers.

30   Amnesty International, "Immigration Cooperation with Libya: the Human rights perspective. AI briefing ahead of the JHA Council 14 April 2005." http://www.amnesty-eu.org/static/documents/2005/JHA_Libya_april12.pdf .

31   For a description of these expulsions and itineraries across the desert, see F. Gatti, ibid., 2005b.

32   Requested on several occasions, the Italian authorities thus far have not presented the list of expulsion orders from the Lampedusa CPTA. During their visit to the CPTA, the LIBE committee could not view the records of arrivals and departures since, the Italian authorities claim, they are not held at the center but at the offices of the Agrigento (Sicily) police.

33   The International Organization for Migration (IOM), commonly mistaken for a branch of the United Nations or an humanitarian organization, has recently come under attack by NGOs including Amnesty International and Human Rights Watch for managing detention centers, running return programs for irregular migrants and asylum seekers, and implementing EU border-regimes. For a study of IOM's activities in Eastern Europe in the field of migration see my IPF research at http://www.policy.hu/andrijasevic/.

34   The video entitled *Lampedusa Scoppia* can be downloaded at http://www.ngvision.org/mediabase/487.

35   When Blue Panorama discontinued its operation of the deportation flights, the private Croatian company Air Adriatic (AA) took over the business. For a press briefing on activists' protests against Blue Panorama see http://www.meltingpot.org/articolo5133.html.

36   The complaint and the accompanying dossier is available at http://www.gisti.org/doc/actions/2005/italie/complaint20-01-2005.pdf.

37   An overview of Amnesty International's documents and reports is available at http://www.amnesty-eu.org/.

38   P6_TA(2005)0138.

39   This data was collected by ARCI (Associazione Ricreativa e Culturale Italiana), the Italian NGO that is the signatory of the complaint with the EC against Italy's collective expulsions, and presented to MEPs during their September mission. Since no official data exist so far, the ARCI dossier is a unique

source of information regarding the numbers of migrants arriving via sea, those removed to other camps or to Libya, and the descriptions of police practices toward migrants. The data was gathered during a permanent monitoring exercise conducted by ARCI in Lampedusa during the months of June, July and August 2005. See http://www.tesseramento.it/immigrazione/documenti/index.ph.

[40] ANAFE – Association nationale d'assistance aux frontières pour les étrangers (France), Asociacion 'Andalucía Acoge' (Spain), APDHA – Asociación Pro Derechos Humanos de Andalucía (Spain), ARCI – Associazione Ricreativa e Cultura Italiana (Italy), Asociaciòn 'Sevilla Acoge' (Spain), ASGI – Associazione per gli Studi Giuridici sull'Immigrazione (Italy), Cimade (France), Federación des Asociaciones SOS Racismo del Estado Español (Spain), Gisti – Groupe d'information et de soutien des immigrés (France), and ICS – Consorzio italiano solidarietà. See footnote 14.

[41] Given the short amount of time that elapsed between the arrival of the migrants and their deportation (at times as little as 24 hours), NGOs claim that it is unlikely that the CPTA authorities examined individually the cases of 1,000 people. Furthermore, they have been deprived of the right to file an appeal due to the decision by the Italian government to remove them.

[42] Conditions of detention fall under the definition of "inhumane and degrading treatment."

[43] "Common Principles on the removal of irregular migrants and rejected asylum seekers," August 2005 by Amnesty International, EU Office; Caritas Europa; Churches' Commission for Migrants on Europe (CCME); European Council for Refugees and Exiles (ECRE); Human Rights Watch Jesuit Refugee Service–Europe (JRS); Platform for International Cooperation on Undocumented Migrants (PICUM); Quaker Council for European Affairs; Save the Children; Cimade (France); Iglesia Evangelica Espanola; Federazione delle Chiese Evangeliche in Italia (FCEI); and SENSOA (Belgium). The NGOs put these principles forward when the Commission Director General for Justice and Home Affairs visited Libya on June 22, 2005 in an attempt to launch cooperation on countering illegal immigration. The Commission nevertheless went ahead and drafted the EU return directive.

[44] These core principles are also to be applied in so-called transit, border and airport zones in the EU. They are: voluntary return should always be the priority; vulnerable persons should be protected against removal (children, seriously ill people, victims of trafficking and pregnant women); persons subject to a removal order should always have access to effective remedies; detention for the purpose of removal should be the last resort; the family unit should be strictly respected; independent monitoring and control bodies should be created; the use of force should comply with Council of Europe recommendations; re-entry bans should be prohibited; and a legal status should be granted to persons who cannot be removed.

[45] The *non-refoulement* principle has been reaffirmed by the EU as the cornerstone of refugee protection. It prohibits the forcible return of anyone to a territory where they would be at risk of serious human rights violations: "No contracting state shall expel or return (*refouler*), a refugee in any manner to the frontiers of territories where his life or freedom would be threatened on account of his race, religion, nationality, membership of a particular social group, or political opinion." This principle makes reference to the lack of individual assessments and to the removal of persons to countries where there exists a serious risk to the physical integrity of those concerned (mentioned in article 19§2 of the European Charter).

[46] Libya lacks the minimum guarantees of refugee protection. Therefore, returning asylum seekers to Libya is in contravention with article II-19-2 of the European Charter of Fundamental Rights, according to which "No one may be removed, expelled or extradited to a State where there is a serious risk that they may be subjected to the death penalty, torture or inhuman or degrading treatment." Italy's obligation to *non-refouleur* to a country lacking minimum guarantees of protection is reinforced by the fact that Italy is a party to the 1951 Refugee Convention, the UN Convention Against Torture and Other Cruel, Inhuman or Degrading Treatment or Punishment, and the European Convention for the Protection of Human Rights and Fundamental Freedoms.

[47] See footnote 31.

[48] EP/LIBE PV/581203EN.

[49] The response by Alessandro Pansa, Director General of the immigration and border police of the Italian Ministry of Interior, delivered to the UN Human Rights Committee during its 85th Session on the 20th October 2005. Notes taken by Claire Rodier, GISTI. http://www.migreurop.org/article909.html.

[50] Since July 2000, Italy and Tunisia have been running joint 'control activities' off the Tunisian coastline. Italian police provide the training courses for Tunisian border guards. However, the Tunisian government rejected Italian funding for the establishment of detention centers, fearing Italian interference in Tunisia's internal affairs. Cuttitta, P. 'Delocalization of migration controls to North Africa,' paper presented at the workshop *The Europeanisation of National Immigration Policies—Varying Developments across Nations and Policy Areas*, European Academy, 1–3 September 2005, Berlin.

[51] While neither Italy nor the IOM have disclosed the content of the project, reports from NGOs and individual experts about the deportation from Lampedusa to Libya acquired nearly weekly regularity after the signing of the IOM-Libyan agreement, suggesting that the pilot project is a repatriation project or a so-called Assisted Voluntary Return (AVR) Program. This information was gathered by the author in Lampedusa during the Asia-Europe Foundation workshop *The Management of Humanitarian Aids and of Transnational Movements of Persons in the Euro-Mediterranean Area and in South-East Asia*, 28–30 August 2005, Lampedusa.

[52] The cooperation between IOM and the Libyan Government was developed within the framework of the 5+5 Regional Dialogue on Migration. The 5+5 Dialogue is an informal forum on migration that brings together the Maghreb countries (Algeria, Libya, Mauritania, Morocco and Tunisia) and the countries of the 'arc Latin' (France, Italy, Malta, Portugal and Spain) to promote the prevention of irregular migration and trafficking in countries of origin, transit and destination. As a partner in the 5+5 Dialogue, IOM organized in cooperation with Libya's People's Committee for Public Security a training session for 100 Libyan officials and police representatives prior to the regional seminar on irregular migration in the western Mediterranean in Tripoli on 8 and 9 June 2004. The focus of the session was on border and migration management and on assisted voluntary return for irregular migrants in Libya. IOM, *Dialogue 5+5. Newsletter*, No. 1 issue, 2004.

[53] EC, ibid., p.15.

[54] The majority of Italy's regions support the closure of the holding centers. In summer 2005, fourteen Provincial Governors and their representatives met at the forum *Mare Aperto* in Bari and drafted a document in which they commit to launching a political-institutional dialogue geared towards changing current Italian immigration law, closing the CPTAs, creating a comprehensive law on asylum, and doing away with administrative detention. The final document is available at http://www.meltingpot.org/articolo5676.html.

References

Amnesty International, *Italy: Temporary stay—Permanent rights: the treatment of foreign nationals detained in 'temporary stay and assistance centres'* (CPTAs), 2005.

Amnesty International, *Libya: time to make human rights a reality*, 2004, AI INDEX MDE 19/002/2004.

AI EU Office, *A letter to Franco Frattini, Commissioner for Justice, Freedom and Security*, Brussels, 21st March 2005, B456, www.amnesty-eu.org.

AI EU Office, *Amnesty International Appeal to the European Union Regarding Expulsions from Italy to Libya*, Brussels, 28th June 2005, B472, www.amnesty-eu.org.

AI EU Office, *Immigration Cooperation with Libya: the Human rights perspective. AI briefing ahead of the Justice and Home Affairs Council, 14 April 2005*. Brussels, http://www.amnestyeu.org/static/documents/2005/JHA_Libya_april12.pdf.

Anderson, B. and O'Connell Davidson, J., *Needs and Desires: Is there a Demand for "Trafficked" Persons?*, Geneva, IOM, 2003.

Andrijasevic, R, "Lampedusa in Focus: Migrants caught between the Libyan desert and the deep sea," *Feminist Review* no. 82:1, 2006, pp.119–124.

Andrijasevic, R. "La traite des femmes d'Europe de l'Est en Italie" *Revue européenne des migrations internationals* Vol. 21(1), pp.155–175, 2005.

ARCI, *Il diario del presidio ARCI a Lampedusa*, 2005a, http://www.tesseramento.it/immigrazione/documenti/index.php.

ARCI, *Lampedusa Watching*, 2005b, http://www.tesseramento.it/immigrazione/documenti/index.php.

Balzacq, T. and Carrera, S. *Migration, Borders and Asylum. Trends and Vulnerabilities in EU Policy*. CEPS: Brussels, 2005.

Boubakri, H. "Transit Migration between Tunisia, Libya and Sub-Saharan Africa: Study Based on Greater Tunis," Regional Conference *Migrants in Transit Countries: Sharing Responsibility for Management and Protection*, Istanbul 30 September–1 October 2004, Council of Europe: MG-RCONF (2004) 6e.

Caritas/Migrantes, *Immigrazione. Dossier Statistico* 2005. Edizioni IDOS, Roma, 2005.

Commission of the European Communities, Proposal for a Directiove of the European Parliament and of the Councic on common standards and procedures in Member States for returning illegality staying third-country nationals. Brussels.

Commission of the European Communities, Communication from the Commission to the European Parliament and the Council. Thematic programme for the cooperation with thirds countries in the areas of migration and asylum. Brussels, 25th January 2006, COM(2006) 26 final.

Corte dei Conti, *Programma controllo 2004. Gestione delle risorse previste in connessione con il fenomeno dell'immigrazione*, 2005, http://www.corteconti.it/Ricerca-e-1/Gli-Atti-d/Controllo-/Documenti/Sezione-ce1/Anno-2005/Adunanza-c/allegati-d3/Relazione.doc.

Council of the European Union, Draft Council Conclusions on initiating dialogue and cooperation with Libya on migration issues, Brussels, May 17, 2005, 9413/1/05 REV 1.

Cuttitta, P. "Delocalization of migration controls to North Africa," paper presented at the workshop *The Europeanisation of National Immigration Policies—Varying Developments across Nations and Policy Areas*, European Academy, 1–3 September 2005, Berlin.

Doctors without Borders (MSF), *Centri di permanenza temporanea e assistenza: autonomia di un fallimento*, Sinnos editrice, 2005.

European Commission, Communication from the Commission to the European Parliament and Council. Thematic Programme for the cooperation with third countries in the area of migration and asylum, COM(206) 26 final, Brussels, 25 January 2006.

European Commission, *Report on the Technical Mission to Libya on Illegal Immigration*, Brussels, 2005.

European Parliament/LIBE, *Report from the LIBE Committee Delegation on the Visit to the Temporary Holding Centre in Lampedusa*, EP/LIBE PV/581203EN.

European Parliament, *European Parliament Resolution on Lampedusa*, 14th April 2005, P6_TA(2005)0138.

Gatti, F. "Io, clandestino a Lampedusa," *L'espresso*, 6th October 2005a.

Gatti, F. "Nel deserto fra Libia e Niger," *L'espresso*, 24th March 2005b.

Hamood, S. *African Transit Migration through Libya to Europe: the Human Costs*. The American University on Cairo, Forced Migration and Refugee Studies. January 2006.

Helton, A. and Birchenough (Kilpadi), P. "Forced Migration in Europe." *Fletcher Forum of World Affairs*, Vol. 20(2), Summer/Fall 1996, pp.89–100.

Human Rights Watch (HRW), *World Report. Events of 2005*. http://hrw.org/wr2k5.

International Federation fir Human Rights (FIDH), *Italy. Right of Asylum in Italy: Access to procedures and treatment of asylum-seekers. Report. International Fact-finding Mission*. No. 419/2, June 2005.

International Organization for Migration (IOM), *Dialogue. 5+5 Newsletter*, No. 1, issue, 2004.

Karakayali, S. and Tsianos, V. "Wilde Schafsjagd in Aigais und die transnationalen "mujahideen." Rastanski Lojia Über Grenzregime an der Südostgrenze Europas," Springerin No. 4, 2004.

Koslowski, R. Economic Globalization, Human Smuggling, and Global Governance, in David Kyle and Rey Koslowski eds, *Global Human Smuggling. Comparative Perspectives*, Baltimore and London, The John Hopkins University Press, 2001, pp.337–358.

Maccanico, Y. "The European Commission Technical Mission to Libya: Exporting Fortress-Europe," *Statewatch bulletin*, Vol. 15, No. 2, March–April 2005.

Mezzadra, S. (ed), *I confini della libertà*. DeriveApprodi, Roma, 2004.

Mezzadra, S. *Diritto di fuga. Migrazioni, cittadinanza, globalizzazione*, Verona, Ombre corte, 2001.

Ministry for Foreign Affairs, Interministerial Committee of Human Rights, *Reply to List of Issues (CCPR/C/84/L/ITA) (Relating to CCPR/C/ITA/2004–5)*, U.N. Human Rights Committee 85th Session, Geneva 17 October–3 November 2005

Noll, G. "Visions of the Exceptional: Legal and Theoretical Issues Raised by Transit Processing Centres and Protection Zones," in *European Journal of Migration and Law* 5: 303–341, 2003.

Pliez, O. "La troisième migratoire, les conséquences de la politique européenne de lutte contre les migrations clandestines," paper written for Asia-Europe Foundation workshop *The Management of Humanitarian Aids and of Transnational Movements of Persons in the Euro-Mediterranean Area and in South-East Asia*, 28–30 August 2005, Lampedusa.

Salt, J. and Stein, J. "Migration as a Business: The Case of Trafficking." *International Migration,* 35(4), 1997, pp.467–491.

Simoncini, A. "Migranti, frontiere, spazi di confine. I lavoratori migranti nell'ordine salariale," *altreragioni*, pp.29–45, 2000.

UNHCR, *Asylum levels and Trends in Industrialized Countries 2004. Overview of Asylum Applications longed in Europe and non-European industrialized countries in 2004.* Population data unit/PGDS, UNHCR Geneva, 2005. http://www.unhcr.ch/statistics.

part two

Ethnic Relations in the Caucasus

'Reliable' and 'Unreliable' Peoples:

The Ingush-Ossetian Conflict and Prospects for Post-Beslan Reconciliation

Ekaterina Sokirianskaia

The only armed ethnic conflict in post-communist Russia, the Ingush–Ossetian conflict over the status of Prigorodny District of North Ossetia was a small-scale regional war that lasted for seven days from October 31 through November 6, 1992, and caused the dislocation of some 30–60,000 people. The conflict received virtually no coverage in the media in 1992 and was quickly forgotten. For the past 14 years, tens of thousands of internally displaced persons (IDPs) from North Ossetia struggling for their survival in substandard conditions in Ingushetia, with no aid from the Russian state, have gone virtually unnoticed by the international humanitarian and development organizations that arrived in the region two years later to assist IDPs from Chechnya.

My policy research project as an International Policy Fellow was designed as an 'early warning report' about the dangerous consequences of protracted displacement caused by conflict. Before I had the chance to publicize my 'warning,' the tragic hostage-taking in the North Ossetian town of Beslan suddenly woke the entire world to the realities of the Ingush-Ossetian conflict. Answers to many of the questions addressed by this policy study are central to a deeper understanding not only of the Ingush-Ossetian conflict, but also a more nuanced policy perspective vis-à-vis Muslim–Christian relations in Russia and interethnic tolerance in the era of the 'war on terror.'

Ekaterina Sokirianskaia is Assistant Professor of Political Science at the Chechen State University in Grozny and works for the Russian human rights organization Memorial in Nazran, Ingushetia. Her research as an International Policy Fellow entitled "Getting Back Home? Toward the Sustainable Return of Ingush Forced Migrants to the Prigorodny District of North Ossetia," is available online at http://pdc.ceu.hu (Source IPF) and www.policy.hu/sokirianskaia

September 1, 2004, Beslan

On the morning of September 1, 2004 at School No.1 in the town of Beslan in the Russian republic of North Ossetia, the parade to celebrate Learning Day was due to take place at 10 a.m. Students and their families gathered in the yard to await the start of the ceremony. The children had come to school in their ceremonial uniform, with flowers and balloons, everyone was in a festive mood, so when armed masked men burst into the schoolyard many at first thought that it was a prize draw, and assumed the shooting was the sound of bursting balloons. When it became clear within a few minutes that this was no joke, the parents and children attempted to flee. Some managed to escape, but the majority were herded into the school.

The terrorists spread the hostages throughout the school building. The bulk of the children and their parents were in the gym. So many people were herded inside that everyone had to sit on the wooden floor with their legs drawn in. It was not possible to lie down or move around the hall.

During the first 24 hours the hostages were allowed to drink. Household buckets for washing the floor were filled with water from the tap and enamel mugs were used to allow the children to drink. Visits to the toilet were made in groups of several people. On the second and third days, water was not allowed. According to several of those I questioned, some children urinated on their clothes and suck the urine. One of the hostages related that he ate the leaves of a houseplant which happened to be nearby.

Meanwhile the relatives of the hostages gathered in groups of up to about 15 people on the square by the town's Palace of Culture, approximately 300 meters from School No.1. It was here that the television cameras had been set up to broadcast reports on the developing situation to Russian and foreign television channels. Many relatives made the journey from distant villages to lend support. When I arrived a few hours after the hostage-taking, I heard the crowd discussing information in the media—that the terrorists who captured the school were from 'the Ingush Dzamaat'. How it was possible to know at that point that the hostage-takers were from an ethnic Ingush group remains unclear. And while the media claimed that the terrorists had expressed no demands, many in the crowd outside the school assumed that the demands concerned the release of Ingush prisoners held in the town of Vladikavkaz.

On September 2, former President of Ingushetia Ruslan Aushev arrived at the school. From among the three presidents invited by the terrorists into the school for negotiations, Aushev was the only one who dared to enter. The incumbent presidents of Ingushetia and North Ossetia—Murat Zyazikov and Alexander Dzasokhov—abstained from visiting the school, as did Doctor Roshal, who cared for hostages during the Moscow Theater Terror in 2002.

Aushev quickly crossed the gym and entered the negotiation room. He said briefly to the hostages, "Don't worry, we'll soon get you all out." The terrorists had gathered women with children of breast-feeding age into a separate room before Aushev's visit, and he was allowed to escort them out. After Aushev left the school, lists with the names of the 26 released hostages were read out. Relatives whose small children were not on the list burst into tears, and some women became hysterical. Soon the crowd began discussing why Aushev was not killed by the terrorists—a fact that, in the opinion of some, confirmed their guess that he was somehow linked to the hostage-takers and that the school had been seized by the Ingush.

According to the hostages who escaped, the gym was mined around its entire edge. Explosive devices were attached to wires slung across the entire length of the hall from one basketball hoop to the other. On September 3 some of these devices exploded at the very beginning of the violent and chaotic events that led to the deaths of over 330 people, 170 of them—children. What caused this, and whether the devices actually exploded before or after the start of the storming of the school, remains unclear.

Several days after the tragic events, Ruslan Aushev explained to journalists that the terrorists had asked him to deliver their demands to the President of Russia. They were written on a piece of paper torn out from a school notebook.

Answers to many of these questions are central to a deeper understanding of Muslim-Christian relations in Russia, and more generally interethnic tolerance in the era of the 'war on terror.'

Across the folded note was written: "To His Excellency President Putin, from Shamil Basayev, Slave of Allah." The demands were to 1) withdraw troops from Chechnya, with the Chechen Republic remaining part of the Commonwealth of Independent States and within the ruble zone, and 2) ensure that peacemaking troops from the international community are brought into Chechnya. The hostages were to be released after Putin's decree satisfying these demands was announced by federal television channels. Aushev said that he passed the note over to the head of the North Ossetian security services. He was sure that the demands "reached the federal center."

Obviously, the horrendous crime in Beslan was linked with the decade-long atrocious war in Chechnya and had nothing to do with the Ingush–Ossetian territorial dispute over the status of Prigorodny District.

After the tragedy in the Northern Ossetian town of Beslan, the local authorities and media deliberately attempted to divert the anger and grief of the people away from the state's failed policies and toward 'unreliable' ethnic groups   Ekaterina Sokirianskaia

Post-Beslan anti-Ingush harassment and violence

Despite the fact that the demands of the terrorists had nothing to do with Ingush territorial claims in the area and, moreover, the group of hostage-takers were not Ingush, but consisted of Chechens, Ingush, Ossetians, and 'individuals of Slavic nationality,' the Beslan events sparked an unprecedented rise in ethnic tensions in the Prigorodny District of North Ossetia. The leading federal and republican printed press, including *Izvestiya*, *North Ossetia*, *Socialist Ossetia*, and *Expert*, published interviews with political scientists and other specialists who implicitly or explicitly linked Belsan with the October–November 1992 Ingush–Ossetian conflict in the district. The authorities did not try to disqualify these myths but instead, during the days immediately following the tragedy, supported groundless links between Belsan and the Ingush–Ossetian conflict of 12 years earlier.

Such speculations had deep resonance in the region, bringing Ingush–Ossetian relations to their lowest point in a decade. The grief and anger of the Ossetian population was successfully re-directed from the federal center and its failed policy in Chechnya towards the neighboring ethnic group. To make matters worse, some well-intentioned Russian non-governmental leaders tried to act as mediators and contacted Ingush public figures and officials urging them to go to Ossetia and apologize for Beslan. Now Ossetians want apologies from the Ingush. On September 4 and 5 all Ingush and Chechen students were asked to withdraw from their programs in North Ossetia and were transferred to other regional universities. Ingush patients were moved from local hospitals. Even women and sick children seeking urgent hospital treatment were harassed by anti-Ingush groups of citizens. In the months between summer 2005 April 2006, nine cases of enforced disappearances of Ingush civilians took place in Prigorodny District. One of the disappeared has been found dead with marks of severe beatings and torture. None of the crimes has been investigated and no one has been arrested or charged with crimes against representatives of the Ingush minority in North Ossetia.

At the same time, the Ingush reaction to the Beslan tragedy received no coverage in the press. The fact that the Ingush government had promptly expressed condolences to the Ossetian people and planned to attend the burial ceremonies (to which they were denied access), that Ingush children had collected money (two million rubles) and toys for the children of Beslan (the convoy with humanitarian aid was stopped at the administrative border and returned back to Ingushetia), the employees of ministries of education and culture allocated their daily salaries to the victims of Beslan, and the elite troops of the Ministry of Internal Affairs in Ingushetia had offered their assistance to Ossetian law enforcement during the hostage-taking crisis remains unknown to the Ossetian public. I was in Ingushetia on the evening of the September 3 and I know that the reaction of the Ingush was identical to that of people everywhere in the world—shock, anger and grief.

'Unreliable peoples' of the Empire

The Beslan tragedy and its aftermath vividly illustrates how easy it is to manipulate the popular notion of collective guilt in the North Caucasus, which in its turn can fuel hatred, violence, and even ethnic cleansing. Combined with the notion of family responsibility and the strictly regulated institution of blood feud still practiced in Dagestan, Ingushetia, North Ossetia and Chechnya—whereby the relatives of a murder victim are allowed to kill the murderer or, if the murderer is dead, a member of his nuclear family—the manipulation of collective guilt can be especially deadly.

Why did Ossetians so easily ascribe collective guilt for Beslan to the Ingush?

While conceding modernist scholarly views tracing the roots of Ingush-Ossetian tensions to the post-Second World War period and namely Stalin's deportation of the Ingush to Central Asia in 1944[1] and annexation of the disputed Prigorodny region to North Ossetia, pre-Stalinist experiences within the context of Russian colonization created stable patterns of relations between Orthodox Christian Ossetians and Muslim Ingush in the Imperial and later Soviet states. Although 18–19th century colonialism did not spur modern Ingush–Ossetian conflict, it did sow the seeds of future animosities by encouraging new patterns of interaction, and promoting the dichotomy of 'reliable' vs. 'unreliable' peoples, which seem to continue playing a prominent role in relations between Russia's federal center and its national peripheries today.

Non-neutral policies of the Empire toward Orthodox versus other peoples during colonial state-building and various mechanisms utilized by communities and 'societies'[2] in response to their integration into the Imperial state profoundly impacted their mutual relations. Colonial perceptions within the context of Russian state-building have been a significant factor in the self-identification and historical construction of the modern Ingush-Ossetian conflict.

The Ingush and Ossetian peoples enjoyed equal footing within the Empire in the early years of colonialism. Many North Caucasian lowland and mountainous societies sought political alliances and protectionism from Russia, especially against the powerful *kabardines*, who at the time controlled most of the fertile lands on the plain (Gakaev: 1999:10; Kodzoev: 2002:153; Tsutsiev: 1998: 20–22). Some societies concluded agreements with Moscow, whereby they offered political and military support to the Russian Empire and its allies, while Russia ensured political endorsement and guaranteed no damage or interference from its side. But by the end of 19th century, after the half-century-long Caucasian War and a major 'pacification' campaign organized by the colonial administrations following the war, the Ingush had been convincingly branded as 'unreliable' people, while the Ossetians were considered to be 'Russia's allies in the Caucasus.' The tempests and turbulence of the Great Empire were mirrored in the relations of Ingush and Ossetian societies, with the modern Ingush-Ossetian conflict the culmination of inconsistent, non-neutral state policy that tended to treat Muslim peoples (including the Ingush) unequally when compared to their Christian neighbors (including Ossetians).

The geopolitical role of religion within the context of Imperial state-building was very conspicuous. Russian state-building was closely linked to Orthodoxy, according to Ossetian ethnographer Tsutsiev, "Orthodoxy in the processes of Russian colonization of the Caucasus was virtually equal to Russian citizenship, becoming a citizen was equal to conversion to Orthodoxy. The confessional identification of non-Russian peoples was a clear criteria of their inter-Imperial stratification. Christian peoples were more reliable... and received status benefits." The Russian state was opposed to the spread of Islam, and some agreements openly stated that 'the allied societies' were obliged to adopt Orthodoxy and resist the spread of the Muslim religion.[3]

During the Caucasian War from 1817 to 1864, Ingush societies did not join the Chechens and Avars in the anti-colonial struggle led by the legendary Imam Shamil and preferred to maintain relations with the colonial administration. Shamil unsuccessfully attempted to convert the Ingush to Islam, as Ingush oral history recounts, "with his sword." As the war persisted, however, Ingush societies became more supportive of the resistance and during the Nazran uprising of 1858,[4] which involved the most bloodshed ever seen in Ingush anti-colonial history, the Ingush called on Shamil's army for help. The Caucasian war resulted in the spread of Sufi Islam to Ingushetia and by 1850 most Ingush societies were Muslim. The famous Chechen prophet-philosopher Khunta Khadzi, who preached peace between peoples and argued against going to war with stronger enemies, was extremely influential among Ingush societies. Khunta Khadzi provided Ingush Muslims with a program of moral behavior under humiliating conditions of colonial subjugation:

> "If they tell you to go to the church, do so: churches are only buildings and in our souls we are Muslims.
> If they make you wear crosses, wear them, as they are only pieces of iron, and in your soul you remain Muslim.
> But! If your women are used or abused, if you are forced to forget your language, culture and custom, rise and fight to death, till the last man!"
>
> *(in Kodzoev: 2002: 167)*

Thus, the Islamization of the Ingush was an immediate reaction to colonial expansion and protracted war. Many Ingush like to emphasize that Imam Shamil was unable to convert them to Islam with his sword, while preacher Khunta Khadzi was successful with his word. This historical fact is central to Ingush self-identification as a peaceful people, who suffered unfair repressions from the state. The values preached by Khunta Khadzi strongly shaped the further development of the Ingush nation. As the war continued, however, many Ingush joined anti-colonial troops. Since then there would always be a more radical fringe of Ingush society who would support Chechens and other Caucasians in their guerilla wars against the Russian State.

Serious Ingush-Ossetian differences crystallized after the defeat of Shamil in the Caucasian War. In the late 1840s-1860s, the policy of 'pacification' implemented in the North Caucasus implied the creation of Cossack settlements inside and around indigenous settlements in strategically important areas, including the resettlement of entire communities (*stanitsy*) of Cossacks from other areas of Russia. Cossack interference into the life of the local community was uneven for 'peaceful' Ossetians and 'unreliable' Ingush. Four Cossack settlements[5] emerged on the territory of the Ossetian societies, while Ossetian villages previously located on the sites of Cossack settlements were moved to the South and North of the Cossack line, to the fertile lowland. Thirteen Cossack settlements[6] were built on the sites of Ingush villages, which encircled Ingushetia and blocked the main thoroughfares connecting the Ingush mountains with the plains. Ingush societies were squeezed out of their most fertile land, locked between the mountains and the Cossacks, and moved as far away as possible from the Military-Georgian Road. The entire central region of Ingushetia was forcefully resettled in 1859–1861 and replaced with Cossack settlements of 200 families each, occupying most of the best fertile land.

> **Although tensions between Muslim Ingush and Orthodox Christian Ossetians are rooted in Stalin's repressions, pre-Stalinist experiences in the context of Russian colonization created stable patterns of relations.**

Non-compliance in the integration process among Ingush was frequent, including military resistance to the regime. The most widespread forms of protest against colonial administration and the deprivation of land were the kinds of abductions and raids that were not uncommon in Caucasian economic practice of the time. Raids and abductions for ransom targeted the representatives of the invading 'out-group'—primarily Russians and Cossacks but increasingly Ossetians, perceived as their allies—and were not considered to be a crime by the 'in-group.' Moreover, such activities were often the only way to get married or earn bread for the family among unemployed, landless young men. Within the framework of the colonial state, this traditional pattern of interaction between mountainous peoples acquired new meaning and resulted in an intense mutual negative stereotyping of the Ingush as 'bandits' and 'hostile tribes' and of the Ossetians to be 'cowards' and 'servants of Russia.' Clearly, the Ossetians saw only one side of the story—the abductions—without seeing the repressive policy of the state and economic deprivation of the Ingush. Meanwhile the Ingush, oblivious of the benefits that colonial state-building had brought to Ossetian societies, considered their behavior undignified for Caucasian men.

Integration into the Russian society was problematic for the Ingush, not only because they had rejected Orthodoxy and converted to Islam, but also because they chose to retain their traditional societies, termed 'free societies' by Russian historians. Free societies expelled feudal lords and retained decentralized egalitarian structures rooted in gerontocracy. Each community was governed by a Council of Elders which consisted of the heads of all families on the basis of customary law—*adat* and *sharia*. It was not possible to strike deals with the elites without the consent of the community elders. Ingush intellectuals were usually religious authorities, educated abroad and critical of the regime. No formal educational system existed in Ingushetia.

By contrast, the adoption of Orthodoxy in Ossetia paved the way for the system of Orthodox schooling, which significantly raised the level of literacy among Ossetians. Educational opportunities resulted in the emergence of strong pro-Russian national elite, opportunities for upward mobility in the army created a new stratum of Ossetian officers loyal to empire. Thus, the Ossetians were inclined to perceive themselves as the winners of colonial state-building, while the Ingush were the losers. The division between 'reliable' and 'unreliable' peoples was internalized by the respective communities—the Ossetians felt included into Imperial state- and identity-building as beneficiaries of the empire, while the Ingush experienced systemic exclusion. The perception of Ossetians as a 'reliable people' was based on two major factors: their relative compliance with the state, and their conversion to Orthodoxy. The perception of Ingush as 'unreliable' was likewise based on two factors: their kin relations to the Chechens (Imperial outcasts) and their adoption of Islam.

Not surprisingly, during the Russian Revolution of 1917 the Ingush and Ossetians took different sides. While Ossetians remained loyal to *the ancien regime*, especially among the military elite, the Ingush largely opposed the regime. Ossetian–Ingush relations had acquired a new dimension: 'pro' versus 'contra' ideology toward the incumbent regime ever since.

On February 23, 1944, all 85,000 Ingush were forced onto unheated cattle trains and deported to Central Asia due to their alleged "cooperation with the Nazis." Over one-fourth perished on the way or subsequently died due to the inhuman conditions of Stalinist exile. The Prigorodny District, overwhelmingly inhabited by ethic Ingush,

was transferred to North Ossetia, and some 25–35,000 Ossetians from North Ossetia and Georgia were resettled there on a 'voluntary/enforced' basis. This meant that each Ossetian district and collective farm (*kolkhoz*) was allocated a certain number of 'volunteers' resettled to the 'new districts.' Refusal to go could entail administrative repression, while settlers were entitled to certain benefits including ownership of the house and cattle herd after five years of work on the Ingush farms. This transfer of ownership resulted in the modern territorial dispute and, as a direct consequence, the Ingush-Ossetian conflict of 1992.

From tension to armed conflict

In 1957 when the 'repressed peoples' were allowed to return from exile and the Chechen–Ingush Republic was restored, the

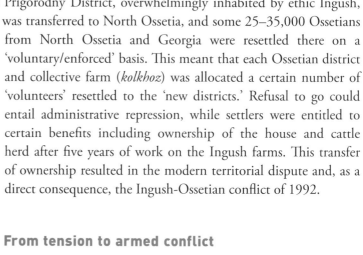

Many of the 40–60,000 Ingush forced migrants who fled the 1992 armed conflict in the Prigorodny District still live in inhuman conditions. The roots of the armed conflict lie in the unresolved ownership disputes precipitated by the Stalinist deportation of the Ingush in 1944. Theories about Ingush involvement in the Beslan tragedy have never been officially dismissed by Russian authorities   Ekaterina Sokirianskaia

Prigorodny District nevertheless remained part of North Ossetia. Upon return, the Ingush found their houses occupied, their cemeteries destroyed, and new people working on their fields. Although the return of the Ingush to the area was actively discouraged by both Moscow and North Ossetian authorities, who created obstacles to Ingush local registration and employment, the Ingush were determined to return to what they considered to be the sacred land of their forefathers. When they returned to their villages they bought the houses that belonged to their families before deportation, and lived illegally (without registration) or bribed officials into registering them. Many integrated well, studied and worked in Vladikavkaz, and despite the tense relationship with Ossetians, the percentage of mixed marriages was rather high.

Nevertheless the "mark of citizens unreliable to the state was fully preserved with respect to the Ingush after [the return from exile] due to the ideological machine that produced daily stereotypes," Tsutsiev states. A representative of Ingush nationality had problems entering higher educational establishments, the army, or civil service and encountered numerous other obstacles. The Ingush, particularly in North Ossetia, remained second-class citizens.

Importantly, following the deportation the authoritarian state prohibited open deliberation or research on issues of deportation, thereby preventing the rehabilitation of social trauma. In fact, the attitude toward the repressed peoples was one of 'pardoned but not forgiven.' A lack of public discussion resulted in the absence of self-reflection on behalf of Ossetian society about their role in the aftermath of deportation in light of the fact that the majority of representatives of other ethnic groups resettled in the houses of the repressed, including Dagestanis and Russians, decided to leave these houses or inexpensively sold them to their original owners. The majority of Ossetians did not return property expropriated from the Ingush. The official Ossetian history includes no mention of the Ingush deportation from the Prigorodny District and the resettlement of the Ossetians to this area in 1944. A newly published volume on the 20th century history of North Ossetia edited by the republic's ex-president Alexander Dzasokhov simply skips this part of Ossetian history (Dzasokhov: 2003). A 2005 calendar published by the North Ossetian Ministry for Nationalities entitled "In Ossetia, as a Unified Family" mentions dozens of nationalities, including 610 Avars, 232 Poles, and 114 Turkmen while completely ignoring the second largest nationality—the 21,000 Ingush.

The outbreak of armed conflict in 1992 was brought on by a number of specific social and political conditions: 1) a weak state and systemic crisis of state governance, 2) a power struggle between the leadership of the former Soviet Union and the leadership of the Russian Federation, 3) the 'nationalization' of politics in the region, 4) the emergence of a free market for arms, and 5) the 'privatization' of law enforcement. Finally, lack of political will and weakness among forces that could counteract the worsening confrontation paved the way to large-scale violence.

Evidently, conflict ensued after a number of private territorial disputes escalated into a series of battles, and the Ossetian interior and Russian federal troops responded by crushing the 'rebel' forces. Russia's Security Council, quoting a group assigned to investigate the events, estimates that 583 people were killed (including 407 Ingush, 105 Ossetians and 17 federal servicemen, with the remainder impossible to identify), over 650 injured (including 168 Ingush and 418 Ossetians), over 3,000 houses damaged, and some 8,000 people immediately affected by the violence. An estimated 30–60,000 people fled the conflict.

Not only did the Ossetian and Ingush press present the events very differently, but also independent reporters working in the area during the war. Over the last 14 years, deeply internalized myths about the conflict that spanned five days in October and November 1992 have snowballed. Truth committees have not been established.

> The Russian state was opposed to the spread of Islam. Some agreements openly stated that the 'allied societies' were obliged to adopt Orthodoxy, which was virtually equal to citizenship in the process of Russian colonization in the Caucasus.

The Ossetian myth of Ingush collective guilt for 'planned action,' premeditated violence and 'treacherous behavior' has become a part of Ossetian popular consciousness and a strong argument against Ingush return. For example, a school principal I interviewed at one of the mixed education schools for Ingush and Ossetian children) in the Prigorodny District said: "Every morning after the first class I check the lists of children who are missing from school. If there are no Ingush names on the list, we can relax and work in peace. But if Ingush children are missing we have to cancel classes and close the school, as this means something terrible will happen." A school teacher from the village of Tarskoe said in an interview: "I went to school with the Ingush, I had many friends among them, and none of them warned me of what was going to happen! How can I live with them after that?!"

Interestingly, similar myths of collective guilt for ethnically charged violence and terrorist attacks have been repeatedly reproduced by both Ossetians and Russians (not to mention other majority populations around the world affected by violence perpetrated by 'outsiders'). For example, the myth actively circulated in Russia that Moscow diaspora Chechens 'knew' about the Nord Ost Theater terror attack in Moscow in 2002 and stopped sending their children to school several days in advance. The popular myth that Ingush and Chechen students in Vladikavkaz did not show up for classes three days before the hostage-taking in Beslan also persists despite the fact that the academic year in Russia starts on September 1, the day the hostage-taking took place.

The social costs of protracted internal displacement

Most of the 30–60,000 forced migrants who fled North Ossetia in 1992 found refuge in the neighboring republics of Ingushetia and Chechnya. In Ingushetia spontaneous residence centers emerged accommodating IDPs from the Prigorodny District, while in Grozny—already home to many Ingush deportees unable to return to Prigorodny—

relatives hosted many Ingush forced migrants. Significant discrepancies in official numbers of Ingush IDPs—the Migration Service of Ingushetia counts 61,000, the Russian Federal Migration Service registered 49,048, and the Chair of the North Ossetian Supreme Soviet puts the figure at 32,782. Such discrepancies are explained by Ingush difficulties in registering their residence in North Ossetia (neither the new houses built or bought by Ingush, nor the families who lived in them, were included in the official register).

Concerned non-state actors and governments provide IDPs around the world with the food, water, and medical care necessary for their survival. In the early 1990s the United Nation's Administrative Coordination Committee developed a conceptual framework aimed to provide for the basic needs of IDPs while at the same time preventing dependency and a loss of working skills by the aid recipient population. Programs integrating relief aid with development, ensuring that IDPs are active participants rather than passive recipients have been widely implemented by international organizations including UNHCR, UNDP, ICRC, WHO, WFP, etc.

For a variety of reasons including the unwillingness of many governments to interfere in Russia's 'internal affairs,' in practice IDPs have spent 14 years in Ingushetia live in inhumane conditions and receive no international support and virtually no humanitarian or medical aid from the Russian state organizations. Although the IDPs reside on Russian territory, federal authorities have not assumed responsibility for those in Ingushetia, resigning them to frustrating years of substandard living conditions and immense poverty.

At the same time, quite impressive progress has been made in respect of return. Thousands of Ingush IDPs have returned to 13 villages of the Republic of North-Ossetia–Alania, which as of the 2002 census was home to 21,442 Ingush. Although the state strategy of reintegrating former combatants into law enforcement agencies is questionable at best, their putting under control has been successful and the physical security of Ingush in North Ossetia has significantly improving in the recent years, with a dramatic reduction in the number of hate crimes (68 in 1999, 19 in 2000, 19 in 2001, 9 in 2002, and 0 in 2003). Although a significant amount of IDP property is still illegally occupied, the Ossetian judiciary has played a major role in the restitution of property and has a record of passing ethnically neutral decisions in favor of IDPs. Basic infrastructure and medical and educational facilities have been restored and in some villages Ingush and Ossetian neighbors visit each other for funerals and weddings, just as they did 13 years ago.

According to the monitoring I regularly carried out in the villages of the Prigorodny District in 2003–2006, the most favorable psychological climate is in villages where Ingush have returned and the settlements are not fragmented into ethnic enclaves, but where Ingush and Ossetian families live on the same street.

Toward lasting peace and sustainable return: Evaluating the options

A number of obstacles continue to prevent a lasting resolution to the Ingush–Ossetian conflict. Throughout the 14 years since the events of October–November 1992, Russian federal authorities have not attempted to propose a *political solution* addressing the underlying cause of the conflict—the territorial dispute. Instead, Russia's policy for resolving the conflict has been to 'liquidate the consequences,' i.e. restore housing and infrastructure and allow IDPs to return while maintaining the political status quo in favor of the Ossetian side. The fact that this status quo was achieved with the assistance of the federal army makes the situation appear even more unfair in the eyes of the Ingush community.

Interestingly the Kremlin, so conscious of subordination, centralization, and state integrity (especially under President Putin), continues to treat the Ossetians and Ingush as two independent nations—one friendly to Russia and the other unfriendly. The division between 'reliable' and 'unreliable' people persists, and nationality policy within the state resembles international relations between allies and antagonists rather than relations between a federal center and its regions.

Moreover, Russian federal policy has failed to promote *good governance and interethnic policymaking* with Ingush political representation. The fact that Ingush returnees have no representation in state institutions has proven to be a serious obstacle to their reintegration. Their exclusion from policymaking has also undermined efforts to *combat discrimination* against returnees in North Ossetia at a time when the territory is overwhelmed with refugees and returnees from two conflicts (South Ossetian refugees from Georgia also remain poorly integrated) and has not seen any *economic solutions* for development and economic revival. Development projects aimed at reducing unemployment and creating conditions for mixed ethnicity work forces would provide strong incentives for reconciliation.

> According to the monitoring I regularly carried out, the best success stories are in villages that are not fragmented into ethnic enclaves but where Ingush and Ossetian families live on the same street

Last but not least, the official policy of media censorship as a way of banning nationalists from the public space has proven unsuccessful. Although it did exclude some hate speech from the mainstream press, hostile messages still made their way to the public. Most importantly, *control of the media* was left to nationalistic elites who failed to promote balanced analyses refuting stereotypes and myths.

The story of IDP return to Prigorodny has its successes and failures. Villages of mixed settlements, where Ingush have returned and live dispersed next to Ossetian neighbors have proven fine examples of post-conflict confidence building. Although some hostility and distrust do remain, relations are on the right track and moving toward sustainable reconciliation.

Dongaron: A Success Story

The village of Dongaron is a striking example of successful transformation from ethic conflict to peaceful reconciliation. The process of Ingush return to Dongaron was completed in 2004.

All 77 applications submitted for return or resettlement were accepted by the local administration, and 33 houses have been rebuilt. Plots of land are being allocated to Ingush returnees who require additional land. There are now 147 families in Dongaron in total, including North Ossetian, Russian, South Ossetian, and 33 Ingush. Refugees from South Ossetia and the inner regions of Georgia are accommodated in 34 flats converted from a former prison. The village has a school educating children from a mixture of ethnic backgrounds, a medical station, and a village club with new library.

Although complete reconciliation requires time, the 'moral-psychological climate' seems healthy. "We do not have any problems with our Ossetian neighbors, we visit each other for tea, and of course weddings and funerals. In recent years there have been no clashes between the youth, they communicate well, although they do not yet party together. In the evenings the Ossetian youngsters get together in the club, and we keep our young people at home to avoid clashes," said Ingush Elder Poshev. The school principal Elisbar Arutunov said: "We have a healthy environment, although some nervousness is created by additional security measures and press." Ingush and the Ossetians line up together for meeting with the local administration, they laugh and crack jokes together, and greet each other in a friendly way. The head of the administration Sozyr Bagalov explained that the main problem is unemployment. "I will tell you something: if you want peace, give us jobs. We do not need to put people around a table in front of each other. We need to put them in an industrial factory, and if they sit at a table, let it be a kitchen table during lunch break," he said. "When someone is unemployed, they have too much time to think about grievances and the status of the Prigorodny District. Let him occupy his time thinking about how to better sell the autumn crops at the market in Vladikavkaz."

Observations and interviews conducted in the ethnically mixed settlement of Kurtat revealed a similarly promising situation.

Tarskoje: A conflict-prone solution

The village of Tarskoje is an example of an unsuccessful post-conflict settlement. A policy of restraint split the village into two ethnic enclaves, de facto creating two separate villages with Ingush living on the right side and Ossetians of the left. Ingush and Ossetian children attend separate schools and there is virtually no communication between the communities. Both sides try not to cross the dividing borderline unless absolutely necessary, and the village administration, library, and club are located on the Ossetian side, restricting Ingush access. In 2004 Ossetian teenagers came to play football on the Ingush side, but the adults forbid the boys from playing together after several weeks. "We decided not to experiment. It will certainly end up badly," said one teacher from the Ossetian school in an interview.

A tense atmosphere pervades the village. Immediately after visitors appear on the Ingush side, militiamen seem to spring from the soil like mushrooms. Driving through the Ossetian side, an unknown car with Islamic prayer beads hanging in the front window is monitored closely by the suspicious looks of the villagers. While attempting to conduct interviews with school teachers in Taskoje together with a foreign journalist, I myself

Before the tragedy in Beslan human rights groups tried to build bridges between children from Ingush and Ossetian schools. The Human Rights Center Memorial carried out small reconciliation projects, which brought Ingush and Ossetian children together in one classroom. After Beslan these projects were suspended ▪ Ekaterina Sokirianskaia

was arrested in Tarkoje and held for three hours in a militia station. The militiamen then summoned two hand-picked teachers to the station, allowed them to talk to us for ten minutes, and escorted us out of the Prigorodny District with two military jeeps in front and behind. The interviews turned out to be interesting nonetheless. A literature teacher from an Ossetian school began the interview cheerfully: "The Ingush are not bandits or terrorists. Terrorists have no nationality," but ended on a much less pacifist note: "All of us have guns in the backyard. We will sell our last cow to buy guns—they will never take us by surprise again." Notably, during the October–November 1992 conflict there was no fighting in Tarskoje, and every Ingush family had already left by the time the Russian and Ossetian troops arrived.

Obviously, there is no lasting peace in Tarskoje. The sustainability of the return is doubtful. This is the situation in the majority of the settlements where Ingush returnees and Ossetian communities form ethnic pockets, such as Chermen, Kartsa, and Kambileevka.

Policy options: Restrict return and create enclaves, or encourage return to places of origin?

The tragedy of Beslan was a severe test for Ossetian-Ingush conflict resolution and Ingush return. An unfortunate consequence of the tragedy has been the decision by Russian authorities to 'temporarily solve' problems of Ingush security by restricting return and dividing Ossetian and Ingush communities into ethnic enclaves. The strategy of enclaves institutionalizes ethnic cleavages, perpetuates the conflict, and increases frustration among the Ingush, who interpret this 'solution' as a defeat—not only does it mean that they loose the Prigorodny District to which they are entitled according to Russia's 'Law on the Rehabilitation of Repressed Peoples,' but it also means that the ethnic cleansing perpetrated against them in 1992 with the support of the federal army has permanent consequences, 'cleansing' them out of the area for good. This new grievance will be another blow to the legitimacy of the federal center in the eyes of the Ingush, confirming their suspicions that they are still being treated as 'unreliable peoples.' In the unstable conditions of the North Caucasus, such grievances can fuel propaganda promoting acts of violence and terrorism.

Peace plan and recommendations

My findings point to the following strategies for government, national and international decision-makers seeking a durable resolution to the Ingush–Ossetian conflict:

To all parties concerned:

1) Acknowledge the importance of resolving the Ingush–Ossetian conflict, which remains a serious destabilizing factor for the entire North Caucasus region, threatens further armed clashes, and creates conditions for the radicalization of youth.

2) Initiate programs aimed at securing a durable peace which include the sustainable return of Ingush IDPs to the Prigorodny District.

To Russian federal policymakers:

1) Seek political solutions to resolve the Ingush–Ossetian conflict. A possible solution to the territorial dispute may include the following elements:

   - The Prigorodny District remains part of North Ossetia. Ossetia recognizes the special status of the district as an area of 'consonsiational' rule.

   - All Ingush IDPs return to the places of their original residence. Those who do not wish to return are provided with full compensation for their lost housing and land.

   - The 'Law on the Rehabilitation of the Repressed Peoples' includes addendum that prescribes a mechanism for the return or compensation of property lost as a result of Stalinist deportation. All Ingush who had property in Prigorodny district before the deportation are assisted in reclaiming it and returning to their historical homeland if they wish.

   - The Prigorodny District Council unites deputies from Ingush and Ossetian communities who proportionally represent their populations. The Council is granted the autonomy, authority, and budget from local taxes sufficient for its needs and elects the head of the district administration on a rotating basis from both Ingush and Ossetian representatives. The villages of mixed settlement create village councils.

   - Ingush are provided due representation in North Ossetian state institutions, including government, parliament, ministries and law enforcement.

   - Former combatants are restricted from occupying leadership posts in the local government.

   - Educational programs in the Ossetian media focus on the crimes against humanity committed by Stalinism and Stalin's statues and portraits are banned from public spaces.

   - A unified federal agency for the resolution of the Ingush–Ossetian conflict is re-established with responsibility for monitoring the return and observance of concluded agreements.

2) Allow for an honest investigation of the tragedy of Beslan and strictly punish in accordance with the law those responsible.

3) Define the borders of the "water protection zone" as soon as possible on the basis of an expert, politically neutral opinion and either begin the process of return to this area or develop a compensation scheme for those houses situated in the water protection zone.

4) Speed up the resolution of the property dispute concerning illegally captured flats in the towns of Vladikavkaz, Oktyabrskoje, Yuzhny, and Ir.

5) End the practice of ethnically segregated education in Prigorodny District schools.

6) Prosecute cases related to the illegal treatment of Ingush prisoners in preliminary detainment in North Ossetia and end the practice of charging Ingush men with 'terrorism' and holding them in Vladikavkaz without legal representation.

7) Transfer the tax inspection authority for the Prigorodny District from Beslan back to the Prigorodny administrative center of Oktyabrskoye.

8) Ban discriminatory practices in North Ossetian institutions including banks (eg. Western Union services), which have been known to engage in a kind of segregated banking whereby services available to Ossetians are restricted for Ingush residents.

9) Provide humanitarian assistance to Ingush IDPs remaining in temporary residence facilities in Ingushetia and grant these facilities official temporary residence center status, providing them with assistance according to the usual scheme practiced by the Russian Ministry of Emergency and migration services.

10) Launch income-generating programs that encourage both new and old enterprises to employ ethnically mixed personnel.

11) Develop programs aimed at youth vocational training and employment in Ingushetia and North Ossetia.

12) Establish recreation centers for youth including sport gyms in the Prigorodny District.

13) Support exchanges focusing on culture, sport, education, and economics between the two republics.

To humanitarian and development organizations:

1) Provide urgent medical and humanitarian assistance in the Prigorodny District to Ingush IDPs as well as refugees from other Caucasus regions.

2) Launch development and income-generating programs in the Prigorodny District targeting Ingush, Ossetian and North Ossetian communities. Specifically, programs should be encouraged that aim to create small collective enterprises involving Ingush and Ossetian employees (kibbutz-like small collective farming, fish farming, and bird factories).

3) Support Caucasus-wide higher education programs for students from conflict zones, including the creation of a western-type liberal university (possibly located in Georgia).

4) Establish programs that counter youth idleness in the Prigorodny District.

5) Continue providing medical and psychological assistance to victims of the Beslan tragedy.

To human rights and peacemaking organizations:

1) Monitor human rights and discrimination in Prigorodny District.

2) Assist the victims of rights abuses in securing redress through judicial institutions.

3) Launch programs aimed at conflict transformation and reconciliation, especially targeting youth. The methodology of peacemaking via positive activities will be most successful.

4) Establish human rights education programs promoting multiculturalism, tolerance and civic and democratic culture that target youth, media reporters, judges and law enforcement officers from the Prigorodny District, Ingushetia, and Ossetia.

Notes

[1] Alexander Dzadziev in an interview with the author in August 2005; Lejla Arapkhanova in an interview with the author in August 2005.

[2] Russian historiography uses the term 'societies' in reference to North Caucasian communities before and during the colonial wars. I will likewise use this term, since I find it more precise and free of ideological connotations (unlike for example '*tribes*').

[3] In 1770 when 24 representatives of Ingush societies signed an agreement with Russia at Barta-bos (the Hill of Agreement) they sent the following letter to the Russian military commandant Nejmich in Kyzlyar: "*Here came to our land the archimandrite Porfiry, in his presence we swore into loyalty and diligence to her imperial majesty. Along with this, according to the state interests this archimandrite took the effort to show us the road of truth according to Christian tradition. We, the kistine people (proto-Ingush societies), herewith undersigned*" Kodzoev: 152. In 1810 another agreement with Russia obliged the Ingush "not to accept the missions of efendies and mullahs or Muslim laws and not to build mosques." (Tsutsiev: 1998:22).

[4] The Nazran uprising broke out in response to the decision of the Russian army to create large settlements on the plains by eliminating small individual households of farmers, which were often located a significant distance from each other. Individual families had to be resettled into big villages (no less than 300 households) which were easier to control. This new setup ran counter to the traditional Ingush economy, lifestyle and rules of land ownership, and the societies sent a delegation to negotiate with the military authorities. The latter arrested four deputies, and in response 5,000 Ingush men attacked the Russian fortress in Nazran. The Ingush called Imam Shamil for military assistance, but Shamil failed to arrive on time and the uprising was suppressed and its organizers executed or sent to labor camps to Siberia (Kodzoev: 165).

[5] Stanitsy Ardonskaja, Arkhonskaja, Nikolaevskaja, Zmejskaja (1838–1845).

[6] Stanitsy Troitskaja (1845), Sunzenskaja (1845), Voznesenovskaja (1847), Tarskaja (1860), Nesterovskaja (1861), Karabulakovskaja (1859), Feldmarshal'skaja (1860), Assinovskaja (1861), Vorontsovo-Dashkovskaja (1861), Galashevskaja, Dattakhskaja, shutors Tarsky and Muzichi (1867).

Conflict in Georgia: Religion and Ethnicity

Archil Gegeshidze

Georgia's peaceful Rose Revolution in 2003 displaced former President Eduard Shevardnadze. During the popular revolution, supporters of current President Mihail Saakashvili marched on parliament carrying roses as a symbol of nonviolence
▪ Archil Gegeshidze

For over a decade Georgian authorities have attempted to characterize Georgia as a nation of extraordinary religious tolerance—a notion most vividly evidenced by Maidani, a patch of land in downtown Tbilisi where a Georgian Orthodox church stands nobly beside an Armenian Apostolic church, a synagogue and a mosque— a scene not uncommon elsewhere in the country. Nevertheless, Georgian modern history is riddled with ethnic conflict fueled by religious differences. Skeptics challenge the government's assertion of a tolerant Georgia as a cynical, propagandistic trick of a central government striving to mold international public opinion in its favor, while at times pursuing ultra-nationalistic policies that infringe upon religious freedom. This is at least partially true. After losing two tug-of-wars with Russia over Abkhazia and South Ossetia, one of Georgia's main policy objectives is to secure international support for the peaceful transfer of these territories back to Georgia. Furthermore, the country's recent quest for a new identity has given rise to several dangerous popular convictions.

Dangerous convictions of a new nation

Following the collapse of communist ideology and the Zviad Gamsakhurdia-led national independence movement, Georgia's identity crisis resulted in the emergence of two popular

International Policy Fellow **Archil Gegeshidze** is a policy researcher with the Georgian Foundation for Strategic and International Studies. He served in the late 1990s as Georgia's Chief Foreign Policy Advisor and Assistant to the Head of State on National Security. Further information about his research is available from the IPF websites: http://pdc.ceu.hu (Source IPF) and www.policy.hu/gegeshidze.

convictions that foreshadowed the course of modern events. First, the conviction that Georgia was in need of 'ethnic purification' because all recent non-Georgian or 'foreign' arrivals living on Georgian land are more loyal to imperial Russia than to Georgia.[1] Prior to the development of Georgian popular discourse promoting civil and human rights as well as the need to guarantee minority rights to self-determination, the 'ethnic purification' discourse launched Gamsakhurdia and his followers to power.

The second conviction nourished by nationalistic sentiments was the idea of Georgian Orthodoxy as the sole religion for 'genuine Georgians.' This outlook had much to do with the important role of the Georgian Orthodox Church in uniting the country in critical times throughout the nation's history. Although Georgians were not altogether ready to immediately flock back to the bosom of the Church after long years of infidelity under the Soviet system, the 'masses' tended to perceive conversion from sinners into believers as the sign and spirit of the times. Being religious, not to mention emulating popular new leaders, had become fashionable.[2]

The 'ethnic purification' and 'genuine Georgian Orthodox' convictions quickly gained popularity. Not surprisingly, in due course both convictions had a significant impact on Georgian policy design, most often with negative consequences.

From ethnic nationalism to ethnic conflict

The official ideology of ethnic nationalism resulted almost immediately in the adoption of policies hostile toward ethnic minorities, most notably the titular ethnic groups in Abkhazia and South Ossetia. Local separatists and their Russian patrons added fuel to the fire in their efforts to pursue goals predetermined by both history and geopolitics.[3] The first serious confrontation took place in South Ossetia. In January 1991 several thousand Georgian troops entered Tskhinvali, an administrative center of South Ossetia, marking the beginning of a year of chaos with sporadic Russian involvement and an escalation into urban warfare. One year later an agreement was reached between the parties bringing about a ceasefire, but the war's consequences were devastating: some 1,000 dead, 100 missing, extensive destruction of homes and infrastructure,[4] and around 30,000 refugees and internally displaced persons (IDPs).[5]

In the meantime, Gamsakhurdia was overthrown by a civil war within Georgia and the former Foreign Minister of the USSR, Eduard Shevardnadze, was invited back from Moscow to stabilize the situation. Nevertheless little progress has been made since 1992 to bring Ossetians and Georgians closer together. Current Georgian President Mikhail Saakashvili's previous attempt in 2004 to break a twelve-year deadlock and take another step to restore Georgia's territorial integrity by undermining the regime in Tskhinvali was misguided,[6] ignoring the fact that only a comprehensive approach to conflict resolution will result in a sustainable peace. Later the approach has changed. Georgia has devised a peace plan implying a three-stage strategy of conflict settlement.[7] The onus is on Georgia, with help from its international partners, to increase the security and confidence of people living in conflict zone, promote economic rehabilitation and development, ensure the right of Ossetians to return to South Ossetia and Georgia proper, and create arrangements guaranteeing South Ossetia's effective autonomy.[8]

Unfortunately the conflict in Abkhazia is comparably more deep-rooted and has had significantly more devastating results both in terms of Georgian nation-building and inter-ethnic relations between Georgians and Abkhaz. During the Russian-backed war in 1992–1993, the Abkhaz defeated the Georgian forces. About 300,000 people lost their homes and the seemingly intractable resentment, grievances and ambitions sparked by the war remain tough obstacles to peace, not to mention the absence of any clear plan for conflict resolution. Unless underlying grievances are addressed, efforts to re-integrate Abkhazia into Georgia are almost certain to lead to violence. Over the past decade inconsistent policies have led to even greater divisions between Abkhaz and Georgians, so that the political positions taken by both sides have diverged radically when compared to their positions immediately following the cessation of hostilities in 1993.[9]

Also viewed as a powder keg of potential violence is Javakheti, a region in southern Georgia populated by Armenians and characterized by widespread poverty and social insecurity, high levels of corruption and organized crime, large-scale illegal storage and possession of firearms, and weak state capacity to address security concerns. In the early 1990s, demonstrations organized by Armenian nationalist organizations calling for secession were not supported by the majority of Javakheti's population.[10] The situation has worsened since 1999, marked by public protests over deteriorating economic conditions, irregular electricity supplies, and growing speculation over the withdrawal of the local Russian military base.[11] Although the central government is currently in control of the situation, the potential for conflict is real.[12]

Over time, however, radical nationalistic attitudes have given way to more liberal views. Georgia's Rose Revolution in 2003 has brought to power political forces that are increasingly aware that only peaceful means will succeed in resolving ethnic differences, and high popular support enables the incumbent authorities to effectively advocate for seeking peaceful political solutions and suppressing ultra-nationalistic sentiments in Georgian society.

Taming religious extremism

Despite general tolerance toward minority religious groups, some Georgians are suspicious of Protestants and the followers of other 'nontraditional' religions and believe that they take advantage of the population's economic hardship by providing economic assistance in exchange for conversion. They argue that foreign Christian missionaries should confine their activities to non-Christian areas, and at times their attempts to 'protect' the country's Church and cultural values turned aggressive in the late 1990s, with hate speech and violent attacks by organized groups of Orthodox Christian vigilantes directed at the members of religious groups including Baptists, Jehovah's Witnesses, Evangelists, Pentecostals, and Hare Krishnas. The authorities failed to respond adequately and at times even cooperated in the attacks, which consequently became more frequent and pervasive, spreading from Tbilisi to many other regions throughout Georgia. The hate speech and attacks faded prior to the November 2003 elections, leading to speculation about how closely the government was controlling the violence. In 2004, there were scattered reports of intimidation and violence against religious minorities, but it was clear that the number of incidents had declined dramatically when compared with previous years.

Georgia's current President, National Security Council Secretary, and Government Ombudsman have effectively advocated for religious freedom and made numerous public speeches and appearances in support of minority religious groups. The Ministry of Internal Affairs and Procuracy have also become more active in the protection of religious freedom by pursuing criminal cases against Orthodox extremists who have continued to attack religious minorities.

Nevertheless, the problem of both verbal and physical harassment of the non-traditional minority religious groups remains, while the Georgian Orthodox Church continues to retain its status as the only religious institution with legal status in Georgia.[13] Numerous parliamentarians objected strongly to a report by the ombudsman calling for equal recognition under the law for all religions. The MPs stated that the historical position of the Georgian Orthodox Church justified its privileged position. In the meantime, the Government passed a law enabling religious groups to register, but the unregistered religious groups still are not officially permitted to rent office space, acquire construction rights, import literature, or represent the international church. Furthermore, the Roman Catholic Church and the Armenian Apostolic Church have been unable to secure the return of churches closed or given to the Georgian Orthodox Church during the Soviet period.

The Ministry of Education now requires all fourth grade students to take a "Religion and Culture" class intended to cover the history of major religions. According to many parents, however, teachers of the class focus solely on the Georgian Orthodox Church, which is hardly surprising considering that the Church has gained a consultative role in all curriculum development.[14]

The above-mentioned cases of religious intolerance should not be viewed as proof of wide-scale Georgian xenophobia or religious nationalism, but more accurately a desperate attempt by the Georgian Orthodox Church to prevail over increasingly influential nontraditional religious denominations.

What next?

Georgia currently finds itself in a unique and critically important moment in its history, when the post-revolutionary political landscape presents a window of opportunity for building a viable democracy and a new state based upon the rule of law. The fate of the new regime will depend upon its ability to upgrade standards for the respect of human rights and ease ethnic tensions—challenges so all-encompassing and profound that they will be

---

Georgia and its Muslims

by Fariz Ismailzade

Georgia's ongoing separatist conflicts are not overtly religious, but the activities of local Muslim communities are often at the center of Tbilisi's discussions on security issues. The leaderships of both separatist regions—Abkhazia and South Ossetia—profess largely Christian Orthodoxy like the majority of Georgians, although the population of Abkhazia is primarily Muslim. The recent political unification of the country's Muslims from various ethnic groups, however, is interpreted by some as a move toward increased self-determination and possibly independence.

Past relations

The majority Christian and Muslim minority populations in Georgia have enjoyed centuries of peaceful coexistence and cooperation in resisting foreign invasions. Since Georgia regained its independence in 1991, however, relations between Christians and Muslims have often been problematic, especially as regards the Turk-Meshetins (Akhiska Turks) deported in the 1940s by Stalin to Central Asia who are currently striving to return to their historic homeland. Despite the fact that the repatriation of Turk-Meshetins was a Council of Europe requirement for Georgia's membership in 1999, Georgian authorities are not aiding and at times hindering this return.

Another Muslim group often seen as posing a threat to Georgian stability and national security is the Chechens settled in the Pankisi Gorge. This group hosted rebels from Chechnya and sparked Russian-Georgian bilateral hostilities in the late 1990s, when the Kremlin began accusing official Tbilisi of assisting Chechen rebels and hiding them in the Gorge and even threatened military intervention if adequate measures were not taken to address the situation. Indeed, due to its links with Chechnya, Pankisi Gorge has become a hotspot for the smuggling of weapons and other illegal goods. Finally, in 1999-2000 former Georgian President Eduard Shevardnadze, eager to stave off Russian invasion and prove to the international community that an independent Tbilisi is capable of controlling its own territory and effectively fighting crime, ordered the army to step in and clean up illegal activities.

Secessionist tendencies among Georgia's Muslim Abkhaz and Ajarian minorities caused the most headaches for Georgia throughout the 1990s. With Russia's help, the Abkhaz have been more successful in their anti-Tbilisi drive, effectively expelling Georgian residents as well as the federal army from Abkhazia in early 1990s and establishing a de-facto independent state. Abkhazia remains the number one security problem for Georgian authorities. Ajaria has not officially declared independence, but during the presidency of Ajarian leader Aslan Abashidze, the territory successfully avoided subordination to the central government. Ajaria's autonomous status was abolished soon after Aslan Abashidze was overthrown in 2004, and Georgia's new political leadership has managed to quell "disobedient" Ajaria.

Meanwhile, Georgia's Muslim Azerbaijanis, who initiated the country's new Muslim Democratic Party, are showing an increasingly frustrated attitude toward Georgian authorities as well as internal strife within their communities, and may prove the largest threat to Georgian stability in the near future. These 600,000 or so ethnic Azerbaijanis live in a compact area in Kvemo-Kartli on the border with Azerbaijan and represent the country's largest ethnic minority. Land privatization is the top priority on the list of policy problems for ethnic Azerbaijanis in Georgia. Land has been neither distributed nor privatized among Azerbaijanis, so they are forced to rent it from ethnic Georgians (or use it with their permission). As a result, ethnic Azerbaijanis believe they are being discriminated against by the government and stage sporadic protests, with several such protests resulting in the death last year of Azerbaijani villagers at the hands of Georgian landowners.

Former President Eduard Shevardnadze's administration did little to address these issues. Nevertheless, ethnic Azerbaijanis chose not to rebel or seek separation from Georgia and, along with their kin in Azerbaijan, they had high expectations that following the Rose Revolution in 2003 the new, more democratic Georgian leadership would solve the Azerbaijani land problem. These hopes were soon dashed when the new administration neglected the land privatization issue and did not place the problems of ethnic minorities high on their political agenda. At the same time, the new regime's fight against corruption, cross-border smuggling and tax evasion has effectively led to what Azerbaijanis perceive as a discriminatory crackdown against Azerbaijanis, with dozens of ethnic Azerbaijani businessmen arrested in 2004. To make matters worse, Azerbaijanis in Georgia traditionally earn profits from agriculture, and the tightened border regulations hinder them from trading and selling their products in Azerbaijan

These tensions, aggravated by the high unemployment rate among ethnic Azerbaijanis in Georgia, have turned this region into a powder-keg for potential conflict, with spontaneous protests a common occurrence.

Current context

On June 20, 2006, the National Assembly of the Azerbaijanis of Georgia invited representatives of Georgia's Muslim minorities to the Turkish city of Erzurum to discuss the establishment of a political party in Georgia. The conference was attended by 80 delegates consisting of ethnic Azerbaijanis, Muslim Ossetians, Chechens (Kistins), Ingush, Turk-Mesheti, Adjar, Abkhaz and Muslim Georgians. As a result of the discussions, a working group was established which will prepare the founding congress of the Muslim Democratic Party of Georgia. According to the final declaration of the conference, the Party will respect the "peace and territorial integrity of Georgia" (the statement was not signed by the Abkhaz delegation).

Both Turkey and Azerbaijan remain major players in Georgia's domestic politics, but both countries would rather encourage Georgian stability and economic cooperation—aims that serve the interests of Georgia's Muslims. Given this international political backdrop, instability involving Muslim minorities in Georgia in the near future is likely to focus on issues of economic discontent vented in the form of small, sporadic protests.

The role of Russia in Georgia's minority relations should not be underestimated given its traditional practice of precipitating unrest among ethnic minorities to exert pressure over former Soviet Republics If Moscow wishes to see the current leadership in Tbilisi weakened, provoking clashes involving Muslim minorities or Armenians and Azerbaijanis in Georgia may succeed in destabilizing the country, especially if Russia chooses to completely withdraw its military base from the Armenian-populated town of Akhalkalaki.

*International Policy Fellow **Fariz Ismailzade** (www.policy.hu/ismailzade) is a political analyst and university lecturer based in Azerbaijan. He is a regular correspondent for various western news services and has worked in Washington, DC at the Center for Strategic and International Studies and the Embassy of Azerbaijan.*

difficult to successfully address without the energetic cooperation of the international community.

Specifically, in striving to ease regional tensions and end ethnic conflict in Georgia, the international community should heed the following lessons learned:

- The lack of coordination between international actors (both international organizations and individual governments) prevents an effective utilization of diplomatic as well as financial resources;

- Multilateral efforts aimed at the political settlement of conflicts, such as the UN Security Council or Friends of the Secretary General on Abkhazia/Georgia, proved to be ineffective due to Russia's veto power; and

- Limited mandates and/or a lack of motivation has meant that United Nations Observer Mission in Georgia and CIS-led Peacekeeping Operations have not brought tangible results.

Policy recommendations for both international actors and Georgia's government:

- Questions of Georgia's accession to the EU and NATO should not undermine cooperation with Russia. Further international pressure via EU-Russia and/or US-Russia dialogue could move Russia toward more constructive bilateral participation in conflict resolution;

- Importantly, the European Union can encourage constructive dialogue toward a settlement by cultivating western liberal values and engaging in conflict mediation with Georgia and Russia;

- Wide-ranging debate on the relation-ship between citizenship, nationalism and ethnic identity should be encouraged in all areas. Meanwhile minorities, including nontraditional religious groups, should be considered in all assistance programs;

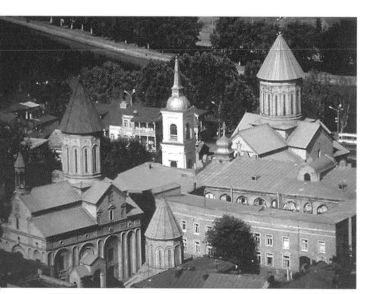

- Last but not least, the needs of those most affected by conflict—often the poorest sectors of society—must be addressed and their voices and well-being should be strengthened through programs designed to boost personal security, civil society, micro-finance, and the leadership of women.

Georgian and Russian churches on the banks of the Kura River, built primarily during the last century. Most incidents of religious intolerance in Georgia are fueled by desperate attempts of the Georgian Orthodox Church to prevail over increasingly influential nontraditional religious denominations.

Notes

1   Ronald Grigor Suny, *The Making of the Georgian Nation*, Indiana University Press, 1994, pp.324–5.

2   Ivlian Khaindrava, *Church in Modern Georgia*, Central Asia and Caucasus, Vol. 5(29), 2003, p.27 (in Russian)

3   For example, prior to the parliamentary elections in 1990 on September 20, the local leadership of South Ossetia initiated a proclamation of full sovereignty within the USSR. Gamsakhurdia's government responded fiercely and abolished the autonomous oblast status of South Ossetia on December 11, 1990. Soon afterward, the direct military confrontation erupted.

4   International Crisis Group, *Georgia: Avoiding War in South Ossetia*, Europe Report #159, Tbilisi-Brussels, 2004, pp.3–4.

5   Pryakhin, Vladimir. *Political-Geographic Quadrangle "Tbilisi-Tskhinvali-Vladikavkaz-Moscow":Prospects for Resolution of Georgian -Ossetian Conflict*, Central Asia and Caucasus, Vol. 5 (29), 2003, p.58 (in Russian)

6   The Georgian approach failed in large part because it was based on a limited analysis of the causes of the conflict. It falsely considered that South Ossetia's de facto president, Eduard Kokoity, had little democratic legitimacy or popular support and that the people would rapidly switch loyalties from Tskhinvali to Tbilisi. The Russian factor was also underestimated, as it was naively believed that Russia would not resist Georgia's attempts to change the *status quo*.

7   The peace plan was developed on the basis of President Saakashvili's initiative made public at the January 26, 2005 Parliamentary Assembly of the Council of Europe. Later, the Plan was supported by the OSCE, EU, U.S. government, etc.

8   International Crisis Group, *Georgia: Avoiding War in South Ossetia*, Europe Report No.159, Tbilisi–Brussels, 2004, pp.3–4.

9   At that time the Abkhaz side willingly negotiated the federal status within Georgia, although there have been various readings of this notion. Currently, the Abkhaz side persistently opposes any effort to include the status issue in negotiations and insists on full independence.

10   Antonenko, O. *Assessment of the Potential Implications of Akhalkalaki Base Closure for the Stability in Southern Georgia—EU Response Capacities*, CPN Briefing Study, September 2001.

11   Javakheti currently hosts one of the largest Russian military bases on Georgian territory. Its closure has already been negotiated with Russia. The military base has been providing significant economic benefits to the residents of Javakheti, including employment, purchases of local agricultural products, assistance with the transit of local goods to Russia and Armenia, illegal economic activity that benefits local political elites, etc. Moreover, due to historical factors, the local Armenian population associates its security guarantees vis-à-vis neighboring Turkey not with the Georgian state, but with the Russian armed forces present on the ground. The region regularly sees hundreds of local residents rallying in protest of the withdrawal of the military base.

12   Gegeshidze, Archil. *Georgia's Regional Vulnerabilities and the Ajaria Crisis*, Insight Turkey, Vol. 6, No. 2.

13   *Georgia—International Religious Freedom Report 2005,* Bureau of Democracy, Human Rights, and Labor, U.S. Department of State, 2006.

14   *Georgia—Country Reports on Human Rights Practices 2005*, Bureau of Democracy, Human Rights, and Labor, U.S. Department of State, March 8, 2006.

Inter-Group Relations and Conflicts in the North Caucasus:
Stereotypes and Realities

Alexey Gunya

I t would be superficial to categorize all conflicts within the context of modern state-building in the North Caucasus as interethnic or religious. Every region is currently plagued by tense internal conflicts over resources, posts, spheres of influence and various power struggles between groups organized around common interests or strategic aims ('strategic groups'). Ethnic antagonisms are not typically the source of inter-group conflict, but rather power struggles between different groups for control over economic resources. A painful adaptation to new economic conditions in the North Caucasus is currently taking place, to a large extent as a result of new competitive networks.

For example, the tragic street fighting in 'peaceful' Kabardino–Balkaria in the town of Nalchik in October 2005 between young men of similar ethnic backgrounds, which led to the deaths of dozens of people, demonstrated that rather than ethnic differences, power relations between states and local societies have a more important role in the development of local conflicts. The attack of government buildings in the Kabardino–Balkaria capital was reportedly in response to Moscow's repeated targeting of what it calls "Islamic extremist groups," including the persecution of practicing Muslims in the region and the wholesale closure of mosques. But perhaps the most influential factor

Alexey Gunya is a senior researcher at the Moscow and Kabardino–Balkarian branches of the Russian Academy of Sciences. Since the early 1990s, he has organized and participated in various expeditions to the mountainous regions of Central Asia and the Caucasus, coordinated international projects concerned with the sustainable development of Caucasian and Central Asian transitional societies. Further information about his research is available from the IPF website: www.policy.hu/gunya.

in the outbreak of such conflicts, often overlooked by contemporary research on Caucasus conflicts and crucial to the search for solutions, has been the practice of 'divide and conquer' so often utilized by Moscow, which in Soviet times involved the carving of North Caucasian lands and peoples into national and ethnic groups. Only recently have anthropologists begun to critically assess stereotypes about nations, religious or ethnic groups inherited from Soviet

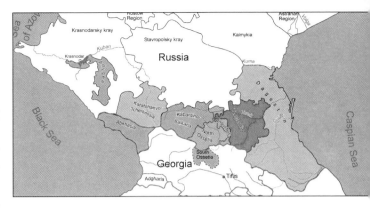

times as constituting 'imposed identities.'[1] Another often-overlooked factor contributing to Caucasus conflict is related to kinship and professional-clan association practices of usurping power by force when engaging in business and political entrepreneurialism.[2]

The North Caucasus is a region with a high diversity of social, economic and cultural forms of development and modes of governance, with each republic characterized by its own development trends and set of problems. Despite persistent stereotypes about a region plagued by conflict, in reality the anarchy so often predicted in most 1990s scholarship about the North Caucasus did not occur. Local conflicts did not become subregional or fundamental, and traditional daily life has been preserved. Inevitable inter-group tension over economic resources may have even played a positive role in certain multiethnic regions where large-scale conflict and violence was once predicted (Dagestan and Karachaevo-Cherkessia being prime examples). In Dagestan, for example, sporadic clashes came to an end during negotiations that managed to establish an economic power balance that "played a stabilizing role for the political system as a whole."[3]

At the same time, the existence of ethnic conflict and dangerous levels of tension in some areas should not be underestimated. The most serious conflicts have occurred in relatively homogenous areas (Chechnya) rather than in regions with multinational (Dagestan, Karachayevo–Cherkessia) or bi-ethnic (Kabardino–Balkaria) populations. Ethnicity as well as religious belonging play an important but not pivotal role in the outbreak of conflict. The creation of a 'market' for ethnic, religious and regional identity is the most important factor contributing to conflicts in the North Caucasus. This includes manipulating the 'price' of individual identities by engaging in ethnic entrepreneurialism to mobilize, seize, and/or redistribute power and resources. The most vivid example of such manoeuvring was the presidential elections in Karachaevo–Cherkessia (1999, 2003), which divided the republic along ethnic lines.

In Caucasus conflicts, ethnic belonging can serve as a 'bargaining chip' for political speculation—a means of mobilizing popular support for the leaders of ethnic groups. Sufficient financial support and promises of more land and resources can often spark the emergence of a new ethnic splinter group that had previously considered itself part of a larger ethnic group, and suddenly strives to define differences between themselves and the larger group.[4] The use of ethnicity as a mobilizing tool is the principal method whereby 'we-group' leaders attain their interests and is therefore an important resource,[5] hotly contested by state and private entrepreneurs alike.

Markers of socio-cultural identification in the Caucasus include the following (according to priority):

1) **Family association** (marriages are often contracted by representatives of different ethnic groups). Family and cognate ties play a dominant role in the practice of usurping power and organizing business and political undertakings.

2) **Religious association.** For example, Russians who adopted Islam become at once 'familiar' to the indigenous population of the Caucasus, while Kabardinians who adopted Christianity are much closer to the non-indigenous Russian-speaking population.

3) **Ethnic affiliation.** For example, the leaders (historians, intellectuals) of two kindred peoples— Karachai and Balkarians—were able to influence public opinion to such an extent that they convinced many among their communities to claim that they are ethnic Alans in a population census in order to boost their chances for increased financial and organizational assistance.

Spotlight on two North Caucasus regions: Kabardino–Balkaria and Karachaevo–Cherkessia

The demarcation of the territories of Kabardino–Balkaria and Karachaevo–Cherkessia, two of the nine North Caucasus regions, was not determined solely on the basis of ethnicity, but primarily according to the groups' efforts to form separate compact settlements while maintaining traditional links between peoples from the mountains and plains in a way that would promote shared development and mutual benefit.

Characteristics of the titular ethnic groups
in Kabardino–Balkaria and Karachaevo–Cherkessia

Name of ethnic group	Language	Share of the ethnic group in the republic's population (%)		Basic form of traditional agriculture	Predominant religion
		1989	2002		
Kabardians	Adyghian group (Caucasian family)	49	55	Arable farming (foothills/ plains)	
Cherkessians		9.7	11.3		
Balkarians		9.6	11		Sunni Islam
Karachai	Turkic group (Altaic family)	31	38.5	Mountain stockbreeding	

In both republics, traditional Soviet methods of political control including ethnic representation, stratification, and centralized Moscow appointment of important positions were used with varying degrees of success. In Kabardino–Balkaria the formation of a single (Kabardinian–Balkarian–Russian) ruling elite led to a rapid adaptation to the new political reality and stable loyalty to the federal center. The leaders of Kabardinian and Balkarian national-democratic independence movements at the beginning of the

1990s were quickly neutralized or co-opted. The shared institution of the Soviet party nomenclatura controlling the leading and all important posts led to political stagnation. Although inter-group tension is at first glance low in Kabardino–Balkaria, the lack of fresh leadership and the suppression of initiative and criticism has led to low rates of development and a great dependence on Moscow.

By contrast, no single ruling elite emerged during both the Soviet and post-Soviet periods in Karachaevo–Cherkessia. Attempts to establish a Moscow-backed ruling elite proved susceptible to popular criticism, as it was linked to the Soviet repression and deportation of the Karachai, not to mention the distortion of information or silence about this dark chapter of Soviet history. The successive changes in government in the 1990s created political instability at regional levels, but this instability was to some extent compensated for by a strengthening of power at district and local levels. The heads of districts, especially in ethnically homogenous areas, have considerably greater administrative powers than the district administrations in Kabardino–Balkaria. Furthermore, the multiparty system in Karachaevo-Cherkessia supports development, competition and criticism. Although the greatest competition has taken place between ethnically-based parties, the level of political openness enjoyed in Karachaevo–Cherkessia—where the mayor of the republic's capital city, Cherkessk, is a Communist in opposition to the region's leadership and press reports detail kinship ties among the elite—is virtually inconceivable in Kabardino–Balkaria.

Preventing inter-group conflict in Kabardino–Balkaria and Karachaevo–Cherkessia

Case studies of Kabardino–Balkaria and Karachaevo–Cherkessia shed light on apparently successful models of conflict prevention in the North Caucasus. A comparison between the two regions reveals the following strategies for conflict prevention employed between different strategic groups:

1) *The creation of joint institutions.* These include joint formal institutions of authority and informal agreements on the redistribution of spheres of influence (quotas, ethnic representation), joint use of land, pastures, markets. In Kabardino–Balkaria, the common strategy of forming a joint elite via interethnic marriages between members of the Kabardian and Balkarian elites highlights the age-old high esteem placed on kinship.

2) *The creation of heterogeneous zones of transition within administrative structures and electoral constituencies, along with the stratification of authority in the upper echelons.* The formation of republics with mixed ethnicities is a deliberate method of regulating conflicts. Examples of ethnic homogenization such as the division of Chechnya and Ingushetia

demonstrate how the 'unmixing' populations can disembed conflict and lead to the outbreak of violence. Conflicts are often based on the production of ideas of inequality between small ethnic groups in situations where ethnic minorities are over-represented in the regional elite.

3) *When conflict appears imminent, the temporary state monopolization of strategic resources or positions (the elimination of local competition and risk).* Moscow's strict control over some positions is also an attempt to lower the salience of ethnic competition.[6] The most blatant example is the state veto on land privatization in Kabardino-Balkaria and the awarding of federal status to a number of territories. But the short-term positive effects of such means of regulating conflicts may be counterproductive in the longer run.

De-emphasizing the importance of ethnicity or religious belonging in fueling conflict allows for a deeper analysis of the important markers of differentiation that can lead to violence, which are often connected to issues of self-identification and aspirations toward the attainment of immediate, often ecomomic, goals.

Notes

[1]   Tishkov V.A. Rekviem po etnosu. Issledovania po sozialno-kulturnoi antropologii. Moscow, Nauka, 2003.

[2]   Galina M. Yemelianova, Kinship, ethnicity and religion in post-Communist societies. Russia's autonomous republic of Kabardino-Balkariya. Ethnicities, Vol. 5(1), pp.51–82.

[3]   Kisriev, E. Formirovanie demokraticheskoi sistemy upravlenia v postkommunisticheskom Dagestane. In: Mestnoe upravlenie mnogoetnicheskimi soobshchestvami v stranah SNG. Ed. Tishkov, V.A. and Filippova, E. Moscow, 2001, pp.71–90.

[4]   Tishkov, V.A. Ibid.

[5]   Zürcher, Christoph and Koehler, January 2003. Potentials of Dis/Order. Explaining Conflict and Stability in the Caucasus and in the Former Yugoslavia. Manchester: Manchester University Press, p.12.

[6]   Coining the term "Soviet people" clearly artificially lowered the value of ethnicity. To a certain extent, the hierarchical structure of identification (for instance, allegiance to both Russia and Balkaria) holds down the price of regional ethnicity.

part three

Political Ideology and Religious Tolerance in Russia

Ideology and Intolerance

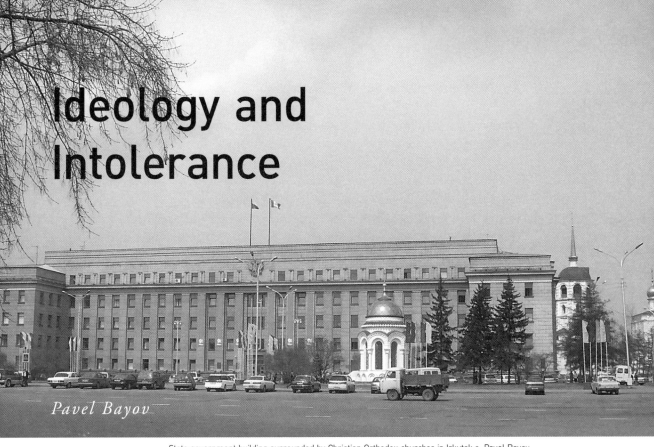

Pavel Bayov

State government building surrounded by Christian Orthodox churches in Irkutsk ▪ Pavel Bayov

Russia's democratic institutions are seriously threatened. Primary sources of this threat are not only the Russian government's abandonment of liberal reforms; nationalistic, 'extreme-right' movements; or the 'authoritarian psychology' of many Russians as elaborated in Theodor Adorno's famous research describing a typical 'authoritarian personality' found in many societies.[1] A far more dangerous threat to Russia's budding democratic institutions, I believe, originates from the Russian Orthodox Church and its hierarchs. The Church has somewhat paradoxically become the torch-bearer of Russia's Communist legacy, subsuming the role of the Communist Party in the monopolization of an often xenophobic 'purely Russian' popular ideology. In the Cold War being waged by the Church, an ideological Iron Curtain is being drawn in an attempt to shut out all 'nontraditional,' 'alien' religions. For example, a common Church slogan promoting its supreme place as Russia's 'official' religion is reminiscent of patriarchal, 'us versus them' Soviet-era propaganda: "This Motherland is our traditional ecumenical territory. Never cross the line!" If we are condemned to witness the emergence of a new authoritarian regime in Russia, it will inevitably be actively engaged with Russia's 'most traditional' Church.

International Policy Fellow **Pavel Bayov** heads the Irkutsk regional government's research and information division for the Cultural Affairs Committee. He also teaches courses on religion, culture and sociology as Associate Professor at Irkutsk State Technical University. Further information about his research is available from the IPF websites: http://pdc.ceu.hu (Source IPF) and www.policy.hu/bayov.

Most disturbing is the overt manner with which the Church lobbies Russia's executive powers and manages to attract more than its fair share of national media praise, while President Vladimir Putin unambiguously demonstrates his religious preferences. In addition to the above-mentioned Communist legacy, the reasons for Russia's cozy Church-state relations and lack of concern for religious freedom are many, including the Orthodox Church's historically jealous rivalry with other confessions, namely Protestantism, Catholicism, and the Russian Old Believers; imperfect Russian legislation and practice protecting religious freedom and ensuring the separation of church and state; and problems of incompetence and weak civil consciousness among media representatives. Last but not least, whether as Cold War arch-enemies or post-Cold War allies, the powerful in Russia and the United States have studied each other's policies for decades. Apparently, as the influence on U.S. policymakers of both the 'war on terror' and the Christian right agenda grows, so does the convenient cooperation between Russian policymakers and Church hierarchs.

A society's protection and even promotion of religious diversity can be an insightful barometer of both civil society and open society. Threats to plurality and social openness also tend to threaten religious freedom. There are some 200 religious confessions and denominations in Russia today (compared with about 250 in the United States), and reducing them to a common demonimator would be a virtually impossible task. The founders of American democracy were fully aware of the importance of the protection of religious freedom when they enshrined this protection in the First Amendment to the American Constitution. Yet in Russia, actual practice runs counter to the legal ban on espousing religious superiority and the affirmation that "all religious organizations are separated from the State and equal before the Law" (see 'Law on Freedom of Worship and Religious Organizations,' Items 3 and 4, 1997). In addition to the extraordinary media attention lavished on the Church and its activities, the above-mentioned legislation is not backed up by any implementation mechanism and is severely limited by the 'fifteen years' rule, according to which a religious organization can be officially registered **only** after it is able to document its existence in Russia for not less then fifteen years (Item 11, 1999 following a review of the 1997 Law by the Constitutional Court).

The current trend in Russia to blame all failed reforms on the so-called 'problem of Liberalism' also serves to strengthen the Russian Church-State monopoly. This 'problem' is discussed broadly in academic circles, media, and among government officials, and the character of the discussion is disturbing. Some experts say that the poor socio-economical situation that Russia currently finds itself in emerged entirely as a result of the 'wrong direction' of reforms undertaken during the last 15 years. By 'wrong direction' the pundits mean, as a rule, the liberalization of the economy. They claim that Russia's failed economic liberalization has proven that Liberalism is not consistent with Russian mentality and traditions and therefore not suitable for Russian society. Moreover, Liberalism and all those associated with Liberalism are primarily responsible for Russia's unsuccessful development and present circumstances.

Blaming Liberalism and Liberals is natural enough. It is a common human reaction, especially by those in power, to blame something or someone else when things become worse and worse. But in Russia I believe the ever-increasing cries of the anti-Liberalists in

Apparently, as the influence on U.S. policymakers of both the 'war on terror' and the Christian right agenda grows, so does the convenient cooperation between Russian policymakers and Church hierarchs.

government, media and academic circles is a semi-coordinated political campaign aimed at creating yet another diversion shielding the Russian executive from criticism about its increasingly authoritarian tendencies (not to mention those of the Church). Certain demands were made by some Russian authorities to a number of well-positioned actors who carry out their mission according to the old rules—they orchestrate an ultimately futile, tragic-comic game of "playing possum" with all of society, including themselves, targeting a Russian elite who now define themselves more by corporate interests than ideological preferences.

Of course what the anti-Liberalists fail (or refuse) to recognize is that true economic liberalization has never occurred in Russia. The same people who blame Liberalism for all of the country's ills claim that the most suitable ideology for Russians is Conservatism. That is, a special, narrowly conceived Russian brand of Conservatism, backed by the Orthodox Church of course, and involving more aggressive politics toward the U.S. and the West and Russia's 'reasonable isolation' (i.e. protectionism in favor of the current economic and political monopolies). The Russian brand of Conservatism even promotes the development of the so-called 'military mind' of the Russian people by introducing education in 'traditional Russian religions' in Russian schools (the assumed connections between traditional religions and military thinking are anyone's guess). Such proposals are seriously considered and discussed even among established and respected academics, political experts, journalists and writers (see for example the proceedings of the Moscow State University sociology conference "Sorokin Readings" held in December 2004).[2]

As the Librarian of Congress and founder of the Kennan Institute for Advanced Russian Studies at the Woodrow Wilson International Center for Scholars James H. Billington once said, "The human ability to create good made democracy possible, but his ability to create evil made it necessary." Recent efforts by the Russian executive and Orthodox Church leadership to consolidate political, economic and religious power has increased the potential for evil in Russia today. Such circumstances make independent policy analysis and the development of Russian democracy and democratic institutions, including those protecting religious freedom, all the more urgent.

Notes

[1]   See, for example, Theodor W. Adorno, Betty Aron, Maria Hertz Levinson, William Morrow, *The Authoritarian Personality (Studies in Prejudice),* W W Norton & Co, 1983.

[2]   *Sorokin Readings.* Proceedings of the 3rd Conference. Moscow: State University Press, 2004.

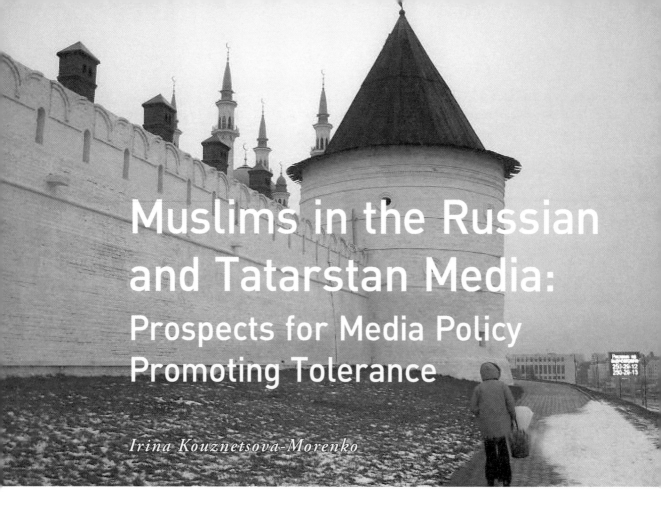

Muslims in the Russian and Tatarstan Media:
Prospects for Media Policy Promoting Tolerance

Irina Kouznetsova-Morenko

As evidenced by the worldwide scandal that erupted following the publication of cartoons depicting the Prophet Mohammed in European newspapers, current media representations of Islam easily become heavily politicized. My International Policy Fellowship research project, which included the first public discussion and cooperative initiative ever organized between journalists and Muslim leaders in the Russian Republic of Tatarstan, revealed the significant role played by the media in fueling intolerance toward Muslims in Russia. Many Russian Muslims now insist that Islamophobia in the Russian media reflects a deliberate policy supported by members of Russian officialdom to provoke a conflict between the followers of the most widely practiced traditional Russian religions—Orthodoxy and Islam.

Muslims make up about 15 percent of the Russian population, and many of them live in Volga region republics of Tatarstan and Bashkortostan. Although the Tatarstan media tends to be more sensitized to Muslim issues than the Russian national media

Irina Kouznetsova Morenko is assistant professor at the Department of History and Sociology of Kazan State Medical University, Russia. Her research activity focuses on issues of social justice, ethnic relations and religion, as well as social aspects of health. **Leissan Salakhatdinova**, sociologist, member of the Tatarstan Union of Journalists is gratefully acknowledged for helping prepare the essay and organizing the roundtable "Islam and Media." Further information about her research is available from the IPF websites: http://pdc.ceu.hu (Source IPF) and www.policy.hu/morenko.

(roughly half of Tatarstan's population are Muslim Tatars), they both fail to adequately represent the role of modern Muslims in Russian social and political life. Ironically, the Tatarstan media's attempt to avoid instigating ethnic and religious tensions by remaining silent on key debates contributes to mutual misunderstanding (for instance the Tatarstan media did not even react when the national press seized on a recent headscarf-related scandal). Rather than promoting democratic dialogue, the Tatarstan media prefers to ward off social tensions by pretending they do not exist.

Such tactics of concealment have profoundly negative consequences. The tendency to take a 'neutral' stance translates into a kind of passive intolerance toward Muslims in practice. The standard mode of operation for the Russian and Tatarstan media in covering any story related to Islam is to reproduce 'facts' devoid of meaningful analysis, relying primarily upon superficial speculation and inaccurate interpretations of Islamic terminology.

The results of a media content analysis show that although purely xenophobic reports concerning Muslims in the Russian media are rare and television broadcasts congratulating Muslim figures and political leaders are common, Islamophobic myths are regularly replicated in media headings and journalistic notes. Foreign Muslims are typically radical, stigmatized characters completely lacking in positive attributes, contributing to a public image of Islam in Russia increasingly associated with threat. The 'image of the enemy' has been constructed—even the once stereotypically pure, feminine, and humble Muslim woman has been transformed into a potential hostage-taker or 'women kamikaze' following the tragic theater hostage-taking in Dubrovka, Moscow in 2002. When Muslim women sought the right to wear their headscarves (hijab) in passport photographs, for example, about a third of media reports described the incident as a threat to national security. Media reports covering the daily life of the Muslim community and various Muslim traditions such as the Kurban Bayram feast (otherwise known as Eid to coincide with the annual hajj pilgimage to Mecca) are characterized by an alarming inter-confessional polarization.

Given this backdrop of public silence or misrepresentation, it should come as no surprise that when several dozen Muslims were arrested in Tatarstan in 2005 on suspicion of associating with the organization Hyzb-ut-Tahri, the republic saw an eruption of spontaneous public protests with relatives of those arrested holding posters demanding, "*Down with Islamophobia in the media!*"

Russian media policy and tolerance

Inciting religious and ethnic dissent is deemed a punishable crime in Russia according to the Constitution and media regulations intended to suppress extremism. Moral and ethical conflicts in journalism are addressed by the Grand Jury of the Russian Union of Journalists, which is guided by Russian and international regulations as well as the professional code of ethics of Russian journalists. Nevertheless, most experts and independent observers acknowledge that media policy and the implementation of media regulation in Russia is not yet elaborated, with Russian codes of journalism ethics consisting mostly of declarations rather than norms of behavior.

Russian policymakers at the federal level not only lack adequate professional capacity to promote democratic dialogue and responsible media policy as a means of easing ethnic and religious tensions, but they also face a unique situation in their dealings with regional leaders in Tatarstan and Bashkortostan. Given the republics' significant Muslim populations, the local governments must form consensus on all relevant policy issues with the local Islamic clergy in the spiritual boards representing Muslim communities. The Muslims of these republics are not yet represented by local civic organizations but only by the clergy—a distinction often criticized by Russian observers at the federal level and completely unrecognized by local Muslim clergymen and journalists. The weakness of civil society in Tatarstan and the lack of open democratic dialogue make it extremely difficult to find innovative solutions to inter-ethnic and inter-religious disputes.

Since the September 11 terrorist attacks in 2001 in the United States, several sensational cases of media-inspired Islamophobia seriously undermined tolerance toward Muslims in Russia. In 2003 the Moscow Muslim Fund Ansar launched a lawsuit against the popular newspaper *Komsomolskaya Pravda* after it published an essay where a passport photo with a headscarf was compared with a photo of a Nazi secret service police cap. In a 2004 lawsuit, Muslims from Saratov and Makhachkala sued the newspaper *Izvestiya* over its coverage about the *Islam.ru* website they maintained. The Moscow City Court ruled in favor of the newspapers.

These lawsuits were intended not only as a protest against concrete publications, but also against the larger phenomenon of Islamophobia in the Russian media. The Russian Muslim server *Islam.ru* regularly monitors media coverage related to Islam in Russia and comments on every instance of Islamophobia. Those bringing the lawsuits clearly believed that the media coverage reflected an intentional Russian policy to provoke conflict between the followers of Orthodoxy and Islam. Public media reports about the lawsuits never mentioned these larger allegations.

The failure to examine and follow up on such allegations highlights not only the active denial of ethnic and religious tensions by the Russian and Tatarstan media (which of course failed to report on the lawsuits at all), but also the low level of engagement by Muslim leaders in Russian national policymaking circles.

In Tatarstan, a number of political institutes are responsible for media policy. At the republic level, the State Religious Affairs Department of the Cabinet of Ministers and the Ministry of Press and Information are responsible. According to Professor Renat Nabiev, Chairman of the State Religious Affairs Department and one of my International Policy Fellowships project mentors, the department faces serious manpower and budgetary problems. The Ministry of Press and Information is engaged in the organizational control of the media to a greater extent. Public journalistic organizations are fragmented and weak, while the Spiritual Board of Muslims is not oriented toward public information campaigns and is staffed by only one part-time public relations person. Given this set of circumstances amid uncertain relations with Russia's federal center, organizations charged with the development of professional media policy in Tatarstan shirk their responsibilities and stagnation predominates. Weak civil society is undoubtedly a major part of the problem—experts evaluate Tatarstan's system of governance to be one of the least developed republican democracies in the country.

Elsewhere in Russia the situation is not quite so dire. Responding to media coverage of the Moscow theater hostage-taking in 2002, the Spiritual Board of Muslims of the Republic of Karelia (a Russian region with a low percentage of Muslims) disseminated a policy paper on regulating the Russian media's coverage of Islamic issues. Thus, *Islam.ru* and Muslim Board of Karelia are good examples of Muslim organizations that unite and empower Muslims to defend their rights in the face of discrimination.

Even in Tatarstan, Islamophobia in media has begun to arouse political reactions (but not yet well-conceived media policies). Following a series of human rights violations on the basis of ethnicity and religion, in January 2006 the Tatarstan Parliament addressed the Russian President and Government requesting that urgent state-level steps be taken to prevent ethnic and religious instability in Russia. Referring to a notorious essay published in *Izvestia* about the Tatar village of *Srednyaya Yelyuzan* in the Penza Region that was stigmatized as a base for Wahabi extremists, Tatarstan's deputies warned against reporting that "instills xenophobia into public thinking." In March 2006, the Tatarstan Parliament rejected the federal draft 'Law on the Fundamentals of State Policy' given their belief that primarily it defends the rights of ethnic Russians only rather than all citizens of Russia. The draft was also criticized by the Tatarstan head of the Muftis Board, Ravil Gaynutdin.

Relations between the Russians and Tatars in Tatarstan have not improved in the last decade, and negative images of Islam in the Russian media only serve to worsen anti-Russian sentiment among Muslims in the republic. Russia's divide-and-rule style 'power hierarchy' is particularly manifested in ethnically diverse regions like Tatarstan

National and Islamic Movements in Tatarstan

by Eduard Ponarin

The revitalization of Islam in Tatarstan dates back to the time of perestroika in the late 1980s—part of the more general process of searching for ideological alternatives involving all peoples of the former Soviet Union. The Islamic rennaissance was an important tool of the Tatar national movement, reinforcing the Tatar population's distinct identity and demands for greater autonomy or independence from Moscow.

During perestroika, Islam was restored largely as a conservative national tradition—a set of popular rites rather than an independent political force. The nationalist movement used Muslim symbols such as green flags and traditional dress to back up political demands with claims of national authenticity. The instrumentalist role of Islam was exemplified by numerous instances of its non-canonical use, such as reciting prayers in theaters or staging theatrical shows devoted to Ramadan and the feast of Sacrifice in stadiums or in the streets near national monuments.

The first public celebration of Ramadan was in Kazan on April 16, 1991. It culminated in a procession of thousands of people to Freedom Square chanting the slogans of the national movement. Since the mid-1990s, such public celebrations of religious holidays have become rare. Religious celebrations today in Tatarstan tend to be more private and local, with little mention in the Russian-language local press, or mere formal greetings published on the occasion of a religious holiday.

A more self-sufficient strand of Islam has emerged, however—one that is independent of both the remnants of the nationalist movement and the local government, and whose followers have recently exhibited political ambitions.

Tatarstan's Islamic rennaissance

As of 1990, there were only 154 Muslim parishes in Tatarstan for about two million Tatars, with most established after former Soviet premier Mikhail Gorbachev's reforms. Of the 55 imams, 41 were older than 60 years of age, only one had university-level theological education, and just eight had secondary (high school level) Muslim education. The year 1990 was a year of great changes. For the first time since the early 20th century, two Muslim secondary schools opened in Tatarstan, breaking the Soviet-era tradition of Tatar religious leaders receiving their education in Central Asia. With significant assistance from rich Muslim nations, the creation of numerous new parishes and the construction of mosques shifted into high gear. The number of (still unregulated) parishes increased from 18 in 1988 to more than 700 in 1992, when the Spiritual Board of Muslims of Tatarstan was established. According to the board's deputy head Valiulla Yakupov, "almost half of the mosques [at the time] were built without any licensing documents from any Muslim authority."

Prior to 1992, Tatarstan's Muslim organizations were subordinated to the Spiritual Board of Muslims of the European part of Russia and Siberia, which is headquarted in the city of Ufa in the Republic of Bashkortostan, and headed by Talgat Tadjutdin. Tatar nationalists played a substantial role in the organization, calling on the Ufa mufti to relocate his headquarters to Kazan, the capital city of Tatarstan, because they believed that the impending secession of Tatarstan from Russia would require independent religious structures. The mufti declined those calls and instead established only a representative office in Kazan.

Eventually, the emergence of an alternative Muslim Spiritual Board based within the republic precipitated a schism among the Muslims of Tatarstan. The acrimony surrounding this split was indirectly related to the abolition of the Council on Religious Affairs in Moscow—a Russian government watchdog organization. After its demise, the receipt and distribution of financial assistance from foreign Muslim countries was left uncontrolled. At the second International Islamic Forum "Islamic Education in East Europe and Muslim States" held in Moscow in the fall of 1992, the leaders of international Muslim organizations concluded agreements with the leaders of the new Russian Muslim organizations to provide financing and teachers and accept local students to Islamic universities abroad. Saudi representatives at the forum reportedly donated fifteen libraries of mostly Salafi (known as Wahabi in Russia) literature and, according to Yakupov, hinted at generous assistance should an alternative organization to the Ufa Muslim headquarters emerge. Disagreement among the Tatar clerics as to how these spoils should be divided greatly contributed to the heat and eventual split of the Muslim community into factions during the establishment of the Tatarstani Muslim Spiritual Board.

Another major factor precipitating that schism was the position of President Shaimiev of Tatarstan, who relied on the support of nationalists to counter Moscow, but became wary of increasingly popular nationalists leaders. He chose to co-opt those nationalists who he deemed less dangerous into his government while seeking to marginalize those he felt he could not trust, especially after he succeeded in securing favorable treaty with Moscow in 1994 guaranteeing several privileges for his republic. Through continued tactics of soft repression of stronger opponents and co-optation of supportive nationalists, President Shaimiev sought to ensure political control over Tatarstan's religious renaissance. Shaimiev chose to support the local Spiritual Board to the detriment of the Ufa mufti Talgat Tadjutdin based outside his republic, orchestrating a campaign against Tadjutdin in the local press and encouraging the seizure of mosques and other premises by the supporters of the new Tatarstani mufti. In January 1995 a Congress of Tatarstani Muslims recognized the new status quo.

It was not long before the head of the newly established religious body, Abdulla Aliulla, discovered how far the republic's leadership would tolerate independent political actors in Tatarstan. His attempt to seize another mosque and a Muslim school in Kazan in the fall of 1995 resulted in a criminal case against him. His leadership position was shaken and, in February 1998, cleric Usman Iskhakov was elected the republic's mufti with Shaimiev's backing. Aliulla condemned the government interference accusing county-level government leaders of handpicking delegates to the Congress of Tatarstani Muslims and instructing them on who they should support. His stance was backed by opposition nationalist parties including Ittifak and Milli Mejlis.

Current context

Appreciating the extent to which his leadership depends upon Shaimiev's support, Usman Iskhakov has consolidated his position as the religious leader of Tatarstan's Muslims. According to the Chairman of the Milli Mejlis Party, Usman Iskhakov "was and remains an obedient tool of the authorities." Shaimiev's domination in religious matters is further exemplified by his personal choice of an imam in 2005 for the newly opened Kul Sharif grand mosque in Kazan. Despite the efforts of local nationalists to unleash a vicious campaign against him on the eve of the elections, steadfast political loyalties have evidently helped Usman Iskhakov to acquire a significant personal fortune and win a second re-election in February 2006.

Eduard Ponarin (www.policy.hu/ponarin) chairs the Faculty of Political Science and Sociology at the European University at St. Petersburg. His International Policy Fellowship project examines current challenges to open societies in Tatarstan.

and Bashkortostan. Relationships with the federal center are characterized as a latent conflict, with the 'ethnic card' often played by local authorities seeking to expand their power base.

Steps toward more tolerant media in Tatarstan and Russia

The roundtable discussions organized within the framework of the IPF project revealed a series of obstacles limiting democratic dialogue and problem resolution regarding Muslims and Islamic issues in the media including the following: 1) the journalistic community does not follow a common code of ethics; 2) local journalists, who are often poorly educated, act as conduits of political statements and policies rather than defenders of freedom

of speech; 3) journalists lack both education and practical experience in understanding and working with Muslims; 4) there are no local institutes assisting in the implementation of media policies and recommendations from the Russian Union of Journalists; and 5) significant prejudice exists in relation to the Muslim clergy.

Tatarstan's journalists noted that sometimes the Muslim clergy communicate in a unilateral way without offering substantial public information, and there is no reliable center that can provide them with information on life of Muslims in Tatarstan. As a result, formal regulations have not led to common practices preventing Islamophobia and religious intolerance in the media. This means that Russian policymakers and Muslim institutions must work together to increase inter-religious and inter-ethnic tolerance as well as the openness of their policymaking processes with these aims. At the level of media professionals, this implies overcoming of journalistic incompetence in highlighting religious issues and relying more heavily on professional journalism ethics. Last but not least, civil society organizations should be strengthened so that they may contribute to tolerance-building initiatives.

The longer term prospects for change will depend upon the willingness of private organizations to introduce special training courses in religious educational institutions as well as for journalists, with the cooperation of journalism faculties and Muslim communities. As a result, Tatarstan's Muslims should be better positioned to engage in constructive cooperation with Russia's regional and central media.

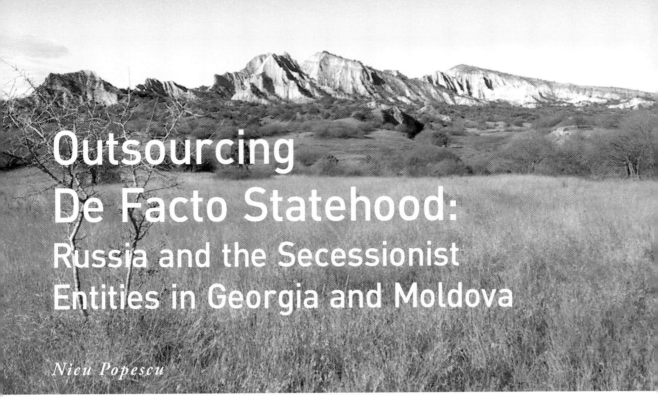

Outsourcing De Facto Statehood:
Russia and the Secessionist Entities in Georgia and Moldova

Nicu Popescu

ussia has been a player during and after the conflicts in the secessionist entities of Abkhazia and South Ossetia in Georgia, the Transnistrian region of Moldova, and Nagorno-Karabakh in Azerbaijan. If before 2004 the Russian government was defensive about its role in these conflicts, by 2006 it has taken a more proactive position.

A 2000 assessment of the situation claimed that in the Commonwealth of Independent States (CIS), Russia's objective is "to maintain rather than enlarge the Russian presence in the region. Moscow tries to save what it still has, rather than extend its political and military platzdarms in its southern neighborhood."[1] The 2000 Foreign Policy Concept of the Russian Federation stated that the top priority of its foreign policy was to "create favorable external conditions for steady development of Russia, for improving its economy."[2]

This is not the case anymore. In his 2005 annual address, President Vladimir Putin stated that it was "certain that Russia should continue its civilizing mission on the Eurasian continent."[3] In 2006 Dmitry Trenin argues that the Russian leadership "came to the conclusion that the withdrawal has ended, and it is time to counter-attack... it is time to re-establish a great power and that the CIS is the space where Russian economic, political, and informational dominance should be established."[4] Russian officialdom has

Nicu Popescu is an International Policy Fellow based at the Centre for European Policy Studies (CEPS) in Brussels. He is also a correspondent for the BBC World Service Romania Section and a PhD candidate at the Central European University in Budapest, Hungary. Further information about his research is available from the IPF websites: http://pdc.ceu.hu (Source IPF) and www.policy.hu/popescu.

decided that the international and domestic context is now ripe to start moving toward this goal. On the domestic front, authorities calculate that by building an image of a Russia under siege by Islamic terrorists and Western-inspired "orange" revolutionaries, the Russian public will rally around their policies.

The 'new thinking' of the Russian Federation was described in an essay for the Wall Street Journal by Sergei Ivanov, Russia's minister of defence and deputy prime minister. He claimed that Russia's two main challenges are "interference in Russia's internal affairs by foreign states, either directly or through structures that they support... [and] violent assault on the constitutional order of some post-Soviet states."[5] No distinction is made between non-governmental organizations (NGOs) and networks used to finance terrorist activities in Russia and Western-funded NGOs engaged in democracy promotion. Both are viewed as categories of foreign organizations that seek to destabilize Russia and its "allies."

President Putin said in the aftermath of the Beslan siege that "the weak get beaten up."[6] This is the new prism through which Russia sees its international relations. International affairs are a fight, and in this fight Russia has to re-establish its regional dominance. Russian policies on Abkhazia, South Ossetia and Transnistria are indicators of this new trend and a means for testing a new foreign policy agenda. Quite logically, Russia's new self-confidence has developed into a new activism that is clearly manifested in its policies towards the secessionist entities in Georgia and Moldova.

In this essay, I attempt to map Russian policies addressing the conflicts in Abkhazia, South Ossetia and Transnistria.[7] Although these conflicts are not necessarily rooted in religion, their resolution would go a long way toward toning down the current level of overblown anti-Islamic official rhetoric in Russia, not to mention the growth of extremism in uncontrolled regions.

Why does Russia feel strong now?

First and foremost, the state of the Russian **economy** encourages the flexing of its political muscles. Russia has seen steady economic growth since 1999 and a significant inflow of cash from high oil and gas prices. Unlike in the 1990s, Russia is not concerned with a lack of resources for pursuing its foreign policy. The 2000 Foreign Policy Concept bluntly stated that Russia's capacity to address the challenges it faced was "aggravated by limited resource support for the foreign policy of the Russian Federation, making it difficult to uphold its foreign economic interests and limiting the scope of its information and cultural influence abroad."[8] A few years later, Putin claimed that "the growth of the economy, political stability and the strengthening of the state have had a beneficial effect on Russia's international position."[9]

A second boost for Russian foreign policy action is the country's **domestic political climate**. An authoritarian government that does not feel challenged in domestic politics is less compromising in its foreign policy.[10] The current elites in Russia have ensured their nearly indisputable political dominance at the expense of democratic pluralism. There is a certain paradox in the Russian elite's depiction of their state as strong, dynamic and pragmatic on the international stage, while internally they often portray Russia as weak, vulnerable and alarmist. In April 2005, the then head of the presidential administration Dmitry Medvedev stated that "if we cannot consolidate the elites, Russia will disappear as a state."[11] Of course such claims of Russia's existential danger and ever-looming external threats to national security serve to bolster public support for the regime.

Thus, Russia's centralization of power and open authoritarianism is not only excused and explained, but deemed necessary and legitimate—the only way to preserve the nation. Such discourse succeeds in undermining all legitimate democratic forces that may challenge the dominance of the Putin administration, creating a black and white political landscape with only non-systemic forces—extremist nationalists and Islamic terrorists—as the challengers. In this context Putin is seen as the lesser of evils. Even Mikhail Khodorkovsky claimed from his jail cell that Putin is "more liberal and more democratic than 70 percent of the population."[12] Thus, the discourse of internal weakness excuses the government's centralization of power.

A third empowering factor for Russia is the current **international political situation**, which plays into the hands of Russian policymakers. Iraq is in a quagmire. The United States is too busy running around in the Afghanistan-Iraq-Iran triangle. The European Union (EU) is perceived as being in a profound and paralyzing crisis following the rejection of its draft Constitution (many Russians fail to understand that the EU crisis is profound but certainly not paralyzing). Both the US and EU need Russia in their attempts to prevent Iran from acquiring nuclear capability for non-peaceful use. In the CIS, the democratic governments that emerged after the 'Rose and Orange revolutions' in Georgia and Ukraine respectively perform with great difficulty. Mikhail Saakashvili's popularity seems to be waning, economic progress is slow, and political centralization seems to be on the rise in Georgia. In Ukraine, Viktor Yushchenko is politically weak, economic performance is declining, and political stability is not yet apparent at the end of the transition tunnel. In contrast to the post-revolutionary states, the regimes in Belarus and Uzbekistan seem as strong as ever.

A fourth factor is **Chechnya**. The defeat of the nationalist secessionist movement in Chechnya means that Russia is no longer fearful of supporting secessionism in other states. Given the strength of the Chechen secessionist movement on its own territory in the 1990s, Russia was at least declaratively supportive of the territorial integrity of other states including Georgia and Moldova. Any precedent of successful secession resulting from violent conflict was seen as questioning the future of Chechnya in Russia. Thus, for most of the 90s Russia hesitated between supporting the secessionist entities in Moldova and Georgia and fears of spillover effects for Russia itself. All this has changed.

The second Chechen war that started in 1999 led to the defeat of the secessionist movement in Chechnya. Certainly, the Chechen guerillas are still a serious security challenge to the internal stability of the Russian Federation, but they are no longer a credible secessionist force. President Putin is right in saying that "there are other regions in the northern Caucasus where the situation is even more worrying than it is in Chechnya."[13] The war in Chechnya is no longer a war for or against the independence of Chechnya or even a truly Chechen conflict anymore, but rather a North Caucasus conflict with profound religious, social and security implications. Russia defeated the nationalist secessionist movement in Chechnya, but ended up with a geographically larger and potentially more destructive security challenge. Whatever the instability in the North Caucasus, Russia feels that the Chechen factor is no longer a constraint on its policies towards the secessionist entities in Georgia and Moldova.[14]

Russia and the conflicts

During the 90s Russia's policies towards the conflicts were largely, although not always openly, supportive of the secessionist forces.

Russian support was directed primarily via conflict settlement mechanisms. Russian-led peacekeeping operations have *de facto* guarded the borders of the secessionist entities, freezing a status quo favorable to the secessionist sides. Peacekeepers[15] allowed the secessionist elites to pursue state building projects while deterring the metropolitan states from attempting to regain control of the regions.[16]

Russia's role in conflict settlement negotiations has also been questioned. Moldova's assessment of the negotiation format in which Russia played the key role was straightforward. President Voronin of Moldova argued that: "The five-party negotiations and the existing peacekeeping mechanism have proven their ineffectiveness, and are not able to lead to a long-lasting solution. The dragging on of the settlement process contributes to the consolidation of the separatist regime, and the promotion of certain mafia-type geopolitical interests, which are foreign to the interests of the population on the two banks of the Dnestr river."[17] Moreover, a resolution of the Georgian Parliament

The author in the field beside a UN peacekeeping plane in Abkhazia

claims that "the Russian Federation does nothing to promote the process of conflict settlement on the territory of Georgia, in fact, the current situation is quite the contrary. A wide range of steps made by Russia currently strengthens the separatist regimes…"[18]

The conflicts in Georgia and Moldova

South Ossetia

The open phase of the conflict in South Ossetia (Georgia) lasted between 1990–1992 and claimed approximately a thousand lives. The conflict ended (following Russian troop intervention) with a ceasefire agreement signed on July 14, 1992, establishing a trilateral peacekeeping operation consisting of Russian, Georgian and South Ossetian troops. A Joint Control Commission (JCC) consisting of Russia, South Ossetia, North Ossetia (a Russian region) and Georgia supervises the security situation and pursues negotiations on conflict settlement. The OSCE oversees the situation, while the EU is an observer in JCC meetings on economic issues.

Transnistria

The conflict in Transnistria (Moldova) lasted for a few months in the spring and summer of 1992. It resulted in some 1000 lost lives and ended with a ceasefire agreement signed on July 21, 1992. The war stopped after the Russian 14th army intervened on behalf of Transnistria and in fact defeated the Moldovan troops. As in South Ossetia, after the ceasefire a trilateral peacekeeping operation was established consisting of militaries from the two conflict parties (Moldova and Transnistria) with Russia as the leading peacekeeper. The OSCE supervises the situation. Negotiations on conflict settlement were pursued in the so-called "five-sided format" which consisted of Moldova and Transnistria as conflict parties and Russia, Ukraine and the OSCE as mediators. In October 2005 the format became "5+2" after the EU and US joined in as observers.

Abkhazia

The conflict in Abkhazia was the most serious of the three as it claimed more than 10,000 lives between 1992–1994. The most intense phase of the conflict lasted from August 1992 to September 1993. The "Declaration on Measures for a Political Settlement of the Georgian-Abkhazian Conflict" was signed in April 1994 in Moscow and an "Agreement on a Cease-Fire and Separation of Forces" (Moscow Agreement) was signed in May 1994.[19] However, outbursts of violence and some guerrilla actions persisted in Abkhazia well after these agreements. There is a Russian-led peacekeeping operation under a Commonwealth of Independent States (CIS) supervised by the United Nations (UN Observer Mission to Georgia or UNOMIG).

However, Russia has not always unambiguously supported the secessionist entities, as is often assumed. Until just a few years ago, Russian policies towards the conflicts oscillated between open support for the secessionists and periods of rapprochement with Georgia and Moldova.

Russian support for Abkhazia and to a certain extent South Ossetia waned in the mid 90s due to two main factors. Firstly, the secessionist challenge posed by Chechnya during the 1994–1996 Chechen war and the subsequent de facto Chechen independence threatened Russia's own territorial integrity. Under such conditions Russia was rather constrained in its potential support for other potentially precedent-setting secessionist movements in the former Soviet Union.

Secondly, in 1994 Georgia joined the CIS, and the CIS Collective Security Treaty and accepted Russian military bases on its territory. Georgia's implicit expectations were that, in exchange, Russia would support its efforts to reassert control over Abkhazia and South Ossetia. Russia's understanding of the deal differed. Russia supported Eduard Shevardnadze to assert himself as the leader of the country in the context of the civil war with supporters of the ousted president Zviad Gamsakhurdia, but did not take a pro-active stance on the issue of Georgia's reunification.

In Moldova, rapprochement with Russia followed the rise to power of the then pro-Russian Communist party in 2001 and lasted until 2003. Moldova's implicit expectation was that a rapprochement with Russia would ensure decisive support for its efforts to resolve the conflict in Transnistria. Therefore Moldova implicitly agreed to follow Moscow's political line in international relations, create favorable, even preferential treatment for Russian businesses, promote Russian language in Moldova and generally promote closer ties with Russia in political, social and economic terms. In exchange, Moldova primarily expected the withdrawal of Russian support for the Transnistrian authorities and the ousting of Russian citizen Igor Smirnov, Transnistria's self-proclaimed president.

From 2001 until 2003 the situation looked promising for Moldova—it seemed as if Moscow policy favored a reunited, friendly Moldova over a pro-Russian Transnistria and an unfriendly Moldova. Russia moved to limit its support for Transnistria in order to promote a settlement of the conflict. Allegedly, the discussions on withdrawing Russian support for the Smirnov-led authorities culminated with talks between Moldova and Russia about which region Smirnov should be appointed to as governor in order to remove him and pave the way toward a conflict settlement.[20] However, this promised withdrawal of support turned out to be only half-hearted. In the end the situation reverted back to square one, with strong Russian support for Transnistria and tense relations with Moldova. The turning point was the failure of the so-called "Kozak Memorandum," a unilateral Russian plan to settle the conflict on largely Russian terms which was rejected by Moldova in November 2003. Since then, Moldovan–Russian relations have irreversibly worsened.

Whatever the oscillations of Russian policies towards the secessionist entities in the nineties, the status quo of Russian support for the de facto states barely faltered and continues to persist. Periodical rapprochement between Russia and Moldova or Georgia did not lead to conflict settlement, as both sides of the deals had erroneous expectations of each other's intentions. Not only did the deals fail, but their failure further complicated relations between Russia on the one hand and Moldova and Georgia on the other. Given such baggage of mutual frustrations and recent Russian internal developments, Russia oscillating experiences, Russia has begun to re-assert its position.

The new activism: Russia's policies toward the secessionist entities

Russian policies towards the secessionist entities are characterized by a stated recognition of the territorial integrity of Moldova and Georgia coupled with contradictory open support for many of the demands of the secessionist entities in practice. The ambiguity of Russian policies creates strong incentives for the separatists to persist in their quest. They are primarily encouraged by the following forms of Russian support:

Political support

Russia pays high-level political attention to the secessionist authorities and has often acted as a bridge between the three self-proclaimed republics which created a community of their own, informally called SNG-2, or even NATO-2.[21] The level of institutionalization of SNG-2 should not be overestimated—it has summits, ministerial meetings and cooperation networks. In fact, most of these summits take place in Moscow and the leaders of the secessionist entities are received by high-level Russian officials.[22] The Russian Foreign Ministry also typically refers to the leaders of the unrecognized successionist entities as "presidents," implying a degree of recognition for the successionist entities.

Other examples of high-level political support include Russian President Putin's meeting with Abkhaz leader Sergei Bagapsh and South Ossetian leader Eduard Kokoity. Apparently, Putin even tried to set up a meeting for them with EU High Representative for CFSP Javier Solana[23] in Sochi in April 2005. Similarly, high-level political support was offered to a presidential candidate in Abkhazia's 2004 elections when the (defeated) candidate Raul Khajimba was campaigning with posters depicting him and president Putin shaking hands.[24]

Passportization

A visible instance of Russian support is the granting of Russian citizenship to the residents of the unrecognized entities. Some 90 percent of the residents of South Ossetia and Abkhazia are said to have Russian passports.[25] The number is considerably smaller in Transnistria, where some 15 percent of the population hold Russian passports. The policy of passportization is a state policy. The passports themselves clearly state that they are issued by the Russian Foreign Ministry.[26] The main objective is to build a legitimate case for Russia's claim to represent the interests of the secessionist entities because they consist of Russian citizens. Thus Russia is creating a political and even legal basis for intervention for the sake of protecting its own "citizens" in the secessionist entities.

The introduction of visa regimes for Georgia in 2001 was another instance of Russian policy driven along the same lines, intended to strengthen the separatist entities while weakening the legitimate states. The residents of South Ossetia and Abkhazia were exempted from the visa regime.

Conflict settlement mechanisms

In the conflict resolution negotiation process, Russia plays a key role, often acting not so much as an unbiased mediator, but rather as an actor negotiating its own interests.

Russia is not opposed to conflict resolution. But it is interested in a settlement that first and foremost serves Russian interests by respecting a number of conditions. The first condition is that the secessionist entities must have a decisive influence over the affairs of the reunified states, even to the detriment of the functionality and viability of an eventual power-sharing arrangement. Second, Russia demands that, in return for serving as the primary external 'guarantor' of peace, it maintain its position as the main power

broker in any power-sharing arrangement. Russia also demands a continued military presence.

Interestingly enough, the main Russian-brokered agreement that came closest to solving a conflict—the "Kozak Memorandum" for Transnistria[27]—met all three of these conditions: 1) high-level influence for the secessionist entity to the point of creating a dysfunctional state, 2) Russia as the main power broker, and 3) continued Russian military presence. When Moldova implicitly accepted these three conditions, progress on a new agreement to settle the conflict had been quick. However, in the end, Moldova backed down due to doubts about the viability of the arrangement, which was clearly highlighted by negative international reactions to the memorandum, including from the US, EU and OSCE. Similarly, Russian proposals to Georgia and Moldova to create "common states" in the late nineties also reflected a level of decentralization that was not likely to work in practice.[28]

Diplomatic support

Russia often supports the secessionist entities in international affairs. For example, three successive annual OSCE Ministerial Council meetings in 2003, 2004 and 2005 failed to adopt common statements due to disagreements between an overwhelming number of OSCE member states on the one hand and Russia on the other. These disagreements were precisely related to the conflicts in Georgia and Moldova and the withdrawal of Russian troops from these countries.

The issue of unsolved conflicts is more and more prominent on the EU-Russia agenda, including in the Road Map for the Space of Common External Security where resolving conflicts in "adjacent" regions is considered a priority.

Support for State-building

Russia has also been crucial in providing support for state and institution building in the secessionist regions. In fact, some of the security institutions of the de facto states

The author with Ukranian Foreign Minister Borys Tarasyuk and Zbigniew Brzezinski

are 'outsourced' to the Russian Federation. 'Outsourcing' or 'contracting out' is used in business jargon to describe a situation when organizational functions of an enterprise are transferred to a third party or country. A similar phenomenon is happening with the 'state' institutions of the successionist entities as they are 'outsourced' to Russia. This is particularly true as regards the 'power structures,' i.e. the ministries of defense and intelligence services.

The local 'security' institutions in Abkhazia, South Ossetia and Transnistria are often headed by Russians or functionaries de facto delegated by state institutions of the Russian Federation. This most often include staff in the local intelligence services and the defense ministries. Examples of Russians de facto delegated to the secessionist entities include ministers of defense Anatoli Barankevich (South Ossetia) and Sultan Sosnaliev (Abkhazia), local intelligence chief Iarovoi (South Ossetia) and minister of interior Mindzaev (South Ossetia).[29] Russian presence is also visible beyond the security services. An Abkhazia prime minister in 2004–2005, Nodar Khashba, came from the Russian ministry of emergency situations. Incumbent Prime Minister Morozov in South Ossetia is also from Russia. The 'outsourcing' of the institutions of the secessionist entities to Russia is most important in South Ossetia, somewhat less in Abkhazia, and relatively little (beyond the security services) in Transnistria. Such arrangements are not necessarily welcome in the secessionist entities themselves, especially in Abkhazia and Transnistria, but are allegedly desired mainly by Russians.[30]

Economic support

Russia plays a key role in the economic sustainability of the secessionist entities. In fact one can credibly make the argument that the *'independence'* of South Ossetia and Abkhazia *depends* on Russia,[31] which is certainly their most important trading partner. Georgian officials claimed that while some of Georgian exports have been banned from entering Russia on grounds of substandard sanitation, similar goods from Abkhazia and South Ossetia continue to be imported, indicating the political manipulation of trade issues in the region.[32]

For years, Transnistrian industry has benefited from Russian subsidies. Transnistria's debt to Gazprom amounts to one billion euros, which means that Transnistria has not paid for its gas consumption in years.[33] In fact, the competitive advantage of Transnistrian industry is based on Russian subsidies.

The socio-economic dimension of Russian support is also important in Abkhazia and South Ossetia. The Russian government not only granted citizenship to an overwhelming majority of residents, but also pays pensions in both territories.[34] These pensions are higher than pensions in Georgia, creating additional incentives for these regions to join the Russian Federation rather than seek a conflict settlement. Russia defends its practice of paying pensions and granting citizenship by citing its humanitarian concerns about the residents of these regions.

Russia is also the main investor in the secessionist regions. Some investments in Transnistrian industry and in Abkhaz tourist infrastructure are justified on economic grounds. However, it is clear that the conflict regions are far from investment havens and many such investments are driven by political imperatives rather than economic logic.

At least some, if not most, of the Russian investments are made because Russian authorities recommended that Russian businessmen offer such investments as a sign of support for the secessionist entities.[35] In a state where businesses are hardly independent from the state, as is the case in Russia, such practices are not difficult to implement.

Economic support for the secessionist entities is coupled with economic pressure on Moldova and Georgia. In 2005, Russia introduced restrictions on meat and vegetables exports from Moldova and Georgia to Russia. In March 2006, Russia banned all Moldovan and Georgian wine and brandy exports to Russia, as well as Georgian mineral water. At the same time, Russia increased gas prices for both countries. Such restrictions did not affect the secessionist entities. In the words of the Russian Ambassador to Moldova: "It is one thing to be a Russian compatriot in Moldova or Kirghizia, and another thing to be a compatriot in Transnistria or Abkhazia."[36] The latter are certainly closer to Moscow than the former.

The status-quo game

Russia's preferred policy is to preserve the status quo, which provides enough room for manoeuvre to assure Russian interests in the conflict areas. Thus, Russia is likely to prevent conflict resolution mechanisms and Western involvement in such schemes. Its main objective is to 'freeze' the conflict, as any attempt to 'defreeze' them is dangerous and counterproductive to Russian interests. Unfortunately, the conflicts are not frozen at all,[37] but only their settlement. The preservation of the status quo can only lead to the deepening and entrenchment of conflicts, escalating tensions while moving away from possible solutions.

The 'Kosovo precedent'

In the context of discussing the Kosovo issue, high-level Russian authorities have come closest to acknowledging that Kosovo may constitute a precedent worth considering in Georgia. President Putin stated in 2006 that "If someone thinks that Kosovo can be granted full independence as a state, then why should the Abkhaz or the South-Ossetian peoples be denied the right to statehood? I am not talking here about how Russia would act. But we know, for example, that Turkey recognized the Republic of Northern Cyprus. I am not saying that Russia would immediately recognize Abkhazia or South Ossetia as independent states, but international life knows such precedents … we need generally accepted, universal principles for resolving these problems."[38] Russia has been moving toward the acceptance of Kosovo's independence, while trying to extract maximum benefit from this possible precedent in the post-Soviet space.

The Kosovo precedent has certainly infused new trends into the politics of the de facto states. The eventual move of Kosovo towards independence, albeit 'conditional,' creates a new *raison d'etre* for the secessionist entities to resist any conflict settlement in the hope that, sooner or later, they will follow Kosovo.[39] For example, the Abkhaz de facto president openly states that "If Kosovo is recognized, Abkhazia will also be recognized in the course of three days. I am absolutely sure of that."[40]

De facto annexation

The overall result of the above-mentioned policies is that the secessionist entities of South Ossetia and Abkhazia are moving toward a situation in which they are de facto incorporated into the Russian Federation. In reality, the secessionist entities 'outsource' not only some of their institutions, but also control over their entities to the Russian Federation. Most of the population in these regions have Russian passports, pensioners receive pensions from the Russian state, the Russian rouble is the used currency, and many of the de facto officials of the secessionist entities are sent "on missions" by the Russian Federation. In addition, there is a process of legislative harmonization between the legal systems of the Russian Federation and those of the secessionist entities.

Reflecting these developments, Moscow's policies towards these secessionist regions looks much like Moscow's policy toward other Russian regions within the Russian Federation. This situation was highly visible during the heavy and high-level intervention of Russia in the Abkhaz presidential elections in 2004. An interviewed expert in Moscow said that "Abkhazia is a de facto continuation of the Krasnodar region" of Russia.[41] The fact that Russia takes over the 'power' structures in the secessionist entities also reseembles Russian regional politics. In the Russian Federation, control over the 'power structures'— ministry of defense, intelligence, prosecutor's office and police—is a competence of the federal center, i.e. Moscow. Russian regions do not control their power institutions, even if they have some degree of self-governance in political and economic matters. The situation in Abkhazia and South Ossetia is similar.

But the secessionist entities are not simply a continuation of Russia. Abkhazia stresses that it wants to be an independent state,[42] not a Russian region. Abkhaz authorities also stress that in the 2004 Abkhaz presidential elections, the Moscow-backed candidate lost the elections. Transnistria does not have a border with Russia and it would be difficult to imagine how would a second 'Kaliningrad' in Transnistria work in practice. Moreover, the interests of the secessionist entities, their domestic policy patterns, and strategic goals may differ from Russia's preferences. Nevertheless, their rapprochement with Russia is not far from a point of no return, especially in Abkhazia and South Ossetia.

International incentives for resolving the secessionist conflicts

In sum, Russia plays a dominant role in the survival and evolution of the secessionist entities in Georgia and Moldova. Despite periods when Russia was rather supportive of the governments of Moldova and Georgia, in recent years Russian policies towards the secessionist entities have become more assertive. This has largely been due to a new feeling of self-confidence among Russian elites inspired by a number of factors, such as economic growth in Russia, consolidation of Putin's "power vertical," the defeat of the Chechen secessionist movement, and the West's problems in Afghanistan, Iraq and Iran. These have all led to a feeling in Moscow that Russia has the resources and the proper international conditions to reassert its dominance in the former Soviet Union. Stepping up support for the secessionist entities is seen as one way to achieve that.

The policies of Russian support for the secessionist entities of the former Soviet Union are a complex web of political, economic, social, humanitarian, security and military activities. These policies include the maintenance of military forces on the ground—not only peacekeepers but also military bases—the training of militaries, provision of economic subsidies, granting of Russian citizenship and passports (the so-called policy of "passportization"), paying pensions, granting preferential trade regimes, ensuring diplomatic and political support on the international stage, interfering in the domestic politics of the unrecognized entities, using conflict settlement mechanisms to freeze conflict resolution processes, delegating Russian state employees to serve in key posts in the unrecognized governments of the secessionist entities, etc. These policies of support are combined with economic and political pressure on the governments of Moldova and Georgia.

As EU and NATO enlargement brings these organizations closer to these conflict areas, their interest in promoting solutions to these conflicts has increased. The international fight against terrorism raises the spectre that the existence of failed states or uncontrolled areas can have repercussions far beyond their respective regions. The stabilization of the Balkans means that the EU and NATO can pay more attention to conflicts which are further afield in the neighborhood. In conjunction with these new international trends, Moldova and Georgia—two of the countries affected by conflict—have become active *demandeurs* of a greater international role in the conflict resolution processes. At the same time, the lack of progress in conflict settlement for more than a decade raises uncomfortable, albeit legitimate, questions about the effectiveness of existing conflict resolution frameworks. In other words, the international community is entering into a phase of reassessing its policies addressing the secessionist conflicts in the former Soviet Union. But the challenge involves not only helping resolve these conflicts, but also dealing with Russia in the process of contributing to conflict resolution.

Taken together, Russian policies toward the secessionist entities often create serious disincentives for conflict settlement. The policy of strengthening the secessionist regimes and weakening legitimate states creates strong incentives for the secessionist entities to maintain the conflicts.

The longer the conflicts continue within the framework of an increasingly assertive Russian foreign policy, the more and more likely it is that the secessionist entities will become de facto parts of the Russian Federation. Moscow's policy toward these regions in many instances resembles its policies towards subjects of the Russian Federation. The paradox of this situation is that, amid the fight for independence, the secessionist entities are 'outsourcing' their de facto independence to another state.

Notes

[1]   Alexei Malashenko, "Post-sovetskie gosudarstva iuga i interesy Moskvy" ("Post-Soviet States of the South and Moscow's Interests"), Pro et Contra Vol 5:3, 2000, Moscow, p.43.

[2]   The Foreign Policy Concept of the Russian Federation, 28 June 2000.

[3]   Vladimir Putin, annual address to the Federal Assembly, 25 April 2005, Moscow, www.kremlin.ru.

[4]   Author's interview with Dmitry Trenin, Moscow, January 13, 2006. For the same argument see Interview with Dmitry Trenin, Strana.ru, January 26, 2006, http://www.strana.ru/stories/02/05/20/2976/271554.html.

5   "The New Russian Doctrine," Sergei Ivanov, The Wall Street Journal, 11 January 2006.

6   Obrashchenie Prezidenta Rossii Vladimira Putina (Statement by President Putin), Rossiiskaya Gazeta, 6 September 2004, http://www.rg.ru/2004/09/06/president.html.

7   The paper does not deal with the Nagorno-Karabakh, a secessionist entity on the territory of Azerbaijan. The character of the conflict, let alone the Russian role in this conflict differs significantly from the other three cases analysed in the paper.

8   Foreign Policy Concept of the Russian Federation, 28 June 2000.

9   Vladimir Putin, annual address to the Federal Assembly, 26 May 2004, Moscow, www.kremlin.ru.

10   An article about China develops the link between internal regime insecurity in non-democratic states and their willingness to compromise in foreign affairs. The essay traces how most compromises made by Chinese leadership in disputes with their neighbours coincide with periods of internal instability in China such as the revolt in Tibet, the legitimacy crisis after the Tiananmen upheaval, and separatist violence in Xinjiang. See Taylor Fravel, "Regime Insecurity and International Cooperation: Explaining China's Compromises in Territorial Disputes," International Security 30:2, 2005, pp.46–83.

11   Interview with Dmitry Medvedev, Expert, 4 April 2005. Downloadable at http://www.kremlin.ru/text/publications/2005/04/86307.shtml.

12   Mikhail Khodorkovsky, "Krizis Liberalizma v Rossii," 29 March 2004, Vedomosti, downloadable at http://khodorkovsky.ru/speech/82.html.

13   Vladimir Putin, transcript of the press conference for the Russian and foreign Media, 31 January 2006, the Kremlin, Moscow.

14   Interview with an expert, Moscow, 12 January 2006.

15   Though UN peacekeeping missions are different in nature and character from Russia's peacekeeping operations, some of their effects have also been criticized. For example, Scott Pegg argued that: " …the specific status quo that the United Nations Peacekeeping Force in Cyprus has helped to freeze is a status quo that the Turkish Cypriot political leadership is quite comfortable with. Thus, whatever its stated objectives may be, one can in some ways view UNFICYP as a midwife present at the birth of the Turkish Cypriot de facto state and as a guardian that helps make its continued existence possible", Pegg, Scott, International Society and the De Facto State, Ashgate, Brookfield, 1998, p.165.

16   Lynch, Dov, 2004: Engaging Eurasia's Separatist States, US Institute of Peace.

17   Moldovan President Vladimir Voronin, Speech addressed to the North Atlantic Council, Brussels, 7 June 2005.

18   Resolution of the Parliament of Georgia Regarding the Current Situation in the Conflict Regions on the Territory of Georgia and Ongoing Peace Operations, 11 November 2005.

19   Agreement on a Cease-Fire and Separation of Forces, signed in Moscow, 14 May 1994, http://www.unomig.org/.

20   Interview with an official, Moscow, January 2006.

21   The Russian for Commonwealth of Independent States (CIS), is Sodruzhestvo Nezavisimyh Gosudartsv, or SNG. But SNG-2 stands for Sodruzhestvo Nepriznanyh Gosudartsv (Community of Unrecognised States). Sometimes the SNG-2 is translated into English as CIS-2, but it does not reflect the play of words between SNG and SNG-2. In addition to Abkhazia, South Ossetia and Transnistria, SNG-2 includes also Nagorno-Karabakh. The second informal name for the group of secessionist entities is NATO-2, which is an acronym for Nagorno-Karabakh, Abkhazia, Transnistria, Ossetia.

22   See Vladimir Socor, "Bagapsh, Kokoity, Smirnov touch base in Moscow," Eurasia Daily Monitor, 28 January 2005. www.jamestown.org.

23   Vladimir Socor, "EU Policy disarray in Georgia and Moldova," Eurasia Daily Monitor, 15 April 2005.

24   For the Russian role in the Abkhaz 2004 elections see "Putin Meddles in Abkhazia Presidential Race," Civil Georgia, 31 August 2004, http://www.civil.ge/eng/article.php?id=7721.

25   In fact Georgia itself has been partly responsible for the situation, as it refused the granting of UN passports to the residents of Abkhazia in the 90s, which resulted in the mass acquisition by Abkhazians of Russian passports as a means to travel. Had Georgia accepted the granting of UN passports to Abkhaz, their necessity to get Russian passport to travel would have been less.

26   The information about the issuing authority on Russian passports in Abkhazia clearly state that they are issued by "MID Rossii," that is the Foreign Ministry of Russia. Author's observation in Sukhumi, March 2006.

27   See text of the "Russian Draft Memorandum on the basic principles of the state structure of a united state in Moldova" (Kozak Memorandum), November 17, 2003, http://eurojournal.org/more. php?id=107_0_1_18_M5.

28   It would be fair to say that not only the Russian Federation supports these type of agreements. The EU supported a Serbia-Montenegro confederation with a level of decentralization that made the common state hardly functional. Moreover, the Republic of Cyprus rejected the Annan Plan in 2004 exactly for the fear that in case of an agreement it will have to share too much power with the self-proclaimed Turkish Republic of Northern Cyprus.

29   Interviews with Georgian officials, Tbilisi, March 2006.

30   Interviews with experts and officials in Sukhumi and Tbilisi, March 2006.

31   Dov Lynch, *Why Georgia Matters*, Chaillot Paper 86, EU ISS, Paris, p.36, www.iss-eu.org.

32   Interviews with Georgian diplomats, Moscow, January 2006; Tbilisi, March 2006.

33   Centre for Strategic Studies and Reforms, *Research Paper on Transnistria* (Chisinau: November 2003), p.28; available at: http://www.cisr-md.org/pdf/0311%20transn-research.pdf.

34   For example in Abkhazia Russia pays some 30,000 pensions. The minimal pension is approximately 30 Euro. Interview with a de facto deputy-prime minister of Abkhazia, Sukhumi, March 2006.

35   Interviews with experts and officials in Sukhumi, Abkhazia, March 2006.

36   See "We arrived to see who wants to be with us" (My priehali ubedista kto hochet byt vmeste s nami), Olvia Press, 6 October 2005, http://olvia.idknet.com/ol46-10-05.htm.

37   See Dov Lynch, 2004, op. cit.

38   President Vladimir Putin, transcript of the Press Conference for the Russian and Foreign Media, January, 31 2006, The Kremlin, Moscow.

39   Interviews with officials and experts in Tiraspol, Transnistria (December 2005) and Sukhumi, Abkhazia, (March 2006).

40   Interview with Sergei Bagapsh, de facto president of Abkhazia, *Svobodnaya Gruzia*, February 28, 2006, published originally in Vremya Novostei.

41   Interview, Moscow, January 13, 2006.

42   Author's interview with Sergei Bagapsh, de facto president of Abkhazia, Sukhumi, March 31, 2006.

part four

Political Identity and Human Rights in Turkey

Islamic Identity and the West: Is Conflict Inevitable?

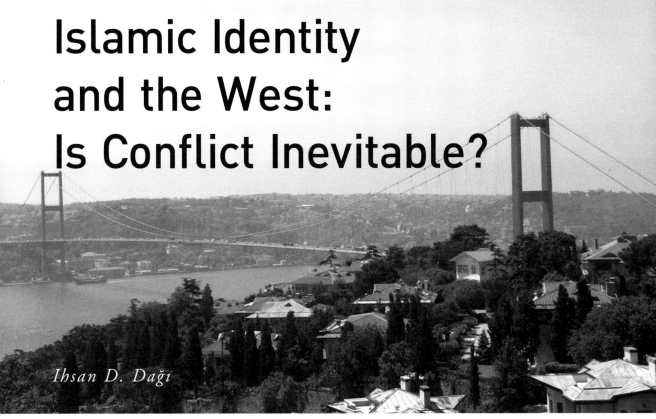

Ihsan D. Dağı

Bridge over the Bosphorus in Istanbul connecting Europe and Asia

The September 11 attacks and ensuing American interventions in Afghanistan and Iraq have reinforced the view that Islam and the West are bound to conflict. However popular this view is among some westerners and Muslims, a contrary development has taken place in Turkey, where Islamic political identity used to be shaped by an opposition to both the West and westernization policies of the Republic. In a unique way, the main body of Turkish Islamists have departed, in recent years, from their conventional anti-westernization position and engaged in a process of "rethinking" the West, westernization and modern/western political values. The changing language of Turkish Islamists presents an important move not only for the spread of modern political values among the Islamic groups in Turkey, but also for a possibility of rapprochement between Islam and the West in the post-September 11 context. The rethinking has been reflected in the identity formation and policy orientation of the Justice and Development Party (JDP), established in 2001 by a group of pro-Islamic politicians, which came to

Ihsan Dağı is Professor of International Relations at Middle East Technical University in Ankara, Turkey. His 2001–2 International Policy Fellowship research, "Islamic Identity and Rethinking the 'Western Question' in Turkey," is available online at www.policy.hu/dagi and http://pdc.ceu.hu (Source IPF).

power in 2002 with a landslide victory. The JDP leadership—by launching an aggressive diplomacy abroad and reformist political strategy at home in order to meet the criteria set by the European Union (EU) for full membership—has demonstrated its departure from an anti-Western Islamic stand. This essay attempts to explain the reasons and outcomes of the transformation of Islamic political identity in Turkey with a view that questions the arguments, widespread both in the West and the Islamic world, for the inevitability of conflict between Islam and the West.

The roots of Turkey's Islamic identity

The last two hundred years of Turkey is all about the history of westernization. When the state fell into decline vis-à-vis the rising European power, the late Ottomans embarked on a process of adopting "western" ways beginning with the westernization of the army, followed by the administration, and eventually into more domestic areas affecting the daily lives of the people.[1] Westernization as a concept and program to "renew" the state and society, in effect, became an identity-constituting orientation.[2]

Western pressures coupled with the policies of westernization as initiated by state elite prompted an Islamic response.[3] After all by the 19th century, the West had penetrated into the Islamic lands politically, militarily and economically. Thus the question of how to stop the advancement of the West was a practical and political issue. In response the West was described as the source of all problems encountered by Muslims; it was evil, degenerating and destroying Islamic civilization. In short, the West was conceived as the absolute 'other,' generating identity debates to which the Islamic thinking had to respond.

However, it was not only the West itself but the wider question of how to respond to the West that raised identity debates. Western civilization was adopted in the Ottoman lands at least since 1839 as a means of catching up and coping with the West. The westernization process and policies, especially with the establishment of the secular Republic in 1923, resulted in the exclusion of Islamic leaders, groups and thought from the centers of the power, eliminating appearances of Islam in the public sphere. In the process of westernization and secularization during the early years of the republican era, the caliphate was abolished, religious orders and institutions were closed down, western civil law was adopted, religious schools and education were banned. No doubt the Kemalist reforms beginning in the 1930s intended to secularize the state marginalized Islam and Islamic groups, and presented a break with the past that was heavily blended with Islam and its social authority. Westernization presuming the possibility of a civilizational shift was, for the Islamists, a rejection of Islam in the renovation of Turkish

state. In short, westernization meant the use of the (modernized) state apparatus to suppress the roles of Islam in social and political realms.

For the Islamists, therefore, the republican reforms made it clear that it was not the West *per se* but the westernizers and the westernization program that swept them away from the centers of political and social order, and left them excluded.[4] Despite the historical references to the "clash of the cross and crescent," opposition to the radical secularization policies of the westernizers in the republican Turkey played a central role in the construction of an Islamic political identity.[5]

Islamic political identity in modern Turkey and the West

Under the single party regime and a strict policy of secularization, an Islamically motivated political movement did not appear until 1950s. Multi-party politics in the 1950s and 1960s enabled Islamic groups to start to express themselves in political processes, but this time within the center-right/conservative Democrat Party and the Justice Party. In the process of restructuring Turkish politics following the 1960 military intervention, Islam's political appeal increased. Its first outright political expression was the emergence of the National View Movement (NVM) under the leadership of Necmettin Erbakan in 1970. The National Salvation Party (NSP), formed by Erbakan with an Islamic orientation, played a key role in the fragmented Turkish politics of 1970 holding around 10 percent popular support.[6]

Issues related to the West and westernization served as a catalyst for the National View Movement's identity formation, public discourse and policies.[7] It differentiated itself from other political movements by taking a critical stand on the westernization of Turkey. The actors, institutions, processes and objectives of westernization were questioned in the name of authenticity, i.e. Islamic civilization, and in the search for power vis-à-vis the West. The NVM leadership believed that westernization was understood by the early republican leaders as a denial of the traditional (read Islamic) values, attitudes and institutions. The impact of westernization on the character of the state and society, traditionally influenced by Islam, was regarded as a more serious problem than that of the West itself. They regarded the attempt to replace Islamic-Ottoman civilization with a western one as the source of the ills of Turkish society. Thus, not only was western domination in Turkey to be eliminated to build a "national order," but also westernization. Erbakan thus proclaimed before the 1995 general elections that once they came to power, they would put an end to the process of westernization.[8]

They believed that historically, culturally and geographically Turkey did not belong to the West, instead it shared its past, values and institutions with the Islamic world—

a world that had to be mobilized to balance the power and pressure of the West.[9] For the NVM, it was westernization policies that resulted in the abandonment of the Islamic world and laid the ground for Turkey to be an all-season ally of the West. The identity, discourse and policy suggestions of the NVM were shaped by its anti-Western stand.

Persistent efforts of the NVM and fragmentation of Turkish politics coupled with deep social and economic problems in the 1990s brought the pro-Islamic Welfare Party (re-named in 1984 after the military regime of 1980–1983) to the forefront of Turkish politics. In the 1995 elections the WP came first holding 21 percent of the votes. After a short-lived coalition government of center-right political parties, Necmettin Erbakan, the leader of the WP, formed a coalition government with the center-right True Path Party. For the first time in the republican history of Turkey, a pro-Islamic political party came to power as a major force, holding a prime ministerial position.[10] This was hard to digest for many, particularly among the traditional state elite including the military.

Search for survival and rapprochement with the West

As a result, the Welfare Party's unexpected success in the 1995 general elections provoked reactions from secularist/Kemalist centers. A "National Policy Paper" prepared by the National Security Council (NSC) described the "reactionary forces" of Islam as the first priority threat to the Turkish state, more dangerous and immediate than the secessionist Kurdish nationalism.[11] The army, aligning with some sectors of civil society, justified by their concern for the future of secularism in the face of the Islamist challenge, launched a campaign against the WP and in effect against the government. Soon after the formation of the Erbakan-led government, the National Security Council, meeting on February 28, 1997, took a number of decisions to "reinforce the secular character of the Turkish state" threatened by the Islamists.[12] As a result of the so-called February 28 process, described by some as a post-modern coup, the government was forced to step down. Yet it did not only aim at the political agents of Islamic movements. In the process, "Islamic capital" was displayed, boycotted and prosecuted to eliminate financial sources for Islamic movements. Islamic non-governmental organizations and foundations were also put under strict control. The popular mayor of Istanbul, Recep Tayyip Erdogan, was prosecuted and imprisoned for inciting hatred among people on religious grounds via a speech he made in Siirt in 1998 in which he read a poem written by Ziya Gokalp, a pan-Turkish sociologist and ideologue of the new republic. In sum, as a result of the February 28 process, the discursive hegemony of Kemalism was reasserted, while Islam's social and economic bases, as well as its political agents, were targeted, resulting in the closure of the WP by the Constitutional Court in 1998 on the grounds that it had become the center of anti-secularist activities.

With the closure of the WP, its parliamentary group joined the Virtue Party (VP), which had been formed by close associates of Erbakan. Yet the anti-westernism of the old days had gone. The party seemed to have abandoned not only its opposition to the West, but also to have adopted western political values such as democracy, human rights and the rule of law as part of its new discourse. Calls for democracy, human rights and the rule of law became the new characteristics of NVM's political strategy after its party was closed down and its leader banned from politics.

In this new language, modern/western values and the West itself as represented by the VP were no more anathema to Islamic political identity. This was symbolized in an ironic way by the decision of Erbakan to take the case of the WP closure and his ban from politics for five years to the European Court of Human Rights (ECHR).

It seemed that the VP sought refuge not only in the West and western institutions like ECHR, but also in the discourse of modern/western values like democracy, human rights and the rule of law. In a parallel move, the NVM's stand on the EU also changed, advocating strongly Turkey's integration into the EU in contrast to its former view of the EU as a Christian club.[13]

The Justice and Development Party:
Limits of Islamism in the age of globalization

When the Virtue Party was closed down in 2001 (again by the Constitutional Court on the same grounds of being a center of anti-secular activities), former mayor of Istanbul Tayyip Erdogan formed a new political party, the Justice and Development Party, with the support of those who were unhappy with the leadership and the discourse of old party. They immediately disassociated themselves from the old leadership and ideology. The JDP won the 2002 elections, receiving 34 percent of the votes whereas its nearest contender—the Republican People's Party—had 19 percent, and the pro-Islamic Felicity Party, still representing the old line of the NVM, received an all-time low of 2.5 percent.[14]

The JDP's organizational network and leadership were to a large extent inherited from the WP and VP. Initially they claimed to form a political party that would go beyond the WP/VP in an attempt to appeal to a wider public, in other words to the "political center."[15] The leadership referred to the Democrat Party of the 1950s, the Justice Party of the 1960s and the Motherland Party of the 1980s—all mass political movements from the center right that gained majority rule in their respective periods—as their political predecessors.[16]

The JDP leadership seemed to have departed not only from the leadership of the NVM but also from its ideology claiming that the party stands for "democratic conservatism."[17] The party program of the JDP, named the "Democracy and Development Program," reflected the priorities of the new movement. While the emphasis on development has always been the legacy of center right politics since 1950, "democracy" was a new element regarded as convenient in relieving the excessive pressure of the judiciary and the military as exemplified in the February 28 process.

Given the pro-Islamic background of its leaders and the newly adapted notion of conservatism, the JDP can best be regarded as a post-Islamist movement; keeping its ties with Islam in the social realm but abandoning it as a political program. Witnessing how Islam's social base, with its educational, commercial and solidarity networks, was disrupted

by the politicization of Islam in the 1990s, they became more interested in keeping Islam's social and economic base intact as the basis of the "conservatism" Erdogan refers to.[18] In the party program and the election declaration, the leadership acknowledged the end of ideologies including Islamism in the age of globalization.[19]

The JDP's position on EU membership and globalization differs significantly from any conventional Islamist stand. EU membership is regarded as a natural outcome of Turkey's modernization; "meeting the Copenhagen political criteria is an important step forward for the modernization of the country."[20] Right after the November 2002 elections, JDP leader Erdogan declared that the government's priority was not to resolve the "headscarf" issue, as would be expected from a pro-Islamic party, but instead to speed up the process to get Turkey into the EU, once called "the Christian Club" by the National View movement.[21] Since its formation, the JDP government has introduced fundamental reforms on the Kurdish issue, human rights and civil-military relations and furthermore made politically risky compromises to resolve the long-standing Cyprus dispute. By desperately seeking the EU membership, the JDP leadership, with its pro-Islamic background, must have explicitly abandoned the idea of an Islamic government in Turkey, as EU membership process practically eliminates such a possibility.[22] It is also unusual to think of an Islamist party approving a globalization process that is believed by many to weaken the "local/national values" and thus erode traditional society—the natural social base for an Islamist movement. An Islamist movement, on the contrary, is fed by the fears of globalization prevalent among the traditional sectors. Rather than leaning toward local and nationalistic reactions, the JDP takes a pro-globalization stand. Anti-globalist tendencies in the party have been overtaken by an analysis that places Turkey not in isolation, but in integration with the external world as a precondition for further democratization, which is expected to open up a broader space for the survival and legitimacy of the party. By continuing the previously accepted IMF program, and by an aggressive privatization policy, the JDP reaffirms its pro-globalization stand.[23] Against opposition to the influx of foreign capital investment in Turkey buying privatized companies or forming partnerships with Turkish companies, Erdogan went public accusing the opponents of foreign capital of being "racist toward foreign capital."[24]

Rethinking the West

As explained, Islamic political identity was traditionally built in opposition to the West, western values and, equally important, to the history of westernization in Turkey. Yet pro-Islamic politicians of the late 1990s, most of whom joined the JDP, realized that they needed the West and modern/western values of democracy, human rights and the rule of law in order to build a broader front against the Kemalist center, and to acquire legitimacy through this new discourse in their confrontation with the radical secularist establishment.

In the face of pressures originating from the military's adamant opposition to the Islamists which influences the attitudes of the judges, high state bureaucracy and mainstream secular media, the JDP embraced the legitimizing power and the virtue of democracy as a means of highlighting 'people power' vis-à-vis state power. They knew that they could survive only in a country that was democratically oriented, respecting civil and political rights, and moreover integrated further into the western world, particularly the EU.[25] This discursive turn, speaking the universal language of political modernity instead of Islam's particularities, also served to secure a place for a moderate Islamic identity.

The Islamists went through similar experiences concerning the value of human rights and the rule of law as they saw their political parties closed down, leaders banned from political activities, and associations and foundations intimidated. In response they moved to embrace the language of civil and political rights that provided both an effective leverage against the pressures of the state, as well as grounds to build international coalitions. Under the pressure of the Kemalist establishment, the Islamists sought to form new alliances with westerners abroad and liberals at home who distanced themselves from the elements of authoritarian regime in Turkey. The search for an international coalition led the Islamists to move westward, where they encountered numerous human rights organizations, the European Union, the European Court of Human Rights and individual states critical of Turkey's human rights record. In the end, the Islamists found themselves on the same side as the westerners, demanding democratization and further guarantees for civil and political rights in Turkey.[26]

The EU emerged as a natural ally to reduce the influence of the army and to establish democratic governance within which Islamic social and political forces would be regarded as a legitimate player. The expectation was that the army's interventions in politics would be significantly lessened as a result of further democratization that had already been put as a precondition for Turkey's entry to the EU; a Kemalist state ideology guarded by the army would not be sustainable in an EU-member Turkey.[27]

Sights set on Europe

As a result, the post-Islamists adopted a new and positive stand on understanding the West, Turkey's membership in the EU, and integration of Turkey into global structures and processes.[28] This was a clear break from their tradition of open "crusade" against the West, deep suspicions about Western values (including democracy and human rights), and criticism of the Turkish history of westernization.

As rejection of the West and westernization was the very basis on which modern Islamist identity was traditionally built, the rapprochement with the West and westernization shakes the very basis of Islamist political identity. What is left is not an Islamist identity as we know it. Transformation of the NVM from the early 1970s to the late 1990s has given birth to a new political party (the JDP) with a liberal, democratic and pro-western orientation and political agenda. A movement that embraces modern political values of democracy, human rights and the rule of law, which advocates integration with the EU, and attracts votes from all segments of society can hardly be called Islamist. It is a case demonstrating that a discursive shift may be followed by identity change under certain circumstances. The Islamists' recent departure from their traditional anti-West and anti-westernization position seems to have transformed the Islamic self of Turkey, opening up new possibilities for the coexistence of Islam and the West.

Notes

[1] Bernard Lewis, *The Emergence of Modern Turkey* (Oxford: Oxford University Press, 1968), pp.45–72; Dankwart A. Rustow, "The Modernization of Turkey in Historical and Comparative Perspective," in Kemal Karpat (ed.), *Social Change and Politics in Turkey: A Structural-Historical Analysis* (Leiden: Brill, 1973), pp.94–95.

[2] Ibid.

[3] See İsmail Kara (ed.), *Türkiye'de İslamcılık Düşüncesi*, Vol. I, (İstanbul, Risale Yayınları, 1986); Şerif Mardin, *The Genesis of Young Ottoman Thought: A Study in the Modernization of Turkish Political Ideas* (Princeton, NJ: Princeton University Press, 1962); Mümtazer Türköne, *Siyasi İdeoloji Olarak İslamcılığın Doğuşu* (İstanbul: İletişim Yayınları, 1991).

[4] Nilüfer Gole, "Secularism and Islamism in Turkey: The Making of Elites and Counter-Elites," *Middle East Journal*, Vol.51, No.1 (1997), pp.46–58.

[5] For a strong statement of anti-westernization in more recent times see Mehmet Doğan, *Batılılaşma İhaneti* (İstanbul, Beyan Yayınları, 1986). For an insider's critique of the Islamists' view of the West see Ahmet Harputlu, "İslamcıların Batı Tahayyülü," *Bilgi ve Düşünce* Vol.1, No.1 (2002), pp.23–27.

[6] Binnaz Toprak, "Politicization of Islam in a Secular State: the National Salvation Party in Turkey," in Said Amir Arjomand (ed.), *From Nationalism to Revolutionary Islam: Essays on Social Movements in the Contemporary Near and Middle East* (Albany, NY: State University of New York Press, 1984).

[7] İhsan D. Dagi, *Kimlik, Söylem ve Siyaset: Doğu-Batı Ayrımında Refah Partisi Geleneği* (Ankara: İmge Yayınevi, 1999), pp.23–25, 42–75.

[8] *Milli Gazete*, December 4, 1995.

[9] Hasan H. Ceylan, (ed.), *Erbakan ve Türkiye'nin Temel Meseleleri* (Ankara: Rehber Yayınları, 1996), pp.99-100; *Milli Gazete*, September 21, 1995.

[10] For an analysis of the WP's ideology and electoral performance in the 1990s see M. Hakan Yavuz, "Political Islam and the Welfare (Refah) Party in Turkey," *Comparative Politics*, Vol. 30, No.1 (1997), pp.63–82; Öniş, (1997), pp.743–766; Haldun Gülalp, "Political Islam in Turkey: The Rise and Fall of the Refah Party," *Muslim World*, Vol. 89, No.1 (1999), pp.24–36; Ahmet Yıldız, "Politico-Religious Discourse of Political Islam in Turkey: The Parties of National Outlook," *Muslim World*, Vol. 93, No. 2 (2003), pp.187–210.

[11] *Hürriyet*, November 4, 1997.

[12] For February 28 decisions of NSC see "Recommendations of the State Council meeting and Comment," *Briefing*, March 10, 1997, p.4. For analyses of the NSC decision see M. Hakan Yavuz, "Cleansing Islam From the Public Sphere," *Journal of International Affairs*, Vol.54, No.1 (2000), pp.21–40; Ümit C. Sakallıoğlu and Menderes Çınarlı, "Turkey 2002: Kemalism, Islamism and Politics in the Light if the February 28 Process," *South Atlantic Quarterly*, Vol.102, No.2/3 (2003), pp.309–32.

13   Yet many questioned the depth of this discursive shift undertaken by the NVM's leadership. As it turned out later the old guards in the movement moved back to their earlier position after the 2002 general elections in which the NVM's moderate and transformed wing came to power with the new formed Justice and Development Party.

14   For analyses of the election results and the JDP see Soli Özel, "Turkey at the Polls: After the Tsunami," *Journal of Democracy*, Vol.14, No.2 (2003), pp.80–94; Ziya Öniş and E. Fuat Keyman, "Turkey at the Polls: A New Path Emerges," *Journal of Democracy*, Vol.14, No.2 (2003), pp.95–108; Ali Çarkoğlu, "Turkey's November Elections: A New Beginning?" *Middle East Review of International Affairs*, Vol. 6, No.4 (2002), pp.30–41; Simten Coşan and Aylin Özman, "Centre-Right Politics in Turkey after the November 2002 General Election: Neo-Liberalism with a Muslim Face," *Contemporary Politics*, Vol.10, No.1 (2004), pp.57–73; Mecham (2004), pp.339–358.

15   Erdoğan, before forming the party, contacted many people including businessmen like Rahmi Koç and a retired general, Atilla Kıyat, see *Sabah*, June 25, 2001; *Sabah*, July 4, 2001.

16   *Milliyet*, July 15, 2001. For an early description of Erdoğan as a moderate politician see Metin Heper, "Islam and Democracy: Toward a Reconciliation?" *Middle East Journal*, Vol.51, No.1 (1997), p.37.

17   Yalçın Akdoğan, *Muhafazakar Demokrasi* (Ankara: AK Parti Yayınları, 2003). The book was forwarded by Recep Tayyip Erdoğan who hailed the publication of the book as an attempt to theorize the JDP's claim to be conservative democrat despite its Islamic origins. The party also organized an international symposium on conservatism and democracy held in Istanbul on January 10-11, 2004 commenced by Erdoğan's speech outlining the conservative stand of the party. For Erdoğan's speech in the symposium see *Uluslararası Muhafazakarlık ve Demokrasi Sempozyumu* (Ankara, AK Parti Yayınları, 2004). pp.7–17.

18   For "social Islam" in Turkey see M. Hakan Yavuz, "Towards an Islamic Liberalism?: The Nurcu Movement of Fettullah Gulen," *Middle East Journal*, Vol.53, No.4 (1999), pp.584–605.

19   *Hürriyet*, July 7, 2001; *Milliyet*, July 15, 2001. See also the party program at www.akparty.org.tr/program, and Erdoğan's speech in the international symposium on conservatism and democracy in *Uluslararası Muhafazakarlık ve Demokrasi Sempozyumu*, pp.7–17.

20   2002 Election Declaration, at http://www.akparti.org.tr/beyanname.doc.

21   Helena Smith, "New breed of politicians start to find their feet," *The Guardian*, March 10, 2003.

22   A popular Islamist intellectual, Ali Bulaç, declared in 1999 that the project of an Islamic state has collapsed, interview with Neşe Düzel, *Radikal*, December 21, 1999. For an analysis of Islamist intellectuals' changing attitude towards globalization, human rights, democracy and the EU membership see İhsan D. Dagi, "Rethinking Human Rights, Democracy, and the West: Post-Islamist Intellectuals in Turkey," *Critique: Critical Middle Eastern Studies*, Vol. 13, No.2 (2004), pp.135–151.

23   Erdoğan's speech in the Center for Strategic and International Studies, Washington DC, January 28, 2002 as commented on by İhsan D. Dagi, "İslami siyasette Batı ufku," *Radikal*, March 3, 2002.

24   "Matbaayi geciktiren kafa sermaye irkciilgi yapiyor", http://hurarsiv.hurriyet.com.tr/goster/haber.aspx?id=3370785&tarih=2005-10–12

25   For an insider view on the need for change in Islamic movements see Yalçın Akdoğan, "Değişimin ve Dönüşümün Teorik Zemini," *Bilgi ve Düşünce*, Vol.1, No.4 (Jan. 2003), pp.12–14.

26   Dagi (2004), pp.140–143.

27   For an early analysis of this kind, see, "Is it Adieu to Ataturk?" *The Economist*, October 16, 1999. For the justification of the Islamists for supporting the EU membership see Ali Bulaç, "Niçin AB," *Zaman*, Dec. 11, 1999; Ali Bulaç, "Türkiye'nin ev ödevleri," *Zaman*, Feb. 16, 2000; Ali Bulaç, "FP, 312 ve demokrasi," *Zaman*, March 25, 2000; Ali Bulaç, "AB tartışması," *Zaman*, March 19, 2002.

28   Ahmet Harputlu, "Türkiye'de İslamcılığın Dönüşümleri ve Yeni Politik Durum," *Bilgi ve Düşünce*, Vol.1, No.4 (Jan. 2003), pp.15–18.

Religion and Conflict: Lessons from the Frontlines of Social Transformation in Women's Human Rights

Nüket Kardam and Yannis Toussulis

A male foreman watches women at work weeding the field in Diyarbakir, the capital of the Kurdish southeast of Turkey • Tim Diirven, Panos

The issue of women's human rights is a central theme in the conflict between secularist and Islamic elites and, more generally, between those espousing 'universal' and 'cultural' views of human rights. There are signs of increased dialogue and conflict resolution on women's human rights issues in at least three countries with major Muslim populations: Turkey, Malaysia and Senegal. These cases could be extended to other countries, such as Morocco, Nigeria and others, but given limited space, this essay focuses on examples from three different geographical areas. What are the types of strategies that are leading to greater dialogue and conflict resolution on women's rights? What can we learn from these experiences?

Activities contributing to greater dialogue on women's rights among parties with opposing or different views are occurring at multiple levels, using multiple strategies and various discursive frameworks (Ertürk, 2004). Two sets of explanations for such changes are evident: 1) governments are changing policies and laws in favor of women's rights as a result of pressure from 'above' (international human rights law, donor pressure and

Nüket Kardam, an IPF senior associate, is Associate Professor at the Graduate School of International Policy Studies, Monterey Institute of International Studies and spends part of each year in her native country, Turkey. Her main areas of expertise are gender and development, international organizations, development theory and practice, and organizational change within donor agencies. Her most recent book is *Turkey's Engagement with Women's Global Human Rights*. **Yannis Toussulis** has served as an adjunct professor in political psychology at the Monterey Institute of International Studies for the past ten years and conducts a private practice in family psychotherapy.

pressure from international networks of nongovernmental organizations), and 'below' due to lobbying by local civil society actors; and 2) individual actors and/or national and local governments with competing world views are striving to change particular cultural and social convention discourses at local community levels opposing women's rights. The case studies below illustrate that global women's human rights norms are necessary but not sufficient for change at local levels, where cultural, religious, or social convention needs to be better understood to fully comprehend the root causes of violence against women. Public awareness needs to be raised about the oppressive nature of certain practices in the name of culture, the positive elements of culture and religion should be highlighted, and alternative masculinities cultivated that are respectful of women's rights.

Women and Islam

Before turning to specific cases, a brief discussion of the polarities and dualisms that prevent effective dialogue may be useful. A discussion of women and Islam cannot be separated from the historical context of Western influence and consequent colonization of most of the Muslim world. The status and rights of Muslim women have been perceived through the dualism of Western civilization and values versus Islamic civilization and values, framing the dialogue in terms of inter-religious and inter-cultural conflict. This perceived opposition has had some unfortunate effects that we must still face and deal with today. The rise of industrialization and capitalism along with the principles of Enlightenment focusing on reason, rationality and individualism are products of Western culture and Christianity, often spread throughout the world through colonialism. The reason and rationality principles of Enlightenment are in fact upheld in Islam, while Arab philosophers such as Avicenna helped transmit Greek philosophy to the Europe of the Middle Ages. Although the dualism between the West and Islam is obviously questionable, the politics of 'us versus the other' has produced a view of the Orient and Islam in stark contrast to Western civilization and values. As Edward Said has pointed out, the West perceives the East as its shadowy, darker 'Other' (Said, 1979). The West is thus defined as the cradle of modernity, human rights (including women's human rights) and superior civilization, while the world of Islam is juxtaposed as being traditional, backward, and in need of 'progress.'

Two major points can be made regarding this analysis: first, the experience of being on the receiving end of Western influence by various degrees of colonization meant that modernity, Western dominance and colonization merged into one in the minds and psyches of Muslim communities. Second, that human rights and especially women's human rights are considered by many Muslims as part of modernity and Western dominance, i.e. something to be shunned and to defend oneself against since this historical experience inevitably created a great deal of resentment and defensiveness along with a search to assert some form of superiority. It is therefore not possible to discuss women's rights in Muslim countries without understanding this historical context and these dualisms because all discussion of women's position and gender issues in the Muslim world have become highly politicized, with criticism of the treatment of women in Islamic cultures viewed a primary element of the rhetoric of colonialism, used to justify domination. In other words, colonial powers used the position of women in Islam as a demonstration of the cultural superiority of the West.

Furthermore, the position of women again became the centerpiece of the rhetoric of independence movements in the colonies, which strove to free themselves of colonial domination while ironically still employing Western rhetoric defining the nation state. The legitimacy of the nation state derived from the rule of the majority with respect for the individual rights of people. The Muslim elite were educated within the framework of western colonial institutions that valued equal individual rights. Thus, no new state could claim to be democratic and respectful of human rights unless it publicly announced that its entire people would be treated equally regardless of race, gender or class, at least on paper. Providing rights to women became a symbol of Westernization, and newly independent states eagerly announced the equality of women with men. But the majority of people in the newly independent states who remained resistant to these top-down, elite modernization efforts came to associate women's rights with the West. Women who claimed to be feminists and their allies were seen as apologists of Western colonial powers and alien to their way of life. Even today, in Afghanistan or Iraq, such 'apologists' are not tolerated but in fact threatened and/or killed (Newsweek, 7 March 2005).

Thus, the call back to Islamic values means a search for an authentic identity that is not influenced, dominated, and shaped by the West. In fact, many have seen the process of Westernization and globalization as turning women into commodities for a consumer culture. The new adaptation of hijab in Turkey in the 1980s, for example, was a demonstration of anti-Western nationalism. Covering also became a sign of resistance to what was perceived as the immoral use of women's bodies in advertising by multinational companies. Yet, oppressive practices that violate women's human rights such as honor crimes are defended in the name of culture, tradition or religion. This situation makes it extremely difficult to avoid polemics and assertions of prejudice over and over again. As one Iranian female author claims, in Iran, as elsewhere in the Muslim world, women who acquired a feminist consciousness in either a Western or an indigenous form have always faced a tension between conflicting components of their identity—their Muslimness is perceived as backward and oppressed, yet authentic and innate; their feminism as progressive and emancipated, yet corrupt and alien (Ziba Mir-Husseini, 1999).

How do we break free of this dilemma, these rigid dualisms and black and white world views that obstruct our understanding of the complexities and multiple realities inherent in the construction of women's identities? How might greater dialogue on women's rights be promoted among parties with opposing views? How might global human rights norms be reconciled with local realities?

Strategies for dialogue

According to Ertürk, multiple levels of intervention and multiple discursive frameworks need to be employed (Ertürk, 2004). At the state level, international human rights law needs to be invoked and states and their agents must observe due diligence to protect, prevent, investigate and punish by law perpetuators of violence against women. Pressure from the international system, by means of international law, international human rights networks, and donor assistance has been highly useful in this area, while civil society advocacy (in many cases supported by donor assistance) has maintained local pressure on the state.

At the community level, involving families and other non-state actors can further legitimize the human rights approach with cultural or a social convention discourse examining the root causes of violence. In such discussions, the oppressive nature of certain practices in the name of culture must be flagged. But since change has to come from within culture, the positive elements of culture and alternative masculinities that are respectful of women's rights should be highlighted. As Ertürk points out, here civil society actors—academics, media, national and international NGO—can play a critical role in collaborating with the state. She emphasizes: "In addition, intellectuals, enlightened community leaders, including religious leaders, who distance themselves from the repressive representation of culture, have an ethical responsibility to work towards reclaiming the space of culture and religion to demonstrate their compatibility with the universal human rights of women" (Ertürk, 2004, p.15). At the individual level, women should be supported via education and dialogue that fosters empowerment and is guaranteed via protective and compensatory mechanisms.

The case studies briefly described below demonstrate how the strategies above can indeed work, and point to the lessons learned form such experiences.

Case studies

Malaysia

In Malaysia, women's activism has focused on the religious interpretation of law. One strategy involves a rethinking of Islamic interpretation and practice or a reclaiming of the space of religion to demonstrate its compatibility with the universal human rights of women (Foley, 2004). This strategy demands equal rights for women and men in all areas of life, with all responsibilities shared, including inside the home. In Malaysia, this strategy is used by a small but significant group of women known as Sisters in Islam. This type of reinterpretation is found in the work of liberal Islamic thinkers such as Amina Wadud, Riffat Hassan, Fatima Mernissi, Abudallahi Ahmed An-Naim, and Fazlur Rahman. The group strives for reform of the Sharia (Islamic law) based on a reinterpretation of the Qur'an, and works in collaboration with international women's networks interested in Sharia reform such as Women Living Under Muslim Laws (WLUML) and the Sisterhood is Global Institute (SIGI). One weakness with their approach and resulting conclusions is that, apart from one member of the group, Amina Wadud, no member of the Sisters are trained theologians. To reinterpret the Qur'an without having an Islamic education is thought to be wrong by many in Malaysia.

In a second strategy, the 'universal' basis of human rights is challenged, and a different conception of human rights from within the culture is advanced which stipulates that women's human rights were conceived on the basis of communitarianism, rather than on the Western liberal tradition of individualism. As Foley (2004, p.70) indicates:

> *In an attempt to come to terms with modernity, Malaysian Muslim women have articulated a conception of rights that rejects the 'Western' notion of individualism and accepts the 'Asian' notion of communitarianism. Communitarianism refers to responsibilities to the family and community having priority over the rights of the individual, whereas individualism reverses this order. The inverted commas are used around Asian and Western because communitarian arguments are also found in the West and this concept is not confined to Asia. It is, however, a perspective legitimated by the current 'Asian values' discourse.*

Photo ▪ Andy Johnstone, Panos

The acceptance of communitarianism by activists is a valuable strategy because it is both culturally appropriate and politically strategic; it helps in gaining access to an audience who will listen because the women speak the language of their culture. The institution of the family is not seen to be threatened—a primary concern for many Asian and Islamic communities.

A third strategy that Malaysian Muslim women have used is the 'equity strategy' dedicated to ending women's oppression based on a 'separate but equal' conception of rights. This strategy complements some aspects in Western feminism as well, but the difference is that Muslim women activists offer their location within a religious discourse, and their use of religious texts to argue their rights. It does not challenge gender roles, but attempts to reclaim women's separate but *equal* rights as wives and mothers within Islam. The attempts for reform are aimed at the Sharia courts and the level of implementation; it is argued that substantive law treats women equitably but in practice this equity is denied. Reform proposals focus on procedural change via efforts such as the retraining of judges to promote their understanding of new rules and procedures so that they can interpret them without gender or class biases and honor requests for female counselors and judges. They also focus on changing the substance of laws by choosing between various legal schools to further benefit women.

In reforming laws and the implementation of the Sharia, women's groups from both equity and equality perspectives work together: the willingness of the Sisters and other organizations to compromise attests to the importance of legal reform to both equity and equality activists (Foley, 2004, p.69). In fact, Sisters in Islam toned down their proposals for reform and worked together with other Muslim women's groups such as the Association for Women Lawyers in proposing reforms to the existing Islamic law.

Turkey

Women's activism in Turkey has effectively employed the promises made by the government to honor international agreements and the required procedures for EU membership to pressure the government for legal reforms furthering greater gender equality. The results include reform of the Civil Code and a new law on domestic violence and honor crimes that favor women. At the same time, at local levels programs by women's organizations such as Women for Women's Rights–New Ways, and the Mother Child Education Foundation focus on basic education, women's empowerment, and education on new laws and their implementation. Such programs are usually delivered in government community centers or schools, and in collaboration with government agencies such as the Social Services Administration. For example, women's human rights education programs such as those offered by Women for Women's Human Rights–New Ways in partnership with the Directorate of Social Services and Children's Protection has led to action plans and strategies for reforming local practices contributing to violence against women and children (Kardam, 2003).

In the area of honor crimes, these multilevel strategies are beginning to take effect. The Directorate of Religious Affairs has issued a ruling and asked all 'imams across Turkey to discuss honor crimes, and proclaim that they are not congruent with Islamic principles.' Women activists have lobbied at the United Nations, including successful efforts in bringing honor crimes to the international agenda and into UN resolutions. At local levels, workshops are being organized where 'masculinities' are being questioned, including ways in which men can maintain their 'honor' without resorting to violence. As women's human rights activist Pervisat (2003) notes:

> *In order to prevent honor killings, it is crucial to redefine the concept of honor within the community. When talking to families, a cultural discourse proves to be very effective. We believe that male members are also victims of the concept of masculinity—they suffer throughout the decision-making process. We try to give men what I call cultural and psychological space where their masculinity is not challenged and they do not feel forced to kill in order to cleanse their honor. To do this, and in order to create space for long-term change, we take advantage of some of the positive aspects of Turkish culture to offer individual men an excuse to avoid violence. These include special occasions and gatherings where nonviolence negotiations are encouraged or where authority figures can act as intermediaries, in which we can make use of traditions of hospitality towards guests or respect for elderly people's recommendations as tools to prevent these crimes.*

Another strategy is to focus on common problems across ideological or cultural divides: Islamist women's organizations are working together with secular women in the area of violence against women, honor killings, the establishment of women's shelters, promoting reform of the Civil Code. The efforts of the Capital City Women's Platform to establish a bridge between 'secular' and 'religious' women's organizations and to develop relationships focusing on particular problems is highly meaningful in terms of overcoming the secular-Islamist polarization in Turkey, for example. Secular and religious women's organizations began to learn from each other so that the former emulated the effective grassroots organizations of the latter, and religious women began to fight for their individual rights including the right to cover their heads on university campuses and government offices, while employing lobbying tactics at national and international levels (such as appealing to the European Commission of Human Rights).

Senegal

In Senegal, until recently female genital cutting was not perceived as oppression, but as a desired and respected tradition among women. The ceremony, usually carried out by older women, brought a modest amount of money and prestige and was a wished-for rite of passage through which girls have demonstrated courage as they pass into womanhood. Those who did not participate were to be shamed and ridiculed.

The end to cutting in many areas of Senegal has come as a result of a number of crucial changes. Individuals in a particular community in Malicounda Bambara in Senegal received a basic education program where they learned communicative and organizational skills. This program was offered by Tostan and funded by UNICEF and the government of Senegal, among others. A group of women who had participated in this program proceeded to persuade the other women in the community, the husbands, and the traditional and religious leaders of the village that such a decision was needed to protect the health of their girl children and to respect human rights (WorldView, p.27):

After an emotional discussion of female genital cutting, the women of Malicounda Bambara went home and discussed the issue among themselves and with their families. They also met with the local imam, or religious leader. That conversation proved to be a breakthrough for more than the women of Maliconda Bambara because 95 percent of Senegal's population is Muslim and its imams are a significant determinant of life throughout the nation.

Thus, the decision came from 'within the culture' and after several months, the village made a public and collective commitment to stop the practice. But neighboring villages sent hostile messages to Malicounda. The women were hurt and depressed, yet defended their position and even traveled to other villages to discuss their commitment with women there. As the health risks were demonstrated as very real, many women

and men participated in the redefinition of female genital cutting as a health threat to women rather than a 'rite of passage into womanhood' and the 'only way to be respectable and find a husband.'

Female genital cutting has been redefined as a health threat to women, but the ceremonies to initiate girls into womanhood have been maintained without the cutting so that culture and traditions remain but harmful practices to women are discarded. Islamic clerics have denounced genital cutting as un-Islamic, and the women who conducted the cutting have been provided with other means of livelihood.

Successful reform based on change from 'within'

As the Turkish and Senegalese cases show, simultaneous action on all levels—international, national and local—seems to be quite effective, but the various strategies have to be tailored accordingly. While support from international actors is necessary, and national level commitment in the form of new laws, policies, and pronouncements by political leaders is important, long-term change and dialogue ultimately requires change from 'within' the culture at the local level. Thus, learning to speak the language of the relevant culture/religion was vital in all three cases. Basic education programs focusing on literacy, human rights, communication and organizational skills can make a big difference in promoting dialogue and conflict resolution at local levels. But such programs need to be nondirective, participatory, and based on proper respect for others.

The cases also show that the dualisms (between the West and Islam, secularism and Islam, universal human rights and rights based on culture and religion) all encourage a black and white worldviews which does not reflect the reality of women's lives. As the Malaysia and Turkey cases demonstrate, women from across ideological divides have begun to work together in common areas of concern, and further possibilities for confluence and dialogue are ripe for exploration. Women's human rights based on individual human rights need to be reconciled with the kinship and family systems, communitarian values, and collective identities within which many women conduct their lives. New alliances with liberal Islamic intellectuals and community leaders as well as human rights activists must be explored. Furthermore, the shaping of masculine identities that encourage the control of women's freedom of movement and sexuality need to be examined carefully and redefined within the local communities themselves.

Existing practices that violate women's rights may perhaps be changed with careful redefinitions (such as the redefinition of masculinities without losing the code of 'honor' or the redefinition of female genital cutting as a health threat to women while maintaining the cultural rite of passage ceremony into womanhood) by working within cultures in participatory, nondirective settings. Thus, women's human rights is one area where current inter-religious, inter-cultural tensions are beginning to be eased, and where lessons may be learned.

References

Berktay, Fatmagül et al (2004), *The Position of Women in Turkey and in the European Union: Achievements, Problems, Prospects,* Istanbul: Ka-Der Press.

Burman, Erica (Summer 2004), "An End to Cutting: Women of Senegal declare a dangerous tradition's end," *WorldView*, pp.23–31.

Ernst, Carl (2003), *Following Muhammad: Rethinking Islam in the Contemporary World,* University of North Carolina Press.

Ertürk, Yakin (2004), *Integration of the Human Rights of Women and the Gender Perspective,* Commission on Human Rights, E/CN.4/2004/66.

"Female Genital Cutting—The Beginning of the End," *Tostan News,* http://www.tostan.orgs/news-fgc.htm.

Foley, Rebecca (2004), "Muslim Women's Challenges to Islamic Law: The Case of Malaysia," *International Feminist Journal of Politics,* Vol. 6, No. 1, March 2004, pp.53–84.

"Iraq's Hidden War," *Newsweek,* 7 March 2005.

Parvizat, Leyla (Fall 2003), "In the Name of Honor," *Human Rights Dialogue.*

Kardam, Nüket (2003), Evaluation of the Women's Human Rights Education Program, http://www.wwhr.org.

Kardam, Nüket (2005), "Violence against Women," *Turkey's Engagement with Women's Human Rights,* London: Ashgate Publishers.

Mir-Husseini, Ziba (1999), *Islam and Gender, The Religious Debate in Contemporary Iran,* Princeton: Princeton University Press.

Said, Edward (1979), *Orientalism,* New York: Vintage.

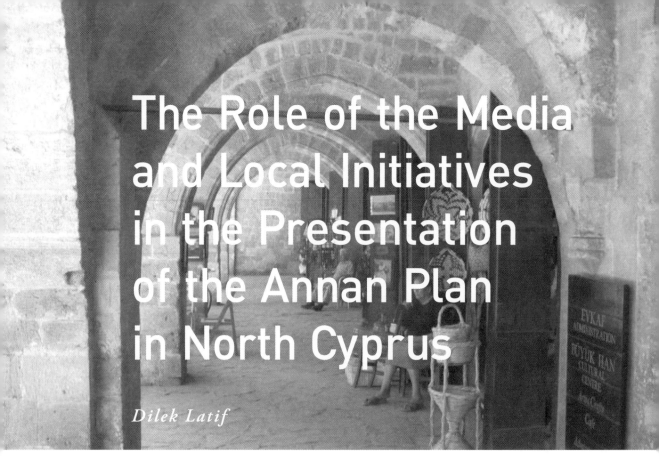

The Role of the Media and Local Initiatives in the Presentation of the Annan Plan in North Cyprus

Dilek Latif

The UN Peace Plan for Cyprus known as the "Annan Plan"[1] has been a significant landmark in the history of the island. This is not only because it constituted the first comprehensive settlement plan to be submitted for public approval. More significantly, its importance is primarily due to the role of the media and local initiatives in presenting the arguments for and against the Plan. Unlike various peace proposals since the 1960s seeking a solution to the Cyprus problem, the Annan Plan has been intensively debated throughout the island among both Turkish and Greek Cypriot communities, the political elite and the media.

The 'Comprehensive Settlement of the Cyprus Problem' was first presented to the parties on November 11, 2002. After fervent negotiations it was initially revised on December 10, 2002, and then again on February 26, 2003. The final version was submitted by the Secretary General to the negotiating teams of both sides on March 31, 2004 in Bürgenstock in Switzerland, where the parties agreed to present it to the people of Cyprus in separate and simultaneous referenda. The comprehensive settlement of the Cyprus problem included "a proposed foundation agreement; proposed constitutions of the Greek Cypriot and Turkish Cypriot constituent States; a proposed treaty on matters related to the new state of affairs in Cyprus; a draft act of adaptation of the terms of accession of the United Cyprus Republic to the European Union; matters to be submitted

Dilek Latif is Senior Lecturer in international relations at the Near East University in Nicosia, North Cyprus and an International Policy Fellowships finalist in 2005.

to the Security Council for decision; and measures to be taken during the April 2004" public referenda.[2]

After the Annan Plan was rejected by the great majority of Greek Cypriots in the April 2004 referendum, which led to its failure as a whole, a widespread belief emerged that the media contributed to the failure of the Plan on the Greek side. Likewise on the Turkish side, the media had a strong impact in supporting the Plan in the referendum. In fact, the media on both sides have played a vital role, albeit in different ways, in shaping public orientation. The specific focus of this essay is the role of the media and local initiatives in the reception of the Annan Plan in North Cyprus.

Catalyst for public dialogue

In the Turkish part of Cyprus, the Annan Plan process has been described as a "media revolution."[3] Since the first version of the Plan was revealed in November 2002 until the referendum was held in April 2004, Turkish Cypriots extensively debated the Plan. For the first time, negotiations between the sides became increasingly transparent as the Plan was leaked very early into the process. The uniqueness of the situation provoked considerable attention and a desire for more information. Following the leaks, the Plan was made available to the media and opened for public discussion.

Over the last two years of negotiations on the Annan Plan, the Turkish Cypriot media was dominated by discussions over the Plan and the eventual referendum. Regular radio talk shows, television broadcasts and the activities of nongovernmental organization (NGO) leaders providing brochures and press releases generated an extraordinarily heated debate on the issue. Daily newspapers supplied translations of the summary of the Plan, whereas various television and radio channels devoted entire days and nights to its various aspects.[4]

In particular, the private media in North Cyprus played a crucial role in mobilizing people to participate in large mass demonstrations, unique in the history of the island, attracting even the attention of the world media. As a consequence, civic initiatives influenced their political leaders and encouraged many to support a settlement along the lines of the Annan Plan. A number of commentators suggested an alternative view as well; that it was the civic initiatives which mobilized the media and then lastly the political elite.

In this period, state-run television and radio channels propagating the official viewpoints lost their monopoly on providing information to the people. Traditionally conservative and nationalist dailies which interpreted the Plan as an unacceptable compromise were also challenged by alternative newspapers that reflected opposing views. In this way, the media became part of the political campaigning for the Plan and the referendum in the North.

As a result, the media was broadly divided into two camps: the pro-Annan Plan/pro-solution camp and the anti-Annan Plan/anti-solution camp. The themes on which they focused, and the information they provided, differed accordingly. The pro-Annan Plan/pro-solution media and their associates presented the Plan as an opportunity that should not be missed for a peaceful settlement and reconciliation in the island.

Slogan from a Turkish Cypriot strike during the Annan Plan negotiations: "Peace in our homeland, peace in the world" K. Atatürk "Peace in Cyprus too" Cypriot–Turk
▪ Dilek Latif

In addition, they highlighted the issue of membership to the European Union and proclaimed that North Cyprus will "unite with the world." The referendum was depicted as an act of self-determination that would reflect the will of the people. The key objectives of the pro-solution media were the recognition of the existence and political equality of the Turkish Cypriots, the creation of a certain and stable future, and increased living standards.

On the other hand, the anti-Annan Plan/anti-solution media focused on the loss of sovereignty and the survival of the Turkish Republic of Northern Cyprus (TRNC). The Plan was presented as full of traps: to vote 'yes' in the referendum would be to vote for self-subjugation and for security to be placed in the hands of foreign powers. The anti-Annan Plan/anti-solution side tried to manipulate the fears of Turkish Cypriots who became refugees as a result of the inter-communal strife in the 1960s and 1970s, by suggesting that the Plan would make them refugees a third or fourth time. Additionally, the dilution of the guarantees and withdrawal of the Turkish troops were arguably overemphasized. Exploiting the fears of the Turkish settlers who came to the island in the post-1974 period, they stressed the repatriation of all settlers back to Turkey.

Opponents of the Plan published a number of booklets, brochures and leaflets. For instance, the Ankara Chamber of Trade published a booklet titled "Annan Plan and Unknown Realities."[5] In the preface, the Annan Plan was described as a document which will destroy the political, social, economic and geographical base of the Turkish Cypriots. The booklet focuses on the territorial arrangements of the Annan Plan and argues that the Plan will leave Turks without any property, and that it aims to annihilate TRNC and the Turkish Cypriot community:

TRNC will give 21 percent of its territory to the Greeks and 65 percent of the arable land, 1,350 working places will be closed down and 15 percent of the population will be unemployed. The total national loss will be 18.3 billion US dollars. A total number of 188 hotels and restaurants will be left to the Greeks which results in a 43 billion US dollars loss. Overall, it was estimated that the TRNC will cost 22 percent of GDP, which amounts to over 200 billion US dollars and a budgeted deficit of 43 million US dollars.[6]

Moreover, the Cyprus Council of the Ankara Chamber (Ankara Baro) published a leaflet "Property Issue in the Annan Plan: Criticisms." Responding to the arguments of Dr. Christian Heinze, the Chief of the Chamber claims that:

Turkish Cypriots living in a Greek property will have to return it back to the original owner before 1974. Those who built houses on Greek property should have to pay the present market value of the land to be able to keep it. The Plan envisaged leaving Turkish Cypriots without property and reducing them to a community with second-class rights. It does not have the potential to contribute to economic development and to reduce unemployment in the North.[7]

Regarding the citizenship rights of Turkish settlers, the leaflet underlines that 35,000 people of Turkish origin should leave the island and not be entitled to the United Cyprus citizenship.

The National Solidarity Council, which is related to the fundamentalist National Peoples Movement, produced a pamphlet entitled "Annan Plan and the Realities not Explained." The pamphlet claims that 'pro-Annanist' parties are in cooperation with Greeks, Americans, and the European Union, and questions whether such a cooperation could be beneficial to Turkish Cypriots. The pamphlet is formulated for the ordinary reader with very simple sentences and many pictures. For example, under the sentence "There will be no sovereign Turkish state but a Greek state" there is a picture of the TRNC flag which is transforming into a Greek flag. In a similar manner, it claims that "there will be no Turkish guarantees but a return to the pre-1974 period, no Turkish soldiers but UN soldiers, no Turkey but Greece and UK." Through such simple sentences it continues: "no territory but migration, no Parliament made of Turks but a mixed Greek Parliament, no compensation but empty promises. 21 percent of the TRNC territory, 75 percent of the productive land and 80 percent of water resources will be given to the Greeks." Throughout the pamphlet, cartoons illustrate that the Annan Plan is a trap to deceive Turkish Cypriots.

Alternatively, the pro-solution group such as the Turkish Cypriot Chamber of Commerce, and strong civic initiatives—the Common Vision of the Turkish Cypriot Civil Society, This Country is Ours Platform, and various NGOs—effectively mobilized the masses during the Annan Plan process, producing and distributing numerous booklets as well. The information stressed that Turkish Cypriots are at an historically important time, and that a solution of the Cyprus problem today is vital:

The Common Vision of the Turkish Cypriot Civil Society on a Solution in Cyprus and EU Membership proposed that the Cyprus problem should be solved before the end of 2002.[8]

Another appeal by a number of NGOs to the President of the TRNC and the political leaders was that the Cyprus problem should be solved before the historic window of opportunity closes.[9]

On behalf of the Common Vision of the Turkish Cypriot Civil Society and This Country is Ours Platform, the Turkish Cypriot Chamber of Commerce in 2003 called the President and the Prime Minister of Turkey to express support and voice their positive views concerning the referendum. The Chamber also pronounced their expectation from Turkey to ensure a 'yes' vote of the Turkish Cypriot President Rauf R. Denktas on March 10, 2003 in the Hague.[10]

Civil society striving for peace

All these documents emphasized that Turkish Cypriots had demonstrated their will for the settlement of the Cyprus conflict and membership for the European Union. As part of civil society in the North, they announced that they will do their best to achieve a 'yes' vote in the referendum.

The struggle between the pro-Annan and anti-Annan forces characterized the December 2004 elections as well. Political parties in favor of a solution advertised in the daily newspapers and chose slogans corresponding to the increasingly vocal expression of the will of people for a solution to the Cyprus conflict and for the membership to the European Union. Conversely, anti-Annan and anti-solution parties used particular language to spread fear in the minds of people and brought the negative sides of the Plan to the forefront.[11]

Although the Turkish Cypriot media and local initiatives were divided and both tried to influence public opinion in the North, the pro-Annan forces were more successful in forming a positive approach towards the Plan and the resolution of the Cyprus conflict. An overwhelming majority of the Turkish Cypriots supported the Annan Plan as demonstrated by a 64.6 percent 'yes' vote in the referendum. Yet, both pro-Annan and anti-Annan media and local initiatives acted rather independently from the official position. It is impossible to prove whether they changed public opinion, but there is a strong conviction that the pro-solution civil society reinforced and solidified public hopes for peace.

Notes

[1] For more information and full text see the official United Nations website of the Secretary-General's comprehensive peace plan for Cyprus *http://www.hri.org/docs/annan/*.

[2] Agenda—The Situation in Cyprus, S/PV.4940 Provisional, Security Council 4940th Meeting, New York, 2 April 2004, p.2.

[3] Interview with Huseyin Guven, Director of News, Bayrak Radyo Televizyonu, 8 January 2005.

[4] The Plan was handled and discussed differently in the Greek part of the island. An intensive and fervent debate on the negative and positive elements of the Plan has not taken place

as in the North. The media concentrated more on the negotiation process rather than the content of the Plan, since there were expectations that the content will face changes.

5   Ankara Ticaret Odasi, *Annan Plani ve Bilinmeyen Gercekler*, Ankara: Gemi Matbaacilik Insaat ve Turizm San.Tic. Ltd.

6   Ibid., pp.3–5.

7   Ankara Barosu Yayinlari, *Annan Plani ve Mulkiyet Rejimi–Elestiriler*.

8   The Common Vision of the Turkish Cypriot Civil Society, *Booklets of 2002*.

9   Turkish Cypriot Chamber of Commerce, TRNC Businessmen Association, North Cyprus Young Businessmen Association, North Cyprus Hoteliers Association, TC Association of University Women, North Cyprus Bank Association, Junior Chamber of North Cyprus.

10 *Letter of the Turkish Cypriot Chamber of Commerce*, 5 March 2003.

11 *Kibris Newspaper*, 13 February 2005, p.3.

part five

Islam and Policy in Central Europe

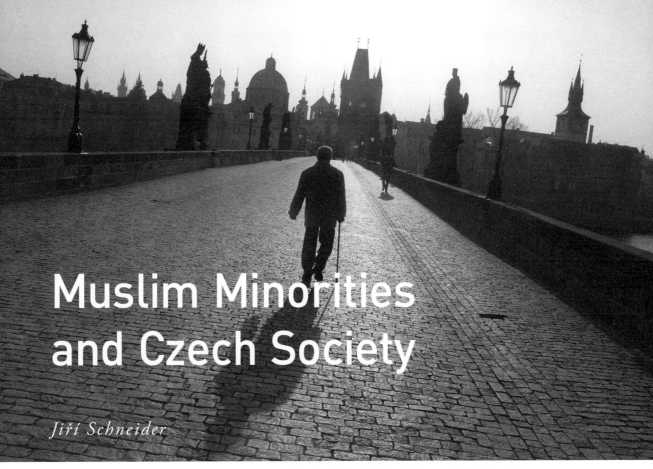

Muslim Minorities and Czech Society

Jiří Schneider

Crossing the Charles Bridge in Prague ▪ Mark Helnley, Panos

uropean events including the Madrid and London terrorist attacks, debate on Turkey's future accession to the European Union, and interethnic tensions in the Netherlands have dramatically changed the way Central Europeans perceive issues related to Islam and Muslims. Although clashes with Muslim minorities in Central Europe are more ideological than actual, themes related to Muslims currently serve as a symbolic playground for a wide range of social fears and frustrations.

Czechs, among the most secular Europeans, have only recently encountered Muslims as neighbors through immigration. During the Cold War, Czech borders as well as the borders of other Soviet bloc countries were closed to Muslim migration. Within this context of shock therapy in cultural diversity, the sharpness of Czech public debates and media coverage on issues related to Islam and Muslims often does not correlate with the scale of real problems on the ground, which tend to concentrate on rather mundane and practical questions about how to better accommodate the everyday life of the Muslim community.

Jiří Schneider, an International Policy Fellow in 2002–3 and current IPF Continuing Fellow, is Program Director of the Prague Security Studies Institute (www.pssi.cz). A lecturer at various American and Czech universities, he was a member of the Czechoslovak parliament and served as Czech Ambassador to Israel from 1995–98. Further information about his research is available from the IPF websites: http://pdc.ceu.hu (Source IPF) and www.policy.hu/schneider.

Muslim minority as a new phenomenon

In relation to populations in many other countries of the European Union, the Muslim community in the Czech Republic is incomparably tiny (approximately 20,000, with some 400 Czech converts among 10 million inhabitants). Nevertheless, the number of Muslims in the Czech Republic has doubled in the past decade and is projected to continue based on the rate that can be extrapolated onto future growth as the country has opened its borders, with most immigrants coming from Arab countries, the Caucasus, and the Balkans. Most Czechs first confronted visible signs of difference such as women wearing veils during the 1990s, when hundreds of Muslim refugees fleeing Balkan wars moved to the Czech Republic. Nevertheless, the Muslim community was not a particularly visible minority and religious differences were not the subject of public dialogue. The primary reason for the relatively rosy state of affairs in the 1990s was the fact that most Muslim immigrants came from the former Yugoslavia and were regarded by the majority population as familiar in terms of both ethnicity and their highly secularized and urbanized lifestyle.

Major points of contention: Islamic centers and registration

Today, several thousand Muslims who are permanent Czech residents or citizens live mostly in big cities. A mosque has yet to be built in the country, and the question of whether to build one has proven extremely contentious in public debates. Muslims have the facilities to gather for worship only in the major urban centers of Prague and Brno. Past attempts to obtain municipality approval for the construction of Islamic centers (for example in various spa locations such as Teplice, Karviná-Darkov, Orlová) have sparked heated public debates about Czech Muslim communities which have awakened and divided local constituencies. All bids except those in Prague and Brno have been denied. In several cases, petitions, polls and public hearings were organized.

Astrological clock, Prague

Virtually no Czech public administrators have experience working with Muslims, so they seek the advice of other religious representatives as "experts" on Islam—a tactic which has further polarized religious communities and congregations. Expressions of tolerance and solidarity (for example one Christian community has offered their chapel to Muslims for prayers) are countered with clear signs of intolerance and bigotry (such as Christian leaders characterizing Europe as a frontline of global conflict and fortress protecting the West from the expansion of Islam).

Although the Czech Constitution guarantees full freedom of religion and religious association, Czech legislation does not provide for a full separation of church (or mosque) and state. To be eligible for state subsidies, religious associations must be registered, and in order to be registered, they must gather petitions from more than 10,000 members (or roughly half of the entire population of the Muslim community in the Czech Republic!). The practical implementation of the rules has been highly discriminatory, since most recognized organizations have fewer members than required, while the Czech Muslim community was unable to complete a petition list and remained a mere citizens' association until it was finally registered in October 2004.

Interestingly, in December 2004 Czech Buddhist Olga Ryantova submitted a petition requesting that the official registration of the Muslim community be reconsidered. The petition included quotations from the Koran implying that Islam is incompatible with human rights and explicitly promotes violence. Similar activities have reportedly been conducted recently by groups related to the Buddhist Diamond Way (Lama Ole Nydahl) in Denmark, Germany and France. To date there has been no official Czech reaction to the petition.

The debate: principal channels and actors

The primary source of information and main forum for Czech debate on issues related to Islam and Muslims is the internet and various discussion groups. The debate is not edited or obviously censored and is generally poorly informed, polarized, emotionally loaded, often aggressive and prejudiced. A worrisome feature of relevant internet-based debates is that, although limited in terms of numbers of participants, their relative anonymity attracts obscure and potentially dangerous extremists.

The anti-Islam camp in the Czech Republic involves Euro-skeptics of all sorts, evangelical Christian fundamentalists, secular liberal feminists, Roman-Catholic traditionalists, opponents of Turkish EU membership, proponents of the separation of church and state who view Islam as a religion of governance, etc. For the sake of illustration, the list below is a combination of opinions proclaimed by the Conservative Club (http://www.konzervativniklub.cz/index_en.php), which tend to promote

Old Town square, Prague

a greater public role for religion, pro-life policies (similar to the Religious Right in the United States), the punishment of wrongdoings after World War I (reconciliation with Germany), and support for Israel. Common arguments tend to be articulated as follows:

- Islamic centers might become hotbeds of terrorism, providing foundations for its financing and logistics,

- Center pulpits would be misused to instigate religious intolerance and violent *jihad*,

- Islam is a synonym for the subordination of women and gender inequality,

- Any concession to the comprehensive aspirations of Islam or giving up general secular jurisdiction would create a parallel Muslim society, and

- Turkish membership in the EU would enable the "Islamization" of Europe.

Islam is defended by official and private Muslim websites (http://www.muslim-inform.cz/, http://www.islam.wz.cz/, http://www.islamweb.cz/, http://ablecd.wz.cz/darkside/). Although they sometimes serve to feed prejudice among critics by promoting open intolerance, hatred and extremism, most of the Czech Muslim websites and contributions promote tolerance and understanding along the lines of the following:

- Christianity, Islam and Judaism share a principal kinship with a common origin (Abraham) and scriptural character of tradition

- Better understanding of diverse cultures would enable Czech society to embrace global opportunities.

Some Czech non-governmental organizations include the promotion of tolerance as an inherent component of their mission. The following examples are selected projects that counter intolerance and promote reconciliation:

- Intercultural Education Project "Variants" (http://www.varianty.cz/) was created in 2002 by non-governmental organization People in Need with the support of EU Phare Program. The project develops tools for high-school education based on respect, equality and diversity, specifically addressing tolerance towards Islam by developing a syllabus including an excellent chapter on Islam using real experiences from Czech Muslims.

- Forum 2000: Bridging the Gaps (http://www.forum2000.cz/) is an umbrella project established by Vaclav Havel in 1997 which aims to bring together representatives of various streams of thinking and perspectives. Notably it has created the tradition of an annual multi-religious assembly with the representatives of several religions including Islam (http://www.forum2000.cz/projects/multireligious_assembly.php). Though positive in its ambition to spark inter-religious dialogue, it has involved mostly top brass international personalities and has failed to have the anticipated impact on local relations to Muslim communities.

- Prague Multicultural Center (http://www.mkc.cz/) is an NGO supported by a broad portfolio of sponsors. Its activities include education, public debate, media monitoring, etc. MCP organized a series of roundtables on the position of women in different cultural and religious frameworks including Islam.

- Youth for Intercultural Understanding (http://www.osmip.cz) was founded in 1998 in Brno by a group of young people who wanted to contribute actively to the process of understanding diverse cultures both "inside" or "outside" Czech society. So far the organization has not addressed the issue of Islam.

Prospects for the future: Media, NGOs, citizens and open dialogue

Due to its multifaceted character, serious public debate on the value-laden issue of Czech relations toward Islam and Muslims requires informed attitudes and the active engagement of knowledgeable individuals unafraid to speak up and argue. It is clear that certain Czech regulations are discriminatory in practice toward Muslims as well as other 'new' religious groups, and these regulations should be reviewed. Less anonymity and more publicity would certainly help to cultivate the debate, which the mainstream media has largely avoided.

One of the key dilemmas for any liberal society is how to conduct a fair and open discourse on critical issues without being labeled as politically incorrect or even extremist, targeted by accusations, harassed or threatened with violence. For a healthy debate to take place, those participating must be assured that their freedom of expression will be safeguarded by state authorities (politicians, law enforcement and judiciary) in the face of threats. Violence motivated or justified by religion should be unequivocally and publicly condemned and denounced, just as in cases involving hate crimes, as such violence undermines the foundations of tolerance. As long as religious incitement to violence exists, it would be unwise to claim that we can deal with it in a strictly secularized discourse. Politicians, public intellectuals, clerics, and celebrities must be invited as citizens to set a benchmark for open and substantive dialogue.

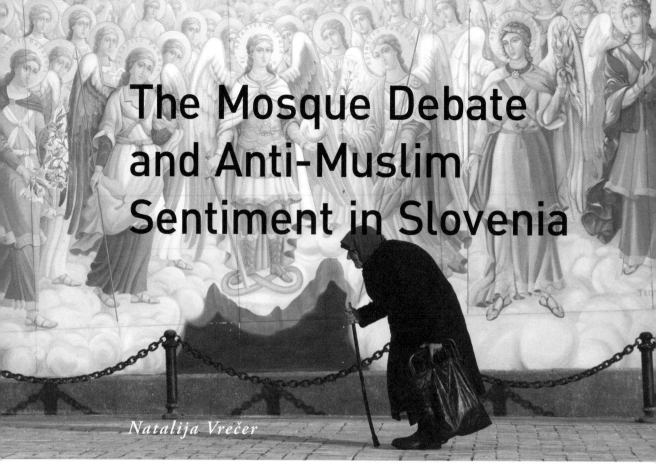

The Mosque Debate and Anti-Muslim Sentiment in Slovenia

Natalija Vrečer

During the First World War, many Muslim soldiers defending Slovenia's northwest border worshipped at a mosque in the Slovenian town of Log pod Mangartom. Toward the end of the war, the mosque burned down. Slovenia's Muslim community has been unsuccessfully trying to build a mosque in the country ever since.

Countless obstacles have blocked the construction of a mosque in Slovenia, a country of less than 2 million people and home to some 60,000 Muslims, including many from Bosnia-Herzegovina who have lived in Slovenia for over three decades.[1] Although freedom of religion is a human right and should be a cornerstone of social inclusion, Slovenia's Muslims must gather for prayers in a small private house in Moste (a district of the Slovenian capital city Ljubljana) and congregate in rented sports halls during times of religious festivals.

A thorough media content analysis of press articles focusing on the absence of a mosque in Slovenia beginning in 1971 (when such articles started to appear) through spring 2005 reveals a shift in the nature of the debate before and after the 9/11 terrorist attacks in New York, with the post-9/11 debate much more heated and xenophobic.

Natalija Vrečer is a researcher focusing on human rights, refugees and migrants with the Slovene Institute for Adult Education. Her 2000–1 International Policy Fellowship project investigated the human costs of temporary refugee protection in Slovenia.

Articles from five Slovenian dailies were analyzed: *Delo* (75 essays), *Dnevnik* (20), *Večer* (4), *Slovenske novice* (6), and *Primorske novice* (1), as well as in the 10 magazines *Mladina* (12), *Mag* (3), *Družina* (2), *Panorama* (2), *Demokracija* (2), *Žurnal* (2), *Start²* (1), *Jana* (1), *Nedeljski dnevnik* (1) and *Mesečnik za kulturo, politiko in gospodarstvo* (1), as well as two articles about the lack of a mosque in Slovenia in the Croatian daily *Vjesnik*. The newspaper *Delo*, in which most of the articles appeared, is Slovenia's most widely read daily. Most of the magazine articles appeared in *Mladina*—a magazine that had a revolutionary role in the breakup of Yugoslavia—although the reviewed articles appeared after the 1990s.

Yugoslav-era mosque in Slovenia?

In 1969, the Muslim community's plan to build a mosque in the Bežigrad area of the capital city Ljubljana was evidently problematic because members of the local population deemed it inappropriate near a cycling and jogging route of "brotherhood and unity" (a slogan of Tito's socialist Yugoslavia intended to encourage ethnic harmony). Such argumentation was quite ridiculous given that the intent of "brotherhood and unity" was to unite rather than divide neighbors of various ethnic and religious backgrounds. By 1974, the Muslim community had proposed 20 locations for a mosque, each time having the proposal shot down by members of local communities. A 1974 essay in *Dnevnik*, for example, reported that residents of the region of Posavje stated that before a mosque was built, the needs of "Slovenians" had to be met in terms of residential, cultural, and leisure centers. In the same year, the Slovenian Commission for Religious Community Relations declared that the delay in building a mosque had become a political problem and that a location for such a building must be approved. Nevertheless, a proposed location near the Ljubljana cemetery Žale was rejected by the Regional Institute for the Preservation of Natural and Cultural Heritage on the basis that it would be out of place.

By 1981, *Vjesnik* declared in the inflated, empty language of "brotherhood and unity" that Slovenians were open and eager to build a mosque. Not surprisingly a mosque was not built, and the media was silent about the issue for the next 15 years.

Renewed media interest in the 1990s

The first relevant article since 1981 was published in *Delo* in 1996 about the increasingly vocal opposition of right wing parties to

The Mosque of Gazi Kasim Pasha (now a Catholic church) and baroque Trinity Column in neighboring Hungary. Built around 1580, it was the main mosque in Hungary until its transformation into a church by the Jesuits after liberation from the Turks ▪ Pietro Cenini

the idea of building mosque in Slovenia. They claimed that the presence of a mosque was contrary to the "Christian culture" of the Slovene nation and Central and Eastern Europe. Arguments against the construction of a minaret claimed that the structure would be too high.

In 1998, for the first time in the analyzed Slovene media, *Panorama* noted that opposition to the construction of a mosque in Slovenia was based on ignorance and amounted to a violation of human rights protecting freedom of religion as well as a violation of the basic ethical standards of European civilization. In 1999, the Muslim community suggested a new location for a mosque in the capital district of Vič on Barje. However, members of the local community argued in the media that many Bosnian Serbs live in that area and that they would be opposed to a mosque. Another supposed reason for the "inappropriateness" of the location was its close proximity to the houses of many Slovenian politicians in Murgle (near the capital district of Vič).

A mosque for Slovenia in the new millennium?

When Osman Đogić became the leader of the Muslim community (*muezzin*) in 2001, he embarked on the effort to build a mosque with more enthusiasm than previous leaders of the Muslim community, and the issue was increasingly the subject of media attention. One of the members of the right-wing party New Slovenia stated that building a mosque would "offend Slovene religious sentiment." Another articulated view was that the *muezzin's* call for prayer would be too loud and that a mosque would be harmful to tourism because it would position Slovenia as more of a "Balkan" nation. The first response of the local population of Vič claimed that those with gardens in the area opposed it, and they were soon joined by those whose homes neighbored the proposed building site. The latter group even stated that the risk of floods in the area, not to mention earthquakes, prevented the construction of a mosque.

It was only following the September 11 attacks in the United States that a new argument against the construction of a mosque appeared, linking Muslims to terrorists. In 2002 many highly emotionally charged letters to the editor about a possible mosque appeared in the daily *Delo*, with letters in favor always eliciting a negative response and vice versa.[3] Opinion pieces and even some letters from politicians stated that "the terrorists" could come to Slovenia if a mosque was built. Newspapers reported in 2003 that the leader of the Slovenian Catholic church at the time Archbishop Franc Rode said that he was against the initiative because a mosque is not only a spiritual and religious center but also a *political* one. In some *Delo* letters to the editor, those against the idea of a mosque in Slovenia compared the peaceful community of Slovenian Muslims to the Turks who invaded Slovenia in the 15th, 16th and 17th centuries, robbing and killing many people. One of the expressly xenophobic articles claimed that larger groups of Muslims would spread diseases. One reporter spoke with Slovenes who said they were afraid that Muslims would reproduce in higher numbers in Slovenia if a mosque was built.

City councillors stated at a 2003 council meeting that the government should be consulted as to whether a mosque should be built in Ljubljana. When one councillor suggested that there should be a popular referendum on the issue, a member of the

Liberal Democratic Party (the leading party at the time) stated that a human rights issue cannot be decided via popular referendum but that freedom of religion must be respected. A number of media reports were published in favor of a mosque as well, including one in which the reporter wrote that "if the Slovenian identity is threatened by one minaret standing beside 10,000 Catholic churches then something is already rotten with this identity." Nevertheless, right-wing party members collected more than 10,000 signatures in favor of a popular referendum. The mayor of Ljubljana, Danica Simšič, considered that the referendum may not be in accordance with the Slovenian constitution and let the constitutional court to decide the matter. The Slovenian Constitutional Court ruled that a public referendum on a human rights issue would contravene the Slovenian constitution. There was no referendum.

In early 2005 another obstacle prevented the construction of a mosque in Vič, namely that part of the land designated for the site was denationalized and returned to the Lazarists of the Catholic order. In March 2005 the media reported that the Lazarists would be satisfied if the municipality compensated them with another plot of land, since they would not want to be responsible for presenting further obstacles to the construction of the first mosque in Slovenia.

Lessons from three decades of 'the mosque debate'

Despite the seemingly never-ending back-and-forth regarding the construction of a mosque in Slovenia, it is heartening to note that while some right-wing politicians and members of the population living in the proximity of proposed sites opposed the construction, Slovenian state institutions have considered such opposition to be a violation of human rights and have not actively prevented various initiatives to build a mosque.

Arguments articulated in the media against a mosque reveal the extent of ignorance, discrimination and xenophobia among many Slovenes toward Muslims, which has prevented the construction of a mosque in the country for three-and-a-half decades. Fortunately, the new, more democratic voices of Slovene media reporters, citizens and courts defending human rights and tolerance are strong. They may well succeed in slowly breaking down the barriers to the rise of the first mosque in Slovenia's recent history.

Notes

[1] This estimation was made by the leader (*mufti*) of the Slovenian Muslims Osman Đogić. According to official statistics, in April 2002 there were 47,888 Muslims in Slovenia, compared with an estimated 31,000 in the 1990s and 3,000 in Tito's Yugoslavia. Because religion was suppressed in socialist times, many people in Yugoslavia did not dare to declare themselves as Muslims. They were permitted to declare themselves Muslims only in the beginning of the sixties.

[2] *Start* magazine ceased publication when Yugoslavia fell apart.

[3] Most of the reporters who wrote about a possible mosque were in favor of its construction. Only one reporter expressed a personal xenophobic opinion. Muslims rarely responded to such articles.

part six

Lessons from the Post-War Balkans

Interethnic Policymaking for Interethnic Tolerance

Islam Yusufi

Meeting chaired by Macedonia's former president, Boris Trajkovsky,
with the author and other minority policymakers

T he development of democratic policymaking processes with equitable representation of ethnic minorities is a crucial challenge on the path toward interethnic tolerance in fragile post-conflict democracies. This lesson was learned during years of Western European democratic consolidation by groups including Swedish-speaking minorities in Finland, the German-speaking minority in Italy's autonomous region of South Tyrol, and Protestants and Catholics in Northern Ireland. In the case of Macedonia, the political participation of the large Albanian minority has been an essential element of an enduring peace. In my work as an International Policy Fellow, I had the chance to interact with minority Macedonian policymakers who had decided that engagement in government work was the only way out of the cycle of interethnic violence that had recently characterized their world.

The right of minorities to participate in the political, economic, social, and cultural life of their country can only be fully realized via participation in decision-making and consultative bodies at national, regional, and local levels. The essence of participation is involvement, both in terms of the opportunity to make substantive contributions to decision-making processes, and in terms of the impact of those contributions.

Islam Yusufi is founder of Analytica, a think tank in Macedonia www.analyticamk.org. Until recently he served as Assistant National Security Adviser to the President of Macedonia. His 2002–4 International Policy Fellowship research, "Security Sector Reform in Southeast Europe" is available online at www.policy. hu/yusufi.

Throughout much of 2001, conflict and general unrest paralyzed much of Macedonia. Until then few minorities had participated in administrative government work. But constitutional and other legal reforms undertaken since the implementation of the Framework Agreement in 2001 have attempted to promote the equitable representation of citizens from minority ethnic groups in the country's public administration, military, police, and public enterprises. While conceptualizing and implementing a coordinated and multi-faceted strategy involving all three branches of government, Macedonian policymakers launched minority training programs which first recruited and trained hundreds of minority police cadets, followed by other recruits. Despite the fact that Macedonia's minorities are not yet equitably represented in the state administration in relation to the overall multiethnic composition of the country, the government's clear commitment to improve the situation has become a critical ingredient driving ethnic reconciliation and democratic consolidation. The initiative has established incentives compelling ethnic communities to make policy choices determining their future coexistence with majority populations.

Western Europe offers a wide range of noteworthy comparative cases from which Macedonia can draw important lessons and adapt according to specific contexts. Innovations in European multiethnic political representation have included the special representation of national minorities via a reserved number of seats in one or both chambers of parliament or in parliamentary committees, various forms of guaranteed participation in legislative processes, formal or informal understandings for allocating decision-making positions such as cabinet and/or court positions to members of national minority groups, mechanisms such as standing directives ensuring that minority interests are considered within relevant ministries, and special measures for minority participation in the civil service. Such initiatives have served as a catalyst to the development of vibrant civil societies in the respective countries.

The current constitution and national laws of Macedonia provide special measures for minority representation in the civil service at all levels, both central and local and, perhaps somewhat surprisingly, not limited to areas populated by minorities. Acknowledging that rule by simple majority is not always equitable in multiethnic societies, special provisions are also included requiring a majority of minority representative votes in addition to overall majorities in decision-making processes.

This effort has obviously served Macedonian political and security interests well: *political interests* by legitimizing the public goods produced by state institutions, and *security interests* by easing interethnic tensions and curbing high unemployment levels. The story, while far from finished, illustrates how deliberate state policies promoting the inclusion of ethnic minorities in the state administration can become an impetus for interethnic reconciliation and grassroots political participation in multiethnic societies.

That said, governments in all of the above-mentioned cases have taken such seemingly altruistic action because it was in their best interest to do so. In multiethnic states a government's continued democratization tends to bolster its legitimacy and vice versa—the legitimization of government policies reinforces political will to forge ahead on the path to democratic maturity.

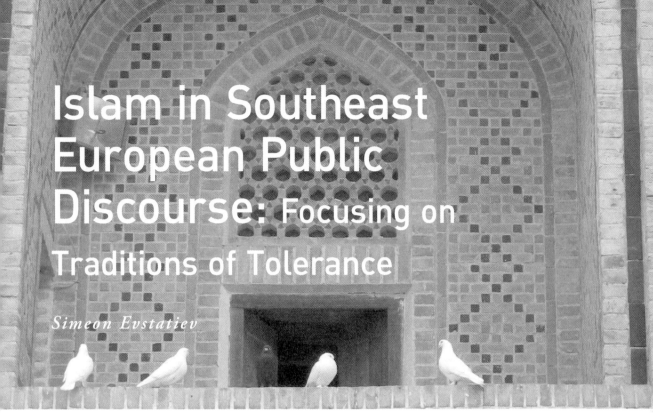

Islam in Southeast European Public Discourse: Focusing on Traditions of Tolerance

Simeon Evstatiev

E ven before the tragedy of September 11, 2001, the western approach to Muslim politics and the 'Islamic factor' in politics has been predominantly selective and crisis-oriented, focusing on the acts of extremists (see for example Esposito, 2003: 69). One of the unfortunate effects of this approach has been that Islam as religion and culture—the faith and the characteristic way of life of many millions of people—has been frequently misperceived and sometimes even identified with terrorism. In recent years, this resulted in the establishment of a destructive image of a militant Islam as opposed to moderate mainstream Islam. Although "religion is obviously central to the political life of peoples around the world, not simply to Muslims" (Eickelman and Piscatori, 1996: 56), the notion of an 'Islamic threat' coming mainly from Arab political regimes and movements has been created in the West. Many observers speak of the alleged incompatibility of Islam and democracy, of the fanaticism of 'Islamic fundamentalists' and of the strong opposition to the secularization and modernization of Middle Eastern societies that have completely different cultural values than those of the West. Despite growing interest among Muslims in the subject of the political role of Muslim identity, many still maintain that there is a single monolithic political doctrine of Islam and that this doctrine is incompatible with pluralist democracy, an idea that first developed in

Simeon Evstatiev teaches Middle Eastern and Islamic History at St. Kliment Ohridski University and serves as Research Director for the Centre for Intercultural Studies and Partnership in Sofia, Bulgaria. His 2005–6 International Policy Fellowship project, "Islam as a Factor in the Design of a European Neighborhood Policy," is available online at www.policy.hu/evstatiev.

the West (see Krämer, 1997: 71). In fact, the re-emergence of Islam in the public sphere is a pluralistic and varied process. Re-Islamization is occuring not only in countries and regions with Muslim majorities such as those in the Middle East and North Africa (MENA), but also among large Muslim minorities in North America and Europe.

In Europe, particularly in the context of EU enlargement, the Wider Europe initiative is facing a broad cultural divide. There is an urgent need for both policymakers and civil society leaders in current and future EU member states to address this divide in advance of the next enlargement in 2007, when the external boundary of the Union will be redrawn toward the Southeast, including significant Muslim communities with long-standing social and cultural links to the MENA region and/or Turkey.

In this context of regional and increasingly globalizing Islam-related challenges, the policy of most Southeast European countries, including Bulgaria, toward the Muslim world and the Islamic factor since the democratization of Southeast Europe in early 1990s has been erratic and virtually non-existent on a conceptual level. Public policies addressing Southeast Europe-MENA relations have been limited, largely reactive and lacking long-term vision. Public interest has been sensation-based, and vague attempts for public discussions on important issues are frequently drowned in stereotypes, misinterpretation and misunderstanding. As a result, Islam is underestimated and misused as a factor in the design of Bulgarian public policy.

This research is based on the assumption that Islam should be a factor in the design of public policies in Southeast Europe, bearing in mind the peculiarities of both domestic Islam and Islamic trends in the Middle East. What is needed now is an adequate understanding of Middle Eastern Islamic and Islamist discourses, debates and social practices and their impact on Muslim communities in the Balkans and their new elites. Furthermore, new initiatives for strengthening civil society should be developed regionally and internationally to foster the formulation of new strategies and the continual

The author surrounded by the Bulgarian Metropolitan Bishop, the head of the Directorate of Religious Affairs, the dean of the Christian Faculty of Theology, and the Grand Mufti of Bulgaria

rethinking of the potential role of Islam in addressing the more trenchant problems of domestic and international affairs.

Bulgarian perceptions of Islam: Traditions of mutual respect versus popular stereotyping

Among the recently acceded and soon-to-accede EU members, Bulgaria is the only country with a substantial Muslim minority (more than 12 percent of the population). In historical and geographical terms, Bulgaria is a natural bridge between Christian and Islamic societies, with Christians and Muslims coexisting in Bulgaria for centuries. However, current political events and the related media depictions have led the Bulgarian public to largely perceive the Middle East as a region fraught with religious and political tensions, violence and war. Bulgarians tend to view some of their Balkan Muslim neighbors in the same light, including Turks and Albanians. Despite mutual understanding characteristic of Bulgaria's ethnically mixed population and everyday communication, the new political elite in Bulgaria exhibit a paradoxical ignorance of Islam as a religion and civilization. Meanwhile the Bulgarian public, once part of the Ottoman Empire, is ambivalent about its Ottoman past. The historical myth of the 'yataghan of Islam' (referring to the traditional Turkish sword) is deeply rooted in Bulgarian consciousness as a result of propaganda carried through the centuries by representatives of the Bulgarian National Revival, followed by a part of the political elite.

Nevertheless, the long relationship between Christians and Muslims in Bulgaria has bred mutual respect as described by the specific Bulgarian term *komshuluk*, meaning good, neighborly, respectful coexistence. The *komshuluk* principles of secular Muslim-Christian interaction (cf. Peev, 1997: 187) were described by prominent twentieth century Bulgarian ethnic psychologist Ivan Hadjiyski as follows: "Even in the philistine towns there were small doors (*komshuluks*) opened in the fences, which were never closed and which made the yards into something like linked vessels; through them the neighbors were providing each other with any kind of assistance," while "widely practiced self-service borrowing turned the owners of many items into only their keepers because the neighbor had the right to enter the yard and take them without asking. The rule was: whatever you want if I have it" (Hadjiyski, 1966: 97).

Showing signs of Christian-Muslim mutual respect during holidays, celebrations, and family occasions is also a Bulgarian tradition. Thus "a common ground is created for mutual respect for the other faith, on which its foreign nature turns into a known difference" (Georgieva, 1994: 225). Although unwritten, it a is widely established rule in Bulgaria that on Easter Christians give red eggs and sweetbread to their Muslim neighbors and friends, while on Kurban Bayram (or Eid festival that takes place during the hajj pilgrimage to Mecca) Muslims give their Christian neighbors meat from the sacrificial animal. At the very least a "Happy Holiday" wish is imperative. Each Easter in days gone by and sometimes today, Muslim children were especially impatient to get the red eggs as gifts, so much so that their mothers and grandmothers sometimes boiled and painted Easter eggs—an intolerable religious symbol from an Islamic law or *sharī'a* point-of-view. Christians and Muslims go out of their way to invite each other to

The author and his wife, Arabist and Islamist Galina Evstatieva, in Egypt with Mohamed Habib, the first deputy of the Supreme Guide of the Muslim Brotherhood.

weddings, birth celebrations and funerals as a sign of trust and respect for the norms of the other's religion and as well as the elements of the human condition common to the followers of all religions—birth, love, marriage and death.

Prior to the establishment of the Communist regime in Bulgaria in 1944, rare instances of state-sanctioned crimes committed against Bulgarian Muslims tended to be fueled by practices of the Bulgarian Orthodox Church (see Eldarov, 2001: 592). Under communism, the Church lost all of its potential for missionary activities and opportunities for the conversion of Bulgaria's Muslim population to Christianity became impossible. Following the transition from a totalitarian to a democratic social system beginning in 1989, the Bulgarian state guaranteed the rights of religious denominations including minority confessional groups through the Constitution and legislation. During the last decade of the twentieth century, when much of the Balkans erupted in interethnic conflict, Bulgarian Christians and Muslims managed to preserve the principles of *komshuluk*. Nevertheless, among the elite as well as the average Bulgarian, ignorance about Islam, both as a doctrine and as a civilization, remained.

At least a part of this ignorance is attributable to the fact that during the 50 years of communist rule, religious instruction was not permitted in mainstream Bulgarian schools. Only in 1997–1998 and 1999–2000 were courses on Christianity and Islam (respectively) reintroduced. The long absence of religious instruction means that there is little experience in Bulgaria in teaching religion in secular schools, especially within the new post-communist context. The problem is exacerbated by the lack of attention paid to school education by the Eastern Orthodox Church and the institutions of the Islamic Community in Bulgaria. The net result is that the teaching of religion is conservative, ethnocentric and dogmatic. The basic moral values of each religion are represented as exclusive, with little or no attention to interfaith relations, either in an ethical/theological or practical/social sense. Thus religious education is cut off from the country's broader social and political development. The most deleterious consequence is that, rather than being a tool for supporting social integration and building bridges of tolerance and dialogue, religious instruction tends to perpetuate if not exacerbate existing divides between Christian and Muslim populations.

It is not an exaggeration to say that the first serious public attempt in Bulgaria to adequately understand Islam was made amid the coverage of the events in the United

States on September 11, 2001. Prominent intellectuals, scholars and writers took an active part in a kind of public awareness campaign, and most of them succeeded in emphasizing the difference between Islam and terrorism. The views of world-renowned thinkers such as Noam Chomsky, Tzvetan Todorov and many others were aired. All forms of media covering the world news extensively and organized regular discussions, seeking the views of political analysts, historians and experts on Middle Eastern and Islamic studies espousing different views. Proponents of a "clash of civilizations" met with the tenacious defenders of intercultural dialogue and understanding. There were also reports of petty backlash—for example, in Bulgaria's second largest city of Plovdiv some youngsters threw stones at mosques, and it was reported that Muslim women were insulted by being called "Taliban" (although their appearance in most cases was so European that the Taliban would be enraged at the sight of them). Nevertheless common sense prevailed, and it can be said that institutions and personalities have become more receptive to ideas of intercultural dialogue and cooperation, while journalists have attempted to be more precise in their discourse about Islam and have begun to ask for expert opinions before resorting to possible stereotyping.

Addressing current Muslim–Christian public policy problems

A central problem for Bulgaria today is the danger that conflictual Christian-Muslim relations on an international level could be internalized on a local social level at a time when new religious public spheres are emerging in Bulgaria. When discussing the 'public sphere' in western and Islamic interpretations, it is important to note significant definitional differences. While western notions of 'public sphere' such as those developed by Habermas (*Öffentlichkeit*) emphasize the "rationality potential" of communicative action and tend to neglect religion (Eickelman and Salvatore, 1994: 6), "the terms *private* and *public* in Islam are not rooted in the heart of Islamic doctrine" (Kadivar, 2003: 660). Private religion can be viewed as a part of public life.

The increased religious activity of the Muslim community in Bulgaria after the fall of communism naturally reflects the international diversity of Islam and the influence of various Islamic religious and ideological centers. Such international linkages were greatly enhanced by recent events which in one way or another associated Islam with international terrorism, fostering the suspicion and distrust of much of Bulgaria's majority population toward their Muslim neighbors. The picture is further complicated by competing power centers within the Bulgarian Muslim community itself. Urgent policy research is needed to more accurately grasp the impact of global developments on the Muslim community in Bulgaria and to initiate a process of interethnic and interfaith dialogue that re-conceptualizes new realities in a constructive way. Among the most policy-relevant types of projects required include interdisciplinary research projects dealing with the intercultural relations from the perspective of religion (concentrating on inter-religious rather than only interethnic coexistence as has been predominantly the case during the last fifteen years) and tolerance-building curricula in public education, youth and media programs. Although the mass education brought about by new communication technologies (such as Internet and desktop publishing) have done away with the censors (Eickelman, 2003: 33), they present a number of new challenges for the work of public policymakers and civil society actors.

During the last decade in Bulgaria several non-governmental organizations (NGOs) have carried out much programmatic work on intercultural relations in general, including the International Center for Minority Studies and Intercultural Relations, the Foundation Interethnic Initiative for Human Rights, the Bulgarian branch of the German Association for Adult Education as well as my affiliation—the Center for Intercultural Studies and Partnership (CISP; www.cisp-bg.org). The Center was established in 2003 by a then-informal group of Bulgarian academics and intellectuals (mostly with backgrounds affiliated with St. Kliment Ohridski University of Sofia) in cooperation with Columbia University in New York and the European Association for Middle Eastern Studies (EURAMES). It should be noted that International Policy Fellowships alumni Plamen Makariev (www.policy.hu/makariev) and Nonka Todorova (www.policy.hu/todorova) are also actively involved with CISP efforts, with Professor Makariev a CISP co-founder. The team at CISP runs a project entitled The Muslim Community in Bulgaria: Facing the Global Challenges sponsored by the Democracy Commission Grant Program at the American Center in Sofia. The project aims to develop specific methodological instruments for measuring various changing influences and attitudes among the Muslim community as well as mainstream public in Bulgaria. The project carries out empirical surveys through focus groups and content analysis focusing on perceptions, prepares policy-relevant analysis, and organizes public debates to discuss survey results and share opinions on the prospects of improving the interfaith and intercultural relations in Bulgaria and regionally.

Given the historical lack of public education in religion in Bulgaria as previously described, one of CISP's major initiatives involves the introduction of issues and themes of inter-religious understanding and tolerance into religious instruction at Bulgarian mainstream schools. This thematic working group has two major goals: the first is reform of the curricula of religious schools/centers, while the second is the introduction of religious instruction into mainstream (secular) schools. The results of the recent research project *Islamic Religious Education in Bulgaria: the Challenges of Partnership* conducted by a team from the University of Sofia affiliated

With Sheikh-al-Azhar in Cairo

with CISP demonstrated an urgent need for cooperation between Islamic educational institutions and mainstream, secular academic institutions if pressing problems of academic quality and independence of Islamic education in Bulgaria and the region are to be addressed.

In cooperation with the Center for the Study of Human Rights at Columbia University in New York, a CISP team is working on the project *Religion And Education: Enhancing Christian-Muslim Understanding In Bulgaria* to develop religious education at mainstream secular schools. The program funded by the United States Institute of Peace and supported by the Bulgarian Ministry of Education and Science. Given the strong relationship between religious identity and political and social peace in Bulgaria and Southeast Europe more generally, it is extremely important that information about different religions be conveyed between groups in ways that maximizes mutual understanding and minimizes stereotyping, or promotes *informed understanding*.

Bearing in mind the importance of the media in shaping public attitudes, CISP has also developed the program *Islam and the Media: Unveiling Prejudices and Overcoming Stereotypes* sponsored by the Matra Program of the Netherlands to enhance the competence of Bulgarian journalists (focusing on local media, particularly in ethnically and religiously mixed regions) to cover Islam as religion and culture, not only by providing more information about Islam but also by uncovering typical ideological manipulations and overcoming prejudices and stereotypes. In Bulgaria, as in the international media, there is a troubling tendency to automatically associate Islam with terrorism.

Emphasizing traditions of religious tolerance in public advocacy and policymaking

Policy analysis and policy design should not simply rely on modernist strategies that identified religion as the problem and proposed "classical" secularism as the solution, avoiding religion's potentially conflictual terrain by virtually banning it from the public sphere. Obviously, this vision of national and international life purified of religious influence has not come to fruition. This reality leads us down a second path, which begins with the potential of religion to contribute to solutions to common problems by working *through* religion. Furthermore, Islam and Islamism in the Middle East should not be viewed solely as reactive response to conflicts wrought by modernizing social and economic changes, but also as a significant modernizing factor within Muslim societies and communities. To better understand this global movement, it is necessary to articulate a new conceptual framework and overcome the separation of religion and politics, of church and state. European policymakers, international donors and civil society leaders should listen more carefully to the internal discourses and debates within Islam and their interaction with the non-Muslim public. Rather than an overly realpolitik struggle over people's imaginations, public interfaith dialogue should involve "a corrective about conventional thinking" (Eickelman and Piscatori, 1996: 9). What is needed is a refocusing of the debate around more authoritative Islamic discourse that more adequately 'translates' intercultural relations as well as European policies toward the Muslim world.

References

Eickelman, Dale F. (2003) "Communication and Control in the Middle East: Publication and its Discontent," *New Media in the Muslim World": The Emerging Public Sphere*.

Eickelman, Dale F. and Armando Salvatore, eds (2004) "Muslim Publics," *Public Islam and the Common Good*, Boston: Brill, pp.3–27.

Eickelman, Dale F. and James Piscatori (1996) *Muslim Politics*. Princeton, New Jersey: Princeton University Press.

Eldarov, Svetlozar (2001) "Bulgarskata Pravoslavna Curkva i bulgarite myusyulmani 1878–1944 [The Bulgarian Orthodox Church and Bulgarian Muslims, 1878–1944]," *Istoriya na myusyulmanskata kultura po bulgarskite zemi* [*History of Muslim Culture in Bulgarian Lands*], edited by Rossitsa Gradeva, *The Fate of Muslim Communities in the Balkans* Vol. 7. pp.592–639. Sofia: IMIR, 2001

Esposito, John L. and François Burgat, eds (2003) "Islam and Civil Society," *Modernizing Islam: Religion in the Public Sphere in Europe and the Middle East,* New Brunswick, New Jersey: Rutgers University Press, pp.69–100.

Georgieva, Tzvetana (1994) "Sujitelstvoto kato sistema vuv vsekidnevniya jivot na hristiyanite i myusyulmanite v Bulgaria" [Co-existence as a System in the Everyday Life of Christians and Muslims in Bulgaria], In *Vruzki na suvmestimost i nesuvmestimost mejdu hrisityani i myusyulmani v Bulgaria*. pp.140–158. Sofia: IMIR.

Hadjiyski, Ivan (1966) *Bit i dushevnost na nashiya narod* [Way of Life and Mentality of Our People], Sofia: Bulgarski pisatel.

Kadivar, Mohsen (2003) "An Introduction to the Public and Private Debate in Islam," *Islam: The Public and Private Spheres. Social Research, an International Quarterly of the Social Sciences*. Vol. 70, No. 3, Fall 2003.

Krämer, Gudrun (1997) "Islamist Notions of Democracy," *Political Islam*, edited by J. Benin and Joe Stork. Berkley, Los Angeles University of California Press, pp.71–82.

Mitev, Peter-Emil (1994) "Vruzki na suvmestimost i nesuvmestimost v ejednevieto mejdu hristiyani i myusyulmani v Bulgaria [Relations of Compatibility and Incompatibility in the Everyday Life between Christians and Muslims in Bulgaria] (Sociological Study), In *Vruzki na suvmestimost i nesuvmestimost mejdu hrisityani i myusyulmani v Bulgaria.*" pp.165–197. Sofia: IMIR.

Peev, Yordan (1997) "Courants Islamiques en Bulgarie", In *Solidarités islamiques, Les Annales de l'autre Islam,* No. 4, INALCO–ERISM, Paris.

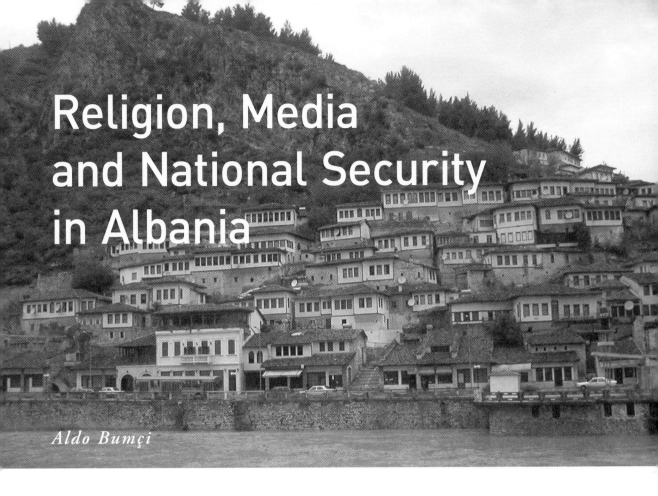

Religion, Media and National Security in Albania

Aldo Bumçi

Following decades of strictly enforced atheism under the Communist regime that fell in 1990, the majority of Albanians are secular, although some 70 percent of citizens would identify themselves as Muslim.[1] The Albanian Muslim religious community is represented by the Albanian Muslim Community (otherwise known as the Albanian Islamic Community)—a government-sanctioned body which oversees Islamic mosques, organizations, and activities in Albania. In recent years, the Albanian media has focused attention and debate on the potential emergence of radical fundamentalism within the Albanian Muslim Community. Many issues raised in the media debate on the potential rise of radical fundamentalism have been securitized—perceived as posing a security threat, or rather a potential threat to the country, if not checked. Albanians in Kosovo and Macedonia have also expressed similar concerns.[2] At times the possible emergence of extremism is articulated as a potential threat, while other reports maintain that there are no signs of fundamentalism or extremism in Albanian society.[3] Yet the debate has reached a level that demands enquiry. In addition to the domestic debate, international developments and their ramifications add fuel to the fire. Although for

Aldo Bumçi was sworn in as Albania's Minister of Justice in September 2005. Formerly he served as the director of the Albanian Institute for International Studies and a professor at Tirana University's Faculty of Social Sciences. His 2001–2 International Policy Fellowship project, "Cross-Border Cooperation Between Albania and Montenegro," is available online at www.policy.hu/bumci.

EU Commissioner Franco Frattini, the author, and Albanian Interior Minister Sokol Olldashi in Brussels © European Community, 2005

the purposes of this research I focus on the Albanian Muslim Community, a more thorough investigation of the topic of religion and national security should focus on all religious communities. I begin by analyzing the nature of perceived security threats as articulated in the media.

The shape of the domestic debate and the way threats are presented

When reporting on the Albanian Muslim Community, local media tend to focus on the following central themes as contributing to a possible 'terrorist threat' in Albania and in need of urgent policy attention. Following a discussion of the perceived concerns, I will turn to the question of their validity based on evidence gathered in interviews.

The influence of foundations from abrod. In the media, the presence and influence of foundations from other Muslim and especially 'Arab' countries is considered to be the major source of concern regarding religious developments in the Muslim Community that may have a negative impact on inter-religious relations and harmony in the country. Islamic foundations and organizations are suspected of imposing unfamiliar religious practices and dangerous ideas, and perhaps even supporting extremist and terrorist activities.

By opening religious schools and courses and targeting mainly the youth, Islamic foundations began educating children about their traditions, and critics have claimed that the foundations were destroying the local, more tolerant Islamic tradition by introducing a conservative version of Islam, which amounted to the 'Arabization' of the specific form of Islam traditionally practiced in Albania. The spread of Wahhabism in particular was presented as an illustration of the fundamentalist nature of these organizations and their teachings, which could create fertile ground for the radicalization of more tolerant 'Albanian' Islam and the emergence of 'Islamic terrorism' in the country. It was also argued that the practice of these foundations to send Albanians to study in religious universities in 'Arab' countries was creating divisions among Albanian Muslims and that the longer term aim of such efforts was to eventually control positions in the Albanian Muslim Community hierarchy. Declarations have also been made claiming that the Albanian Muslim Community has grown dependent on the funds provided by the foreign foundations, which in turn has weakened its authority.

Another concern related to the activity of religious foundations is the possibility that they could serve as front organizations organizing or financing terrorist and extremist activities. For example, the arrest and extradition of several members of the *Islamic Jihad* working for various religious foundations in 1998 and the closing of the Al-Haramain Foundation branch in Albania were part of a larger action taken by Saudi Arabian and US authorities to close Al-Haramain branches in five countries because it had provided financial and logistic support to the Al-Qaeda network. As a consequence, the media reported on the lack of proper control over religious foundations in Albania.

Albanian students who have studied in religious universities abroad. Another issue that has been articulated in the press is related to the Albanian students who have studied religion abroad and particularly in 'Arab' countries. As described above, possible threats to Albanian religious life have been largely perceived as coming from outside Albania. But the return of Albanian students who had studied in other Muslim countries meant that what used to be considered an external influence now also had the potential of originating from local Islamic foundations. First of all, Albanian students were sent to study abroad by the different Islamic foundations that operated in the country, which was an issue of concern considering the way foundations were perceived. The countries and universities where the Islamic foundations based in Albania primarily sent students are perceived as the countries that harbor the most Islamic radicalism. Media reports as well as former state officials criticized some of the education received abroad for teaching not only Islamic studies but also military training. Thus, the majority of the Albanians who had studied in Arab countries were stereotyped as being religious extremists and fundamentalists bent on 'Arabizing' and radicalizing 'Albanian Islam' and usurping the Albanian Muslim Community hierarchy under their control.

The two rival groups within the Albanian Muslim Community. Albanian students who had studied abroad are indeed demanding representation in the institutions of the Albanian Muslim Community, leading vulnerable officials of the Community to depict their opponents as extremists in the media. The first group of Community leaders are mainly represented by the traditional and moderate older generation of religious teachers and imams associated with the Albanian tradition, i.e. graduates of the religious school system following the so-called 'Turkish' school. The second group is represented, at least according to the media, as comprising primarily young, radical students who have studied abroad mostly in Arab countries or those who have taken courses organized and sponsored by various Islamic foundations in Albania. Media reports and prosecutors have even linked this group of 'extremists' and the struggle for control within the community to the unsolved killing of the organization's General Secretary Salih Tivar. Apart from its ideological aspect, the clash has been presented as largely a struggle for control over the management of the Community assets.

International developments and the risk of creating artificial internal cleavages. Internet and other international media reports promulgating ideas about the existence of a global religious conflict between Islam and Christianity have deepened anti-western feelings among many Albanian Muslims. Thus an 'Islam versus the West' cleavage has been created that translates into a strengthening of the religious dividing lines in the Balkans, especially in Bosnia, where people who shared the same culture were instigated into building separate ethnic identities through the instrumentalization of religion. Boosting religious identities can serve to weaken national identities and create symbols of division that serve the interests of leaders in search of popular support. For Albania, a multi-confessional society, religious instrumentalization could have catastrophic impact as it could affect both the tradition of tolerance as well as the process of state and nation building.[4]

External appearances. The unfamiliar external appearance of some believers with long beards or headscarves are portrayed by the media as further evidence of the foreign, fundamentalist Muslim tradition brought to the country from abroad. In a few isolated cases, school directors have prohibited young students from attending classes with headscarves.

Politics and religion. Another facet of Albanian media discourse and declarations about a 'terrorist threat' relates to certain policies adopted by the Democratic Party Government which ruled in 1992–96 due to allegations that the Party, and especially the former head of the intelligence service Bashkim Gazidede and former President Sali Berisha, pursued policies that welcomed Islamic religious foundations and even suspected terrorists to the country.

Analyzing the perceived concerns

Based primarily on interviews conducted with current and former representatives of the Albanian Muslim Community, religious individuals including imams and muftis, representatives of the Albanian Committee of Cults, and a number of essays and publications, it is possible to identify the factors that have fueled the above-mentioned concerns articulated in the Albanian media:

International Developments. It is important to place concerns of radical fundamentalism within the Albanian Muslim Community in a broader international context. The importance of international events on Albania's internal political scene cannot be overstated; for example the collapse of communist regimes in the former Warsaw Pact countries had a decisive affect on the collapse of communism in Albania, even though Albania had left the Warsaw Pact long before and had pursued a policy of isolation. One could argue that the domestic debate that has emerged in Albania surrounding the Albanian Muslim Community would have not emerged, at least in its current shape, had we not witnessed the dramatic international terrorist acts that have taken place in recent years. Like other countries, Albania has taken measures to strengthen internal security and border control and has contributed troops in both Afghanistan and Iraq. The danger for Albania is not so much the possibility of a terrorist attack, but rather the nature of debate that has emerged in Albania related to the Albanian Muslim Community and the danger of religious radicalization among its members.

The ways in which the Albanian media portrays the process of importing and implanting of religious radicalization to Albania is simplistic, feeds off incomparable

The Etehem Bay Mosque, built in the early 1800s. During communist rule the mosque was closed until January 1991, when ten thousand people attended prayer service despite opposition among weakening communist authorities

international media reports and fuels local tensions. As put by Arber Xhaferri, "Due to the globalizing intensity and potential of this propaganda, cultures, mentalities and experiences of small nations have been jeopardized."[5] It is essential that Albanians avoid the kind of stereotyping that seems to be growing. John Esposito, one of the world's most prominent scholars on Middle East and Islam, has noted that "a focus on 'Islamic fundamentalism' as a global threat has reinforced the tendency to equate violence with Islam, to fail to distinguish between the illegitimate use of religion by individuals and the faith and practice of the majority of the world's Muslims who, like adherents of other religious traditions, wish to live in peace."[6] At the same time, what is presented by the international and local media as a Muslim–Christian religious conflict in most cases has nothing to do with religion. As Fred Halliday observes, despite the tendency to present the region of the Middle East as peculiar, it shares many post-colonial and developing world characteristics including a conflictual and violent relationship with former colonial powers.[7] This set of circumstances has no relevance to the case of Albania.

Foundations. Generally speaking, Albanians take pride in a national tradition of religious tolerance and moderation. The religious revival following the collapse of communism was not a cause for concern, as indigenous religious communities that survived communism were part of this tradition. This is why 'threats' are publicly perceived as originating only from external actors. Nevertheless, the simplistic, black-and-white media picture of Islamic foundations in Albania is far from the reality.

Various foundations were established in Albania following a long period of Communist rule that had a devastating effect on religious life and institutions in the country. While the end of the communist regime heralded the beginning of a new era, the bleak economic conditions of the early 1990s meant that the indigenous Muslim community lacked the necessary resources to rebuild mosques and religious schools, not to mention qualified human resources to lead the various activities of religious life (for example the Albanian-language version of the Quran was available in the country only after 1990). The assistance provided by foreign donors was important in the revival of Albania's religious life, as well as in charity work helping orphanages, building centers of sanitation, etc.

Islamic foundations have come under the spotlight of public scrutiny primarily following several high-profile cases indicating that they were used to hide extremist and terrorist individuals who were later identified and extradited. Several foundations were closed after they had been shown to be providing financial and logistic support to terrorist networks. International reports on the role of Saudi Arabian-funded schools and organizations spreading Wahhabi teachings in other parts of the world have also contributed to a general distrust about the presence of foundations because "the ideologies of the Mujaheedin and Taliban were bred in Pakistani schools founded by Saudi Arabia."[8]

Furthermore, the inability of the Albanian state to provide proper oversight and control has, in a way, increased apprehensions about the role of various foundations. Due to the particular conditions of weak post-communist Albanian institutions, no institution was charged with a clear and well-defined responsibility to regulate foundation activities. Registration procedures for religious foundations were similar to those of other non-governmental organizations operating in the country. The Albanian Committee of Cults, whose status was upgraded from the Secretariat that existed before, does not enjoy any legal authority for controling the activity of foundations. The Committee is informed by the foundations of their activities via an informal practice that has developed mainly due to the need for foundations to maintain good relations with a state agency.[9] The Committee is understaffed and underfunded. Various ministries and the intelligence services also have some formal work with the foundations such as various registrations, etc. but no agency is fully responsible for oversight.

In addition to the state agencies, the foundations have had to cooperate with the Albanian Muslim Community, since the rationale of their presence was linked to the assistance that would have been provided to its members. The Albanian Muslim Community should have taken the lead in this cooperation, but this proved difficult due to the disadvantaged position of the local religious structures vis-à-vis foreign foundations. The local community eventually grew dependent on foreign financial assistance as well as religious knowledge and scholarship. Thus, the foundations sometimes facilitated students' study abroad without receiving the consent of the local community. Some argue that the lack of Community transparency forced many foundations to limit their cooperation.

The number of Islamic foundations operating in Albania as well as their activities have declined in recent years. Measures taken by Saudi Arabia and the US against the Al-Haramein foundation have resulted in a reduction of funds, while the identification and extradition of certain individuals working for these foundations has contributed to better monitoring of their activities. It should be stressed that those foundations involved in such extremist activities are a small minority—over 20 such foundations have operated in Albania, and those accused of instigating violence constitute only a few of them.[10]

What is most worrying is the tendency of the Albanian public to associate the entire Muslim Community with the problems linked to some foundations. The media contributes to such associations by showing everyday pictures of believers praying alongside stories related to terrorism, for example. Either intentionally or unintentionally, such presentations convey the wrong messages. It is the sole responsibility of the state to allow foundations access to and permission to work in the country. The state should provide the required legal framework to ensure better monitoring of foundations and to ensure that they cooperate with the Albanian Muslim Community.[11] Furthermore, the state could reduce tensions within the Muslim community as well as its over-reliance on foundations if it focuses on the urgent problem of property restitution for the Muslim Community.

Albanian students who have studied abroad. In the early 1990s, Albania was in a great need of qualified personnel to work in different institutions of the Muslim community, teach in madrassas, and preach in the mosques as imams. In order to address these needs, Albanians were sent to study religion only in Arab countries or Turkey. The only other option for those who choose to pursue a religious career would be to join a religious institution in Albania, but these institutions remain underdeveloped. Given this situation, the mere practice of studying at a foreign religious school is a natural process and cannot be identified as a threat. The group of students who choose this path is diverse, they cannot be categorized as the new 'class enemies.'

The Albanian Muslim Community has attempted to send students to countries that follow the Albanian Islamic tradition—the Hanafi School in Islamic Law—or a similar tradition. Agreements have been signed with Turkey, Egypt, Libya, Jordan and Malaysia to cooperate in student exchange programs. Likewise, the community strives to staff its madrassas and community institutions with teachers and leaders from Albania and/or countries following a similar Islamic tradition. At the same time, students have been sent by foundations to study in Saudi Arabia and other states that do not follow a similar Islamic tradition, without informing the local community. As mentioned in the first section, former state officials have made declarations more than once stating that some of these students have studied in semi-military schools.[12] If true, this would be critical information, but as is usually the case with intelligence service declarations, they are difficult to verify or scrutinize via normal public channels. While as a researcher I could not verify the former Intelligence Service information, it is worth mentioning that the Albanian Embassy in Saudi Arabia and other embassies in countries tagged for training terrorists stated that they had no contact or information about any Albanian studying there.

Some of the measures proposed by those interviewed include channeling the processing of all study abroad scholarships via the Albanian Muslim Community and ensuring that the best students from Albanian madrassas can receive them. This would mean that students would first acquire some religious education in Albania and presumably be in a better position to judge and filter the information received abroad. These proposals sound sensible, but in a democratic country a person has

EU Commissioner Franco Frattini, Albanian Interior Minister Sokol Olldashi, and the author at the EC
© European Community, 2005

the right to study wherever he or she chooses to do so. Moreover, it is entirely possible that a person could embrace radical ideas even in countries that follow the Albanian tradition such as Turkey or Egypt. As John Esposito notes, contrary to popular assumptions, the strength of Islamic movements "is not so much in the religious faculties and humanities as in science, engineering education, law and medicine...Many leaders of these movements have earned their doctorates in Western universities."[13] Furthermore, in a globalized world people become familiar with radical movements via internet and the media. While such instances may be exceptions, a desire to reduce the risk of radicalization should not interfere with an institutionalized policy on scholarships and universities that is based on equity and democratic principles.

The best guarantee against the emergence of religious extremism and radicalism in Albania is a strong Albanian Muslim Community comprised of well-educated religious scholars and possessing the necessary financial resources to act independently and uphold religious traditions based on tolerance.

The Albanian Muslim Community. Divisions within the Albanian Muslim Community appeared most pronounced in the late 1990s, and have since diminished. Nevertheless, the differences or the conflict, depending on how they are perceived, within the Albanian Muslim Community have been made public through various official declarations depicting their opponents as extremists. National authorities have identified the issue as significant enough to specifically call on Albanian Muslims to leave aside their differences.[14] A major source of the clashes resulted from the fact that Albania did not offer formal religious education under communism, leading to a situation in which the young Albanian students who had studied abroad or those that had taken courses from various foundation were critical of the Community's older leaders, whom they viewed as unprepared and unqualified to hold to their positions. The young generation has been educated in religious universities and speaks foreign languages, including Arabic. While

arguments about the lack of sufficient religious knowledge are grounded to some extent, the old generation emphasizes the fact that the young generation should acquire what they call "the school of life." As Ervin Hatibi put it in a meeting commemorating the eightieth anniversary of the establishment of the Albanian Muslim Community, "it would be unjustifiable not to look back at this legacy to see how the forerunners have addressed these issues... former graduates of madrassas, the last witnesses and successors of that Islamic spirit of reformation and moderation, of that generation of religious scholars and activists that established the Albanian Muslim Community in 1923."[15] While the older generation bears and conveys this tradition, the younger generation represents the future of the Albanian Muslim Community. Labeling Albanian students who have graduated abroad as radicals and extremists is a mistake.

As has been reported in the media, many conflicts that emerged in various local branches of the Muslim Community as well as in the central structures are related to property following allegations of mismanagement of the Community's property and the need to increase transparency. Some have argued that most important source of the conflict has been economic rather than ideological or generational. The unresolved problem of land restitution and compensation in Albania, even 13 years after the collapse of the communist regime, is a grave national problem. Thus the associated sensitivities go far beyond religious sentiment. The restitution of property is central to the Muslim Community's goal of achieving greater financial independence from foreign donors. The state could greatly contribute by making efforts to return a sizeable portion of the Community's property. Although it is the Community that is ultimately entitled to the management of its own property, the state could assist in the peaceful settlement of related disputes by requiring improved transparency related to deals involving former state property.

> **The best guarantee against the emergence of religious extremism and radicalism in Albania is a strong Albanian Muslim Community able to act independently and uphold religious traditions based on tolerance.**

Another problem associated with the tensions within the Muslim Community is related to the statute that regulates the Community's daily affairs and accusations of nepotism in nominations, unjustifiable dismissals, and a lack of adherence to provisions of the statute. Again, the state could diffuse the situation by preparing legislation regulating relations between the state and religious communities, in cooperation with religious communities.

Media representation of the Albanian Muslim Community —a threat in itself

Though a much more systematic study could be conducted, the results of a brief study monitoring the Albanian print media highlight the negative implications of biased reporting about the Albanian Muslim Community. The way media outlets frame events and project them to the public has a significant impact on the way we perceive the world around us. In Albania, media coverage and the representation of events evolving in the Albanian Muslim Community has revealed both professional coverage presenting various points-of-view as well as biased and negative reporting. Although it is therefore unfair to generalize, patterns of negative representation are worrying.

Most disturbing are frequent media associations of Islam with above-mentioned generalizations as well as words such as 'terrorists' and 'fundamentalists,' as in the case of students who have graduated abroad, or by associating particular items of news such as information on foundations with images of ordinary believers. While such representations are partially attributed to the lack of knowledge and professionalism in the media, the desire to 'make a scoop' and increase the circulation of a newspaper, it is also attributed to an unfriendly attitude toward Albanian Muslims and Islam. All those interviewed expressed indignation about biased media presentations and coverage. There are two major negative implications resulting from such misrepresentations: the pitting of certain groups against Islam in Albania and generalized comparisons of the Muslim Community with the institutions of other religious communities in the country.

Furthermore, when such essays appear in a particular media, they are not perceived by the public as being accidental; conspiracy theories abound. Thus the image of an 'unfriendly other' that is against Islam in Albania begins to take shape. In this way the media, through its representations, generates new public concern and indignation that did not exist before. Those interested in the manipulation of religion for other purposes capitalize on exactly these feelings to mobilize their followers. To make matters worse, in a country where Muslims already feel marginalized or at least slighted (the Community has not yet been allowed to build a mosque in the capital, for example), it is easy to stir resentment about what is perceived to be the intentional demonization of Islam when compared with other religions. The adoption of a journalism code of ethics by the media concerning the coverage of religious subjects could be helpful.

Politics and religion

Although politics in Albania has tended to steer clear of exploiting religious divisions, there is always a risk of political opponents developing a framework of negative religious connotations. Whether it involves current, former or aspiring Albanian politicians, portraying members or leaders of opposition parties as tolerant toward Islamic extremists is a dangerous practice. Arguments provided in the past, such as membership in the Islamic Conference or the presence of individuals with links to terrorist organizations in the country, are without merit and cannot be supported. Political relations between Albania and the West (both the US and EU members states) during the period when Albania joined the Conference was extremely good, with frequent diplomatic visits and significant levels of financial assistance provided to Albania, not to mention the fact that the US assisted in the establishment of an anti-terror office by the Albanian Intelligence Service at the time. And the fact that individuals or organizations linked with terrorist networks have been residing in Albania does not automatically imply complicity by the Albanian government any more than it would any western government.

The need for greater openness

Finally, it can be argued that Albania's public discussion about developments within its Muslim Community have been spurred primarily by two factors: 1) the communist destruction of religious memory and tradition, and 2) a lack of openness on the part of religious institutions and the media to report on different aspects of religious life.

Communist rule and the total ban on religious life meant that generations grew up in an environment devoid of daily contact with everyday religious practices. Of course, religious life in terms of faith did continue, as reflected in the religious revival after the collapse of communism. However, this is different from the daily religious practices and customs, which were totally banned. Thus in the early 1990s, a significant portion of the population had grown unaccustomed to religious practices. People were not used to see religious people with long beards, women wearing headscarves and other aspects of religious life. Combined with international developments and media representations seen on television, apprehension developed and certain normal aspects of religious life were perceived as indicators of threat.

Furthermore, public ignorance and a lack of information about what happens in religious institutions has fueled intolerance. In this context, more openness could be achieved in terms of relations between religious institutions and the wider public.[16] The media too should show more interest in covering the positive aspects of religious life. Television programs could be organized that focus on madrassas and other institutions to inform the public and dissipate unfounded concerns. Public seminars could also be organized that bring together media and representatives of religious communities.

Policy recommendations

A strong Albanian Muslim Community

A strong Albanian Muslim Community that is able to support itself without substantial foreign support is the best guarantee against any form of potential radicalization. To strengthen the Albanian Muslim Community measures in two main directions should be taken: 1) the state should pay particular attention to the issue of property restitution, so that Albanian Muslim Community can achieve a substantial degree of financial independence, and 2) the labeling of Albanian students who have studied abroad and namely in 'Arab' countries as radicals and extremists is a mistake. While individuals who endorse radical ideas may be among such students, they do not represent the majority of Albanians who have studied religion abroad. It is exactly the educated young that embody the best values of the Albanian Muslim Community, and who will carry on the work and defend against forms of radicalization.

Media code of ethics

The ways in which the Albanian media have represented the debate surrounding the Albanian Muslim Community has created negative stereotypes–such as nurturing perceptions about the existence of an 'unfriendly other' among Albanian Muslims and fostering comparisons between different religious communities. In order to avoid creating artificial problems, the media should adopt a code of ethics and avoid using language and reporting offensive to believers. Moreover, seminars and trainings should be organized that bring together media and religious community representatives.

Improved relations between the state and religious communities

The government should take a number of measures to regulate and maintain relations with religious communities in an institutionalized context. It should adopt legislation and sign agreements with the respective religious communities as demanded by the constitutions, and provide the Committee of Cults with the proper legal basis and sufficient human resources to perform its duties.

Notes

[1] Most Albanian Muslims are either associated with the Bektashi school (a particularly liberal form of Shi'a Sufism), or a moderate form of Sunni Islam.

[2] Arbër Xhaferri, "Hakerat e Mapave," *Shekulli*, February 21, 2004; Veton Surroi, "Shqipëria, feja dhe globalizmi," *Korrieri*, May 22, 2004; Kim Mehmeti, quoted in Pirro Misha, "Tolerancë fetare apo papërgjegjshmëri;" Isa Blumi, *Islami Politik ndër Shqiptarët: A po vijnë Talibanët në Ballkan*, KIPRED, Prishtinë, June, 2003; Declaration of the Kosova Muslim Community, Korrieri, February 20, 2004.

[3] Artan Fuga, "A rrezikohemi nga integralizmi fetar në Shqipëri," 24 November, *Koha Jonë*.

[4] Arbër Xhaferri, "Hakerat e Mapave," *Shekulli*, 21 February 2004; Veton Surroi, "Shqipëria, feja dhe globalizmi", *Korrieri*, 22 May, 2004.

[5] Arber Xhaferri, "Religion, Politics and Albanians," in *Religions and Civilizations in the new Millennium—the Albanian Case*, Albanian Center for Human Rights, November 2003.

[6] John Esposito, "Political Islam: Beyond the Green Menace," *Current History*, January 1994, p.24.

[7] Fred Halliday, *Islam and the Myth of Confrontation*, I.B. Tauris, London, 1995, pp.27–30.

[8] Sina Ali Muscati, "Reconstructing 'Evil': A Critical Assessment of the Post-September 11 Political Discourse," *Journal of Muslim Minority Affairs*, Vol. 23, No. 2, October 2003, p.262; Isa Blumi, *Islami Politik ndër Shqiptarët: A po vijnë Talibanët në Ballkan*, KIPRED, Prishtinë, June, 2003.

[9] Interview with representatives of the Albanian Committee of Cults, 2003.

[10] Xhavit Shala, National Security and the Challenges of Integration, Albanian Center for Studies on National Security, Tiranë 2003, pp.100–101 In this publication 6 foundations are mentioned as involved or allegedly involved in unlawful activities.

[11] This opinion was shared by all those interviewed, whether imams, ordinary believers and representatives of the Albanian Muslim Community.

[12] F. Klosi (Former Head of Albanian Intelligence Service): "Të rinjtë më shkolla gjysëm ushtarake," Korrieri, 21 January 2003; Xhavit Shala, *National Security and the Challenges of Integration*, Qendra Shqiptare e Studimeve per Sigurine Kombetare, Tirane, 2003, p.104.

[13] John L. Esposito, "Political Islam, Beyond the Green Menace," *Current History*, January 1994.

[14] "Muslimanet të lënë ndarjet," *Korrieri,* 25 June, 2004, p.5.

[15] Ervin Hatibi, "Mëvetësia e Myslimanëve Shqiptarë," *Shekulli*, 28 December, 2003, p.15.

[16] Ervin Hatibi, "Per nje manifest civil te myslimaneve shqiptare," *Shekulli*, 4 September, 2003, p.15.

Stumbling Block on the Road to Democracy:
Security Sector Reform in Serbia

Mladen Momčilović

The Gendarmerie in Northern Serbia in training in 2003. The unit was made up of various anti-terrorist special forces including the notorious Red Berets, accused of war crimes in Croatia, Bosnia and Kosovo and disbanded after some of their members were arrested for the murders of Prime Minister Zoran Djindjic and former President Ivan Stambolic

▪ Andrew Testa, Panos

After the disintegration of Yugoslavia erupted in violence in 1991, ordinary people were forced to confront daily the tragedies and dilemmas brought by war and its divisions. Today, Serbia and Montenegro hosts more than half a million displaced people—the largest refugee population in Europe. This reality, combined with the rough road to democratization and possibilities for Serbia's further disintegration assuming that Kosovo and/or Montenegro split, ensures that the country remains the 'black sheep' of the Balkans for the foreseeable future.

Some democracy indicators for Serbia, including measures of political freedom, began improving after the downfall of the Milosevic regime in late 2000, only to slip back dramatically following the assassination of the pro-reform Serbian prime minister Zoran Djindjic in March 2003. Democratization efforts have stalled as political stability

Mladen Momčilović (former IPF Manager of Recruitment and Training) is Parliament Program Manager for the Belgrade office of the USAID-funded National Democratic Institute for International Affairs (NDI). He served for two years as Deputy Director of NDI Serbia's Security Sector Reform Program. He has also worked as Managing Editor of the East European Constitutional Review (EECR) at the Constitutional and Legal Policy Institute in Budapest.

is compromised and corruption remains rampant. In the meantime, the security sector[1] has remained virtually untouched, with proposed reforms held hostage by elite vested interests.

Although Serbia is not the only country that has been slow down the road of transition, there is a real danger that the inability to push reforms forward will result in a backsliding of political and economic development. Serbia and Montenegro's official declaration of its commitment to join international security organizations including NATO and the Partnership for Peace (PfP), not to mention the ever-so-distant hope of eventual European Union accession, means nothing without a commitment to not only restructure but thoroughly reform the country's security sector.

Security sector reform and democratic and economic development

It should come as no surprise that the countries in Central and Eastern Europe that represent transition success stories all first participated in the NATO or PfP processes of security sector reform. Experience shows that serious security sector reform begins to yield results only when the government backing such reform is also open to parliamentary oversight and budgetary transparency regarding their own affairs.

A primary mission of the National Democratic Institute's Serbia Security Sector Reform Program (SSR) has been to educate a variety of stakeholders about the longer term benefits of immediately costly security sector reforms. While the SSR is only one piece of the reform puzzle, it can be crucial to the development of a healthy institutional environment furthering democratic ideals as well as economic development. Serbia is unlikely to improve its overall economic prospects until its leadership commits to the development and effective implementation of *democratic reform plans* within the security sector, which must include the closure of excess facilities and the creation of social programs for officers who lose their jobs. Currently, citizens are paying an unreasonably high premium for an excessively large military force with mostly obsolete equipment and questionable readiness. Not surprisingly, the Army's popularity has been declining sharply since the violent change of regime in 2003.

A mass burial of Kosovar Albanians who were killed during the war in 1999 and transported to mass graves in Serbia. The Serbian government was slow to release the bodies back to their families for burial ▪ Andrew Testa, Panos

Defaced poster of ex-President Slobodan Milosevic
▪ Andrew Testa , Panos

Crucial steps for Serbia in implementing security sector reform

While the main obstacles to security sector reform in Serbia are daunting—namely the unwillingness of the major stakeholders to undertake reforms and cooperate with the Hague Tribunal's war crimes investigations, the pervasiveness of corruption in Serbia, and the lack of concrete security sector reform planning—those working on the ground have learned to hone their skills in the *art of the possible*. Much networking and lobbying and numerous public events intended to inform and educate policymakers have yielded key allies, sparked an avalanche of pro-reform events, and united a sizable local SSR assistance network.

The lack of willingness on the part of the major security stakeholders to open up the sector to reform and their poor cooperation with the Hague Tribunal are major stumbling blocks. While the lack of transparency is blocking substantial Western assistance from those who have experience in building democratically accountable and civilian-led security institutions, the lack of cooperation with the war crimes tribunal is preventing existing assistance schemes from exercising effective oversight of the sector and providing technical assistance to the self-reform efforts of army and police units. A deadlock has been created, and any future political instability threatens to critically weaken pro-reform stakeholders and their efforts while strengthening potential transitional losers within the security sector, who for the time being are firmly standing their ground and threatening to push the country back into its pre-2000 isolation.

Furthermore, the lack of well-developed action plans for the reform of Serbia and Montenegro's security sector along with rampant corruption in the sector are blocking progress. The Union Parliament has yet to develop a normative doctrine—a new legal framework for controlling the defense sector. The diverging threat assessments developed by Serbia versus Montenegro has resulted in the country's inability to even draft a common national security concept. Despite the fact that a defense strategy was adopted in 2004, developing a comprehensive Union security concept has proven virtually impossible given the fact that the republics retain their own security information services and police forces. Montenegro's recent referendum in which voters narrowly elected for independence from Serbia can only make matters more difficult.

Nevertheless, SSR efforts have led former Minister of Defense Boris Tadic to strengthen civilian control over the armed forces by placing the General Staff and the army's intelligence agencies under the authority of the Ministry, while current Minister Prvoslav Davinic has established some relations with parliamentarians and opened military bases to visits by parliamentarians. The Committee on Defense in the Federal Assembly, one of the SSR program's major partners, unfortunately only exercises limited oversight over the defense sector. For example, the Committee was permitted to scrutinize and ratify only a few line items in the 2005 defense budget. A detailed defense budget and multi-layered audit process for defense spending remain elusive goals for the Union and Republican parliaments. The Ministry of Defense and Armed Forces have yet to convert their old budgeting system to a multi-year, program-based system that is both transparent and accountable. Corruption is so pervasive in the security sector that it seriously erodes citizen and investor confidence not only in issues of security, but in the overall economy

---

In May 2005, a graphic video portraying a uniformed Serbian paramilitary unit executing six civilian men aired on Serbian television. The video forced a reluctant government in Belgrade to confront wartime atrocities, including the 1995 Srebrenica massacre in which Serb soldiers killed more than 7,000 Bosnian Muslim men and boys.

"It was important to react immediately on the basis of this video, which was shocking and terrible for all of us," said Serbian Prime Minister Vojislav Kostunica on June 2, 2005, as he announced the arrest of several soldiers who appeared in the video.

The videotape, dated June 25, 1995, begins with an Orthodox priest blessing members of a Serbian military unit, which has since been identified as the Scorpions, a group directed by Serbia's Ministry of the Interior. The video then cuts to an extended section (there is no audio) in which a group of these red-bereted troops force six men in civilian clothing, their hands bound, out of an army truck onto a country road, where they are made to lie face down. When other soldiers arrive, they march the six men into a grassy area off the road where they execute four of them, shooting them in the back. At gunpoint, the soldiers force the two remaining men to drag the bodies off to a nearby white shack. Later, the two men are made to lie down on the floor of the building where they are also shot.

According to the *Observer* newspaper in London and other sources, the murders took place east of Sarajevo. The cameraman was a Serbian known by his nickname, Bugar. Soon after, someone made 20 copies of the tape to give to members of the Scorpions. The commander of the unit, Slobodan Medic, ordered the tapes destroyed, but one copy survived and was hidden outside Serbia for years. Then in a trial of Scorpions in 2003, where they were accused of killing 19 ethnic Albanian civilians, one mentioned the existence of the videotape. Natasha Kandic, who heads Belgrade's Humanitarian Law Center, managed to track down the man with the tape.

Kandic released it to Serbian prosecutors, The Hague tribunal, and Serb television. Among those immediately arrested was Scorpion commander Slobodan Medic. Now, Kandic says, Serbia must arrest General Ratko Mladic, the Serb military commander wanted on charges of genocide for the Srebrenica massacre.

From a report by FRONTLINE/World, a national public television series in the United States that turns its lens on the global community, covering countries and cultures rarely seen on American television. The report with a video clip is available at http://www.pbs.org/frontlineworld/blog/2005/07/srebrenica_the_1.html

and government institutions. Improving anti-corruption enforcement mechanisms and developing stronger regional anti-corruption networks should help improve Serbia and Montenegro's capacity to combat corruption.

Although the Ministry of Defense is slowly turning the political rhetoric of reform and including the need for civilian control over the armed forces into real steps, sustained reform is unlikely without Ministry capacity to plan and react strategically, and strategic behavior demands informed decision makers. Yet, the capacity of the Ministry to carry out *applied policy research* and analysis to inform decision-making is extremely low, and what capacity does exist is highly centralized, poorly managed, and ultimately of little operational value. The Ministry of Defense is constantly seeking strategic, timely research and analysis and is in principle prepared to pay for it, but does not know how to handle the process of managing applied policy research. Experience in setting research priorities, tendering research, facilitating the research process, and assuring that the product is delivered at the operational level where it is most useful is virtually absent.

Implementing International Policy Fellowships experience in security sector reform

Given this backdrop, the SSR program facilitated the first initiative aimed at strengthening the policy research capacity of the Ministry of Defense with assistance from a major international think thank. Applying my experience with the International Policy Fellowships (IPF) program of the Soros foundations network facilitating fellows' policymaking efforts has time and time again proven to be extraordinarily valuable when applied to the SSR reform efforts. Knowledge gained via IPF trainings and ways of doing things has become my everyday way of thinking in supporting local policymaking activities. While many donors are often too large and too bureaucratic to sufficiently detect and respond to the real needs of local communities, Soros foundations network involvement in the Balkans and especially Serbia and Montenegro over the past ten years has had grassroots impact.

Taking this one step further, regional networking among policy researchers and experts can go a long way toward finding solutions to common problems. For example, IPF fellow Islam Yusufi's pioneering security sector reform work in Macedonia has tackled similar problems, and his initiatives not only in Macedonia but in the region as a whole can serve as an example to other practitioners and institutions involved in security sector reform while fostering security sector policy debate and donor strategies.

The process of security sector reform is ongoing, and surely one of the most vital areas to be addressed in the region. Bringing together context-specific experiences and perspectives from different countries and utilizing shared conclusions and solutions will go a long way toward jointly identifying and tackling the reform challenges that many of us face on the road through post-communist reforms.

Note

[1] The "security sector" typically includes the armed forces, police, paramilitary forces, intelligence services, judicial and penal institutions, and the elected and appointed civil authorities with responsibility for security sector control and oversight.

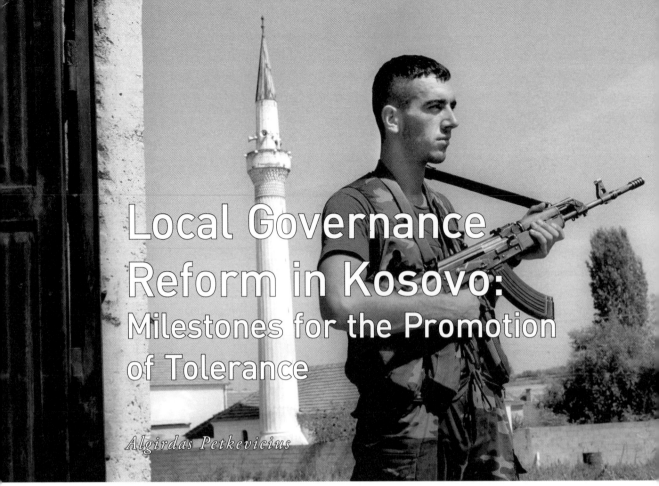

An Albanian fighter during the Kosovo conflict stands guard in the village of Dobrosin. The war in Kosovo between Albanian separatists and Serbian and Yugoslav security forces lasted from 1996 through 1999 ▪ Andrew Testa, Panos

Local Governance Reform in Kosovo: Milestones for the Promotion of Tolerance

Algirdas Petkevicius

T he objective of this research is to present and briefly analyze the prospects for local governance reform in Kosovo, emphasizing the impact of this reform on the promotion of ethnic tolerance. Alternative views are presented as to how this reform could contribute to the improvement of relations between the Albanian, Serb and other ethnicities in Kosovo.

Directions of Kosovo local government reform

One of the objectives of ongoing local governance reform in Kosovo is "the integration of all communities into the democratic structures of Kosovo."[1] Local governance reform is therefore a crucial element of Kosovo peacekeeping efforts. Persistent problems of

Algirdas Petkevicius is Local Government Officer with the Organization for Security and Cooperation in Europe's Mission to Georgia. He has worked with the OSCE since 2004 in its local offices including Kosovo. Prior to his OSCE engagement, Algirdas worked with the Lithuanian Ministry of Public Administration Reforms and Local Authorities and as an independent consultant. Further information about his research is available from the IPF websites: http://pdc.ceu.hu (Source IPF) and www.policy.hu/petkevicius.

governance in the territory including 1) the high degree of centralization in governance, 2) the large size of existing municipal units (the reason why many villages and areas are not represented in the Municipal Assemblies), and 3) the presence of different ethnic communities within certain municipalities plagued by ethnic tension make local governance reform all the more urgent.[2]

While alternative solutions for decentralizing Kosovo's governance have been many, ranging from a possible increase in the number of existing municipalities to the creation of pilot sub-municipal units, the most recent solution adopted by the Kosovo Government has been the creation of five new pilot municipalities with the same rights and functions as the existing 30 municipal units.[3] In addition, all Kosovo municipalities should acquire an increased range of functions in the fields of transport, environmental protection, energy supply, local economic development and other fields. The portfolio of the reforms (including the transfer of additional competencies to the municipalities) is expected to be completed by 2008, with new pilot municipal units becoming fully operational and a more decentralized model of governance fully applied.[4] This portfolio is subject to approval by the Parliament of Kosovo.

The planned municipal governance reform is intending to decentralize a significant share of governmental affairs to the municipalities. In this way each municipality, as a service provider to all the residents within its jurisdiction, should acquire an increased responsibility for ensuring the same level of services to different ethnic communities. The hope is that the provision of equal quality services to all residents will help promote ethnic tolerance at local levels.

Multi-lingual education and other initiatives are also important for the promotion of ethnic tolerance but are not within the scope of this essay.

Ethnic considerations in reforms

Local governance reform in Kosovo has always been dominated by an interethnic agenda with tense relations between the municipalities with predominantly Serb populations and the Kosovo Provisional Institutions of Self-Government (PISG). Attempts to improve governance and service provision have been undermined by the possibility that, in case decentralization proceeds and/or new municipalities with the predominating Serb population are set up, the Serb municipalities may ignore the PISG and become the tools of Belgrade policy.

In general, the Kosovo government's commitment to promoting local economic development promises to boost ethnic tolerance as new jobs are created and the representatives of various ethnic communities begin work. At the same time, solutions proposed by the Serb Government include wide-ranging autonomy for all Serb settlements across Kosovo, such as the autonomy in judicial affairs, natural and mineral resources and other fields traditionally belonging to the realm of the central government.[5] There is little chance that these solutions would be acceptable to the Kosovo government.

While it is not possible to foresee the final outcomes of the reform, it is clear that a gradual approach will prevail. Plans to create several pilot sub-municipal units in 2005 include the town of Gracanica, with a predominantly Serb population living within the municipality of Pristina—the capital of UNMIK-administered Kosovo. It remains to be seen whether this trend will develop.

Local governance reform as a tool for increased tolerance

Local governments may play a significant role in promoting interethnic tolerance. A good example is the municipality of Kamenica in Kosovo, with the efforts of the municipal administration to boost tolerance between ethnicities by promoting open dialogue, innovative security arrangements, and other programs widely recognized as a good practice.

Apart from the creation of certain pilot municipal units that may provide some ethnic communities in Kosovo with the possibility of managing their own affairs in a more efficient way, ethnic tolerance must also be encouraged by improving communications between the central and regional authorities, exchanging transparent information more frequently, translating official documents into all official languages, and fostering the safe freedom of movement of Serbs in Kosovo.

Serb municipalities (especially those in the northern parts of Kosovo) frequently assert that they do not receive timely and correct information from the Kosovo governmental institutions (namely the Ministry of Finance) and that centralized funds for capital investment distributed by the PISG are allocated without due transparency. The lack of available data on the level of investment resources that have been allocated for the municipal capital investment projects throughout Kosovo (such information is not available from the Ministry of Finance website and is not distributed in paper copies), frequently fosters allegations that funds were distributed on the basis of ethnic considerations. Thus the development and regular update of key PISG ministries websites, as well as improved document translation and information communication practices appear necessary.

Translation. It is clear that further efforts are necessary to promote the use of official languages (Albanian and Serb in particular) in municipal work.[6] As mentioned, PISG institutions have inadequate capacities for ensuring that public documents are adequately translated into all official languages in Kosovo. Legal and other official documents, both at the central and municipal levels are frequently translated incorrectly. The reasons for this appear to be technical rather than political. As stated by Ulrich Steinle and Senad Sabovic, "Despite the still relatively heated political

An American NATO KFOR peacekeeping soldier
from a company of the 1/160 Infantry on patrol in 2005
in the ethnically mixed village of Zegra in Kosovo
■ Andrew Testa, Panos

Sufism: Kosovar Albanian Dervishes dance during festivities to celebrate the coming of spring ▪ Andrew Testa, Panos

situation in Kosovo when it comes to inter-ethnic relations, … problems with the translation of legal texts derive not so much from political differences, but apparently from shortcomings that we can generally label as 'technical.'"[7] The use of various languages in municipal practice differs depending on their location. Possible measures that could be taken to rectify the situation include an increased reliance on private service providers for translation, increased quality checks, and the training of translators.

Safe freedom of movement. Efforts to promote the safe freedom of movement of ethnic minorities in Kosovo have also been of particular concern to the international community. Following the March riots in 2004, these concerns increased and led the OSCE to conclude that "additional measures are required in order to rebuild the trust and to improve security for minorities."[8] While it is recognized that the international KFOR (Kosovo Force) may provisionally ease tensions, efforts on the side of both the Albanian and Serb communities are also necessary. The municipal administrations can definitely play a vital role in easing tensions related to the lack of freedom of movement by organizing regular meetings and discussions, promoting ethnic tolerance, helping coordinate the work of municipal Community Committees, and remedying discriminatory practices in employment.

International community initiatives

In addition to security arrangements provided by the international KFOR (Kosovo Force), the international donor community in Kosovo has undertaken significant initiatives aimed at the promotion of the dialogue between different ethnicities. A good example is the OSCE Mission program bringing together the representatives of different ethnic communities to discuss sensitive issues at seminars, conferences and roundtable discussions and ensure that security arrangements are in place to create good preconditions for their participation.

Significant tolerance-building programs supported by international donors also focus on legislative reform and capacity building support to structures such as Community Committees that deal directly with discrimination and human rights issues.

While significant in scope and aspirations, the efforts of the international community in Kosovo could be even more effective if they also supported programs promoting the transparency and availability of public information along with translation units within Kosovo minitries and municipalities.

Recommendations

It appears inevitable that greater decentralization and territorial administrative reform will take place, bringing Kosovo's governance more in line with most European territorial-administrative systems. Increased decentralization can provide municipal administrations with more opportunities for bringing citizens together for the resolution of local affairs. The work of the municipal Community Committees should be further strengthened, if they are to respond adequately to the concerns of various ethnic communities and, together with international actors, oversee the fair distribution of finances and jobs for different communities. An obvious potential advantage of the territorial-administrative redivision of Kosovo is increased trust on the part of residents served by the municipal administrations, while possible disadvantages might include the introduction of additional languages in municipal work and municipal isolation or separation.

A brief review of local governance reform in Kosovo and the increased roles that the municipal administrations may play in an effort to strengthen ethnic tolerance reveals that further decentralization or territorial-administrative reform may empower municipal administrations with new opportunities to play a vital role in easing ethnic tensions. By strengthening interethnic dialogue, improving the delivery of equal services to all residents, solving translation problems, and strengthening the work of the Community Committees, the international community may succeed in supporting local governing structures to ensure the future peace and security of Kosovo.

Kosovar children in 1999 on a climbing frame in a refugee camp in Macedonia look over the Shar mountains toward their homeland ▪ Andrew Testa, Panos

Notes

1   *Governmental work program on reform of local government*, adopted by the Kosovo Government on February 22, 2005.

2   This issue is perceived to be of greater importance by the international community than by Kosovo institutions. See the Appendices for a chart outlining the ethnic composition of Kosovo's population.

3   See the Appendices for a 2005 list of pilot municipal units to be established.

4   See the Appendices for a list of competencies to be decentralized to the municipalities by 2008.

5   See "A plan for the political solution to the situation in Kosovo and Metohija," Ministry of Foreign Affairs of Serbia and Montenegro, http://www.mfa.gov.yu/Facts/plan_kim_e.html.

6   Steinle, Ulrich, Sabovic, Senad, *"Lost in Translation" or How to Make Three Languages Speak One Legislative Voice* // Assembly Support Initiative Newsletter, No. 15, February 2005.

7   Stoyanova, Anna, *Assessment of Language Policy Implementation in Municipal Practices* // Assembly Support Initiative Newsletter, No. 15, February 2005.

8   "Human Rights Challenges Following the March Riots," Department of Human Rights and Rule of Law, Organization for Security and Cooperation in Europe, Mission in Kosovo, 2004, p.6.

Appendices

Ethnic composition of the population of Kosovo local governments (from OSCE Mission in Kosovo municipal profiles, the most recent data available, and various sources):

Municipalities	Albanian population (%)	Serb population (%)	Roma population (%)	Others (%)
Prishtine/Pristina	97.4	2.2	0.1	1.8
Gjilan/Gnjilane	89.4	9.5	0.2	0.8
Gjakovë/Đakovica	95.5	6	0.4	Egyptians/Ashkali – 4
Viti/Vitina	94	5.5		
Prizren/Prizren	81.6	0.09	2.3	Bosniaks – 9.6 Turks – 6.4
Istog/Istok	92	1.2		Roma/Egyptian – 3.9 Bosniak – 2.9
Klinë/Klina	96.5	0.17	3.3	
Podujevë/Podujevo	99.1		1.067 (including Ashkali)	
Vushtrri/Vucitern	95.4	4	1.2	Ashkali – 3.9
Kamenice/Kamenica	82.5	16.6	0.8	
Noveberde/Novobrdo	61.3	37.3		0.1

Municipalities	Albanian population (%)	Serb population (%)	Roma population (%)	Others (%)
Pejë/Peć	86.3	1.2	1.9	Egyptian – 4.9 Bosniak – 5.4
Deçan/Dečani	98.6			Bosniaks – 0.1 Others – 1.3
Obiliq/Obilić	84	12	2	Ashkali – 1.71 Gorani, Bosniak – 0.3
Fushë Kosovë/ Kosovo Polje	85	8	1	Ashkali – 5.6 Others – 0.5
Mitrovice/ Mitrovica	n/a	n/a	n/a	n/a
Skenderaj/Srbica	100			
Leposavić/ Leposaviq	n/a	n/a	n/a	n/a
Zubin Potok /Zubin Potok	5.4	93.9		
Zvečan /Zveçan	2.1	72.6		
Lipjan/Lipljan	83.3	12.2		Croats – 0.5 Others – 2.6
Shtime/Štimlje	97.41		0.14	Ashkali – 2.4
Gllogovc / Glogovac	100			
Suharekë/ SuvaReka	99.45		0.57	
Dragash/Dragaš	n/a	n/a	n/a	n/a
Rahovec/ Orahovac	97.1	1.7		1.1
Malishevë/ Mališevo	99.9		0.1	
Shtërpcë/Štrpce	33	66.7	0.2	
Kaçanik /Kačanik	100		0.02	
Ferizaj /Uroševac	97.4	0.1		

The establishment of the following pilot municipal units was elaborated by the Kosovo government's program "On the Reform of Local Government" adopted on February 22, 2005.

Pilot municipality, in which a pilot municipal unit is to be created	Pilot municipal unit to be created
Pristina	Gracanica
Decani	Junik
Gjilan	Partesh
Prizren	Mamusha
Kacanik	Hani Elesi

According to the government program "On the Reform of Local Government," the following competencies are to be transferred to the municipalities by 2008:

Executive powers:

- Local economic development
- Protection of cultural heritage
- Building permits
- Local social welfare institutions
- Local infrastructure
- Street names
- Local Transport (bus, taxi)
- Primary and secondary education facilities
- Primary health care facilities
- Sports and cultural facilities
- Emergency response and firefighting

Delegated authority:

- Civil status registration and documentation
- Business registration and licensing
- Social assistance payments
- Public utility services
- Municipal property land
- Environmental protection
- Forestry protection

From the Archives

Recent publications

Related OSI publications

http://www.soros.org/resources/articles_publications/global_listing

Open Society Justice Initiative · *Ethnic Profiling in the Moscow Metro* · June 2006

Open Society Justice Initiative · *Justice Initiatives: Ethnic Profiling by Police in Europe* · June 2005

OSI Iraq Revenue Watch · *Protecting the Future: Constitutional Safeguard for Iraq's Oil Revenues* · May 2005

OSI US Programs, Gara LaMarche · *Immigrant Communities in the Crossfire* · February 2005

OSI EU Monitoring and Advocacy Program · *Muslims in the UK: Policies for Engaged Citizens* · November 2004

Open Society Justice Initiative · *Racial Discrimination in Administrative Justice* · August 2004

OSI EU Monitoring and Advocacy Program (EUMAP), Zamila Bunglawala · *Aspirations and Reality: British Muslims and the Labour Market* · July 2004

Center for Policy Studies publications edited by IPF fellows and associates

http://cps.ceu.hu/books.php

Nationalism after Communism: Lessons Learned (2004)
Edited by Ivan Krastev (1999–2000) and Alina Mungiu-Pippidi (1999–2000)

Reinventing Media: Media Policy Reform in East Central Europe (2003)
Edited by Peter Bajomi-Lazar (2000–1) and Miklos Sukosd (IPF Mentor 2002–3)
Conceptualization and English editing by Pamela Kilpadi (IPF Program Manager)

Society and Genetic Information: Codes and Laws in the Genetic Era (2003)
Edited by Judit Sandor (2002–2003)

Reshaping Globalization: Multilateral Dialogues and New Policy Initiatives (2003)
Co-edited by Violetta Zentai (IPF Advisory Board)

Center for Policy Studies Policy Documentation Center
International Policy Fellowships policy studies

http://pdc.ceu.hu/view/source/International_Policy_Fellowships.html

Yaman Akdeniz • *Internet governance: toward modernisation of the policy process in Turkey*

Bojan Aleksov • *Religious education in Serbia*

Mukhtar Ahmad Ali • *Transparency and freedom of information in Pakistan*

Syed Mohammad Ali • *Enhancing effectiveness of Pakistan's poverty reduction*

Nurlan Almaganbetov • *The impact of land reform on economic development in rural Kazakhstan*

Abdel Mahdi Alsoudi • *The impact of US aid policy on democracy and political reform in the Arab World*

Rutvica Andrijasevic • *How to balance rights and responsibilities on asylum at the EU's Southern border of Italy and Libya*

Fatima Fouad Abo Al Asrar • *Democratic governance in a tribal system*

Asomudin Atoev • *Intellectual property rights and the internet in Central Asia*

Sabit Bagirov • *Azerbaijan's oil revenues: ways of reducing the risk of ineffective use*

Florian Bieber • *Balancing political participation and minority rights: the experience of the former Yugoslavia*

Aldo Bumci • *Cross-border cooperation between Albania and Montenegro*

Ihsan Dagi • *Islamic political identity in Turkey: rethinking the West and westernization*

Simeon Evstatiev • *Islam and secularism as a challenge to wider Europe: a Balkan policy perspective*

Archil Gegeshidze • *Georgia in the wider Europe context: bridging divergent interpretations*

Alexei Gunya • *From democracy to disorder? Comparing governing strategies in the North Caucasus*

Yelena Istileulova • *Gender inequalities in SMEs and governmental structures in Kazakhstan*

Mukhtar Aziz Kansi • *An appraisal of social services delivery for children in Pakistan*

Izabella Karlowicz • *The difficult birth of the fourth estate: media development and democracy assistance in the post-conflict Balkans*

Galiya Khassanova • *Women in democratic institutions in Kazakhstan*

Irina Kouznetsova-Morenko • *Islam in mass-media space of Russia and Tatarstan: policy and social analysis*

Mehr Latif • *The politics of participation: evidence from five districts in Pakistan*

Plamen Makariev · *Education of Moslem-minority children in the Balkans. Overcoming the cultural gap*

Zhanna Nauryzbayeva · *Expertise as a driving force of policy-making: the case of pension reform in Kazakhstan*

Semsa Ozar · *Barriers to women's micro and small enterprise success in Turkey*

Saad Abdullah Paracha · *Devolution plan in Pakistan: context, implementation and issues*

Eduard Ponarin · *National movements and Islamic movements in Tatarstan*

Sabina Qureshi · *Pakistan: education and gender policy. Girls' education: a lifeline to development*

Ahmad Idrees Rahmani · *The role of religious institutions in community governance affairs: how are communities governed beyond the district level?*

Ruben Safrastyan · *Armenian-Turkish relations: from interstate dispute to neighborliness*

Syed Tauqir Hussain Shah · *Madrassahs in Pakistan: a threat to enlightened and moderate Pakistan?*

Ekaterina Sokirianskaia · *Getting back home? Towards sustainable return of Ingush forced migrants and lasting peace in Prigorodny district of North Ossetia*

George Tarkhan-Mouravi · *A "realistic" approach to regional security in the South Caucasus*

Nonka Todorova · *Legal framework of state-church relationship in Serbia and Montenegro, Macedonia, and Bulgaria today: between European standards and national continuity*

Fauzia Yazdani · *Women's representation in local government in Pakistan: impact analysis and future policy implications*

Islam Yusufi · *Security sector reform in South East Europe*

Policy Documentation Center—other related studies
http://pdc.ceu.hu

Asbed Kotchikian · *Border Politics: the geopolitical implications of opening the Turkish–Armenian border*

Irakli Mchedlishvili · *Georgia and Caucasus: search for the principles for the regional security concept*

Centre for Eastern Studies · *Kosovo—the question of final status*

Centre for Eastern Studies · *Relations between Turkey and the European Union*

Centre for Eastern Studies · *Chechnya and Russia: the significance of the Chechen problem for contemporary Russia*

Centre for Eastern Studies · *North Caucasus: the Russian Gordian knot*

Centre for Eastern Studies · *Tajikistan: the trial period*

Centre for Eastern Studies · *Uzbekistan: the major source of instability in Central Asia*

Related International Policy Fellow publications available from the IPF website

Bojan Aleksov · www.policy.hu/aleksov
Perception of Islamization in the Serbian National Discourse (2005)
Religious Education in Serbia (2004)

Abdel Mahdi Alsoudi · www.policy.hu/alsoudi
Anti-Americanism in the Arab world (2005)
Islam and Democracy in the Arab world (2003)

Florian Bieber · www.policy.hu/bieber
Dozens of relevant publications on ethnic relations in the Balkans (2001–2006)

Simeon Evstatiev · www.policy.hu/evstatiev
Islam, the Balkans, and the European 'Neighbourhood' Project (2005)

Archil Gegeshidze · www.policy.hu/gegeshidze
Georgia's Regional Vulnerabilities and the Ajaria Crisis (2004)
Georgia within the New Wider Europe Context: Towards Bridging Divergent Interpretations (2006)

Ivan Krastev · www.policy.hu/krastev
The Anti-American Century? (2004)

Plamen Makariev · www.policy.hu/makariev
Education of Moslem-Minority Children in the Balkans. Overcoming the Cultural Gap (2002)
Frameworks for Intercultural Understanding. Islam as a Challenge (2001)

Nicolae Popescu · www.policy.hu/npopescu
The EU and South Caucasus: Learning Lessons from Moldova and Ukraine (2006)
Settling conflicts in the Neighbourhood: the EU and Moldova (2005)

Ahmad Idrees Rahmani · www.policy.hu/rahmani
The Role of Religious Institutions in Local Governance and Provision of Social Services in Afghanistan (2005)

Nana Sumbadze · www.policy.hu/sumbadze
Issue of repatriation of Muslim Meskhetians (2002)
The Problem of Muslim population of southern Georgia: prospects of deportation and the local resistance (2002)

Mihai Surdu (co-author) · www.policy.hu/surdu; www.soros.org/resources
Broadening the Agenda: The Status of Romani Women in Romania (2006)

George Tarkhan-Mouravi · www.policy.hu/mouravi
A "Realistic" Approach to Regional Security in the South Caucasus (2001)
Number of publications on repatriation of Muslim Meskhetians in Georgia (2001–3)

Nonka Todorova · www.policy.hu/todorova
Legal Framework of State-Church Relationships in Serbia and Montenegro, Macedonia, and Bulgaria Today: Between European Standards and National Continuity (2005)

Islam Yusufi · www.policy.hu/yusufi
Number of policy documents and occasional papers on the issues of security and security sector reform in Southeast Europe (2001–5)

Current International Policy Fellows with related projects

Promoting Open Muslim Societies Working Group

Ibrahim Al-Marashi · www.policy.hu/almarashi
Ethno-Sectarian Discourse in the Iraqi Media

Nazila Ghanea-Hercock · www.policy.hu/ghanea
Enhancing the Protection of the Rights of Migrant Workers in the Countries of the Gulf Cooperation Council

Majid Mohammadi · www.policy.hu/mohammadi
Judicial Reform in the Twentieth Century Middle East

Haroon Rafique · www.policy.hu/rafique
Gender Budgeting in Pakistan: Issues and Policy Interventions.

The Challenge of Wider Europe Working Group

Elena Klitsounova · www.policy.hu/klitsounova
Making European Human Rights Policy Attractive and Effective for Russia

Combating Open Society Threats Working Group

Victoria Antonova · www.policy.hu/antonova
Diversity Management and Concepts of Multiculturalism in Russia

Alexey Gunya · www.policy.hu/gunya
From Democracy to Disorder? Comparative Analysis of Governance Strategies in Kabardino–Balkaria and Karachai–Cherkessia (North Caucasus)

Eduard Ponarin · www.policy.hu/ponarin
Challenges to Open Society in Tatarstan

Azamat Temirkulov · www.policy.hu/temirkulov
'Traditional' Social Legacies, State Building and Democratization: The Case of Kyrgyzstan

Photo Archives